Dog Soldier Justice:

The Ordeal of Susanna Alderdice in the Kansas Indian War

Jeff Broome

Foreword to the Bison Books edition by John H. Monnett

With a new preface by the author

University of Nebraska Press
Lincoln and London

Library of Congress Cataloging-in-Publication Data

Broome, James Jefferson.
Dog Soldier justice: the ordeal of Susanna Alderdice
in the Kansas Indian war / Jeff Broome;
foreword to the Bison Books edition by John H. Monnett;
with a new preface by the author.
p. cm.
Includes bibliographical references and index.
ISBN 978-0-8032-2288-5 (paper: alk. paper)
1. Cheyenne Indians—Wars, 1868–1869.
2. Cheyenne Indians—Wars—Kansas.
3. Alderdice, Susanna, 1840–1869—Captivity, 1869.
4. Indian captivities—Kansas. 5. Women pioneers—
Kansas—Biography. 6. Frontier and pioneer life—Kansas.
7. Frontier and pioneer life—Great Plains.
8. Indians of North America—Wars—Great Plains.
9. Indians of North America—Wars—1866–1895. I. Title.
E83.866.B86 2009
978′.02—dc22
2009011401

Foreword

Jeff Broome's *Dog Soldier Justice: The Ordeal of Susanna Alderdice in the Kansas Indian War* is a brave effort for a twenty-first-century historian striving to add a significant dimension to the historiography of America's Indian wars. First published locally in 2003 by the Lincoln County (Kansas) Historical Society, the book gives rare voice to civilian pioneer settlers living in the Indian country of the central plains. Rarer still, those pioneer voices are exclusive in Broome's book. But the story and tragic fate of one of those settlers—Susanna Alderdice, whom Broome has chosen to focus upon—are by no means unique.

Born Susanna Ziegler in 1840 in Ohio, this young woman moved with her family to the Missouri-Kansas border during the early 1850s. No record exists as to whether or not her family suffered hardship during the turmoil that was "Bleeding Kansas" at the end of that decade, but in 1860 Susanna married James Daily and moved to Clay County, Missouri, today a suburb of Kansas City. Soon the couple pushed west to the frontier town of Salina, Kansas, perhaps to escape border violence. A loyal Unionist, James enlisted in the 17th Kansas Volunteer Infantry when the Civil War broke out but succumbed to typhus at Fort Leavenworth in 1864. When James died he left Susanna with two small children, John and Willis.

By 1866 Susanna had met and married Thomas Alderdice, a "galvanized" Yankee who had fought in a Confederate Mississippi regiment during the Civil War until his capture and parole, after which he came north and joined a U.S. Volunteer unit. In 1866 the couple moved to a homestead claim along the Saline River, close to Spillman Creek in Lincoln County, Kansas—the farthest line of Euro-American settlement on the Kansas prairie. To the west lay the buffalo ranges and quite a different civilization, the civilization of the Cheyennes, Pawnees, and roving bands of Lakotas and

Kiowas. Soon the Alderdice family would run headlong into that violent line of demarcation.

By 1868 both Tom Alderdice and Susanna's brother Eli Ziegler would be veterans of combat with the Cheyennes and Lakotas, both serving as scouts under Maj. George Forsyth at the famous Battle of Beecher Island in September of that year. During that fateful year of intense Indian warfare on the Kansas plains, the Alderdice homestead was raided by Cheyenne Dog Soldiers. Several warriors took Susanna captive, while three of her now four children were left for dead. Young Willis eventually recovered. The youngest child, Alice, would later perish in captivity, as would Susanna herself in order to prevent her rescue by the 5th Cavalry during the melee of the Battle of Summit Springs on July 11, 1869, in Colorado Territory. Another captive—Maria Weichel, a German immigrant to Kansas—was rescued, barely alive.

The argument has been advanced that Susanna Alderdice was simply one of many pioneer women who suffered similar fates in the American West. Why study her? Why is she important? Collectively, these women are all symbols—metaphors that illuminate the idea that the wars of American westward expansion and Indian resistance to that expansion were indeed total wars. It is important to study such women individually since the story of each is often more meaningful if placed at the personal level as a case study. Susanna Alderdice's story is a tribute to all such Euro-American women on the western frontier.

Susanna Alderdice was ultimately a victim not only of Indians defending their lands but of federal land policy that resulted in Kansas growing too quickly. Eager to seize rich lands east of the ninetieth meridian before those areas of adequate rainfall were all claimed under the new Homestead Act of 1862, the Alderdices and many others (including an ever growing number of European immigrants, Scandinavians, Czechs, Russians, and Poles) surged westward from the Missouri borderlands and the Mississippi Valley following the

Civil War. In no other place on the Great Plains was the physical integrity of the natural habitat more drastically altered in such a short space of time as in Kansas during the decade of the 1860s and the early 1870s. The census of 1870 reveals a nationwide population increase of 239.9 percent over the course of the 1860s. During the same time, the population density in Kansas rose from 1.3 persons per square mile in 1860 to 4.5 persons per square mile by the end of the decade.[1]

This rapid agricultural expansion had devastating consequences. Unlike Red Cloud's War in Dakota's Powder River Country in the late 1860s, many more whites collided with Indians in prime buffalo ranges in Kansas. Prior to 1866 the Indians had legitimate claims to much of the land in Kansas, especially after the Treaty of the Little Arkansas was nullified by Kansas voters and thus never ratified by Congress. But for many pioneers the homestead laws held sway over Indian claims. According to the Treaties of Medicine Lodge (1867), which relinquished Cheyenne and Arapaho claims in Kansas and established the Cheyenne and Arapaho Indian Reservation in Indian Territory (Oklahoma), the Cheyennes agreed not to hunt buffalo above the Arkansas River. Consequently, the herds congregated above the Arkansas to escape hunting pressure from the reservation Indians. Whites rather than Indians benefited from the larder. With farm expansion the herds became even more concentrated in valleys, where they were easily hunted by the ever increasing numbers of homesteaders. This all too rapid rearrangement of the landscape helped collapse native equestrian life ways almost immediately.

For the Cheyenne Dog Soldier warrior society, used as they were to hunting above the Arkansas along the Republican River and the South Platte, this situation was simply too much change too fast. They would leave their new reservation by early 1868 and move north into the bulk of the advancing white expansion. The rapid depletion of their landscape helps explain the brutal intensity of the war that followed their breaking of the 1867 treaty. Prior to the Treaties of Medicine Lodge, 1867 was the bloodiest year in Kansas history in terms of numbers of whites killed by Indians—an estimated 128 people, including soldiers and civilians. But in terms of actual acts of brutality committed against settlers, a result of a surge in homestead claims shortly after the treaty went into effect, 1868 and 1869 may have been even worse.[2]

Susanna Alderdice was captured in May 1869. Although captivity had been an integral part of the social systems of feuding French and English colonists and their Indian allies on the Atlantic coast during the eighteenth century, and an accepted possible fate for many, the pioneers who migrated to the Great Plains in the nineteenth century mostly came from regions where Indians had been eliminated or assimilated. Others came from Europe and had never seen an Indian. They did not carry with them personal experiences of captivity but rather the cultural baggage of horrifying stories learned in childhood—what American history has dubbed "Puritan captivity myths." These childhood nightmare tales only intensified some settlers' fears and made the uncertainty of captivity all the more terrible. Sexual abuse was frequent, as it was for captives in colonial America. If an Indian camp was attacked, death could come at any time, as it did for Susanna Alderdice. For the Indians of the plains, however, a significant reason for captivity, at least regarding whites, was to acquire hostages for future possible negotiation.

Unlike examples from colonial society, captivity narratives from the West are often silent in the secondary literature. Possibly due to the high visibility of Indian nations in the West in modern times, the subject is often too hypersensitive for many researchers.[3] Indeed, in the twenty-first century hypersensitivity regarding exploitation of Indian peoples everywhere and their sometimes violent responses to the Euro-American westward movement, while perfectly understandable from an Indian perspective, often impedes a complete understanding of the era of Indian resistance in

American history. Captivity was often brutal, and there is no way to sugarcoat that reality. But one must keep in mind that brutality was also practiced by whites against Indians as well.

Jeff Broome recognizes these principles in *Dog Soldier Justice*. He spent many hours in the recesses of the National Archives in Washington painstakingly perusing the voluminous files of the federal Indian depredation claims (mostly contained in RG 123), garnering the stories of scores of pioneer settlers like the Alderdices. As a result, he has compiled in *Dog Soldier Justice* the most complete record to date of the Indian raids in Kansas during 1868 and 1869. State and federal depredation claims can often be misleading and exaggerated because of some victims' attempts to recover as much financial compensation as possible for their property loss. However, Broome found that many of these claims documents nevertheless reveal poignant stories of settlers on the western frontier who were always promised support from their government for their life-threatening task of advancing Euro-American civilization. These settlers were just as often as not ultimately forsaken by the government in their endeavors.

Today the study of the era of Indian resistance, and with it the study of white pioneer reminiscences, has faded somewhat into the shadows of a broader and more inclusive "ethnohistory" of Indian peoples. Decolonization efforts further diminish the reality that Indians and Euro-Americans do have an almost five-hundred-year period of "shared history" in the Americas that does significantly affect the present and the future. To achieve a full understanding of the impact of that shared history, the experiences of *all* participants must be analyzed. In an essay titled "America's Blurred Vision: A Review Essay on Indian-White Histories," Native American historian David Fridtjof Halaas asserts that over the past two or three decades it has not only been unpopular but unwise to write about the period of Indian resistance in American history in terms other than pro-Indian. "Ubiquitous in these histories," he states, is the "obligatory litany of sins committed by white missionaries, Indian Agents, politicians, military leaders, and Protestant reformers . . . to write otherwise [is] to invite charges of racism."[4] Much ethnohistory, unfortunately, is premised on Halaas's statement. Halaas urges historians to follow the example of Native American scholar Father Francis Paul Prucha in fighting for a principle that should have been methodologically established long ago: "the right to see beyond simplistic moral judgments and to write to *understand* [emphasis mine], not condemn, the actions of both whites and Indians" in American history.[5]

How can we "understand" settlers such as Susanna Alderdice? Can we condemn her and her family for their ignorance of Indian religious beliefs and culture when they came west? Certainly we can not, for this story is not one of a "conflict of cultures." The Kansas Indian War between 1867 and 1869 was a war over land—its conquest versus its defense. Questions of sovereignty and differing visions for the future economic use of the land called Kansas were concepts understood by whites and Indians alike. The Cheyennes recognized the "right of conquest," for they had evicted others in the past. The war was also, to some degree, one of religious conviction and practice. Many middle-class whites who came of age moving west during the 1860s were products of a religious revival now called the Second Great Awakening. Farmers especially thought of themselves as God's chosen people, the prophets of Euro-American civilization in the "wilderness." They viewed the Kansas prairies as resources in the raw placed before them to "make fruitful" as the Bible dictated. Any civilization that did not transform the plains into a productive agricultural subregion of the continent surely did not possess God's sanction to own it. Pioneer farm families such as the Alderdices were convinced of their right to conquer lands that nonagricultural Indians had, in the past, conquered from other nonagricultural Indians.

Ideally, as with other periods of conflict in American history that present such paradoxes between antagonists, the era of Indian resistance should be examined according to Prucha's vision by synthesizing all sides of the story within the same study. Sadly, this goal has not yet been achieved to any significant degree. The differences between ethnohistorical methodology and traditional historical methodology, fueled by the hypersensitivity of the subject matter, still prevent a complete bilateral understanding of this significant topic. The United States is unique among imperial nations (since the dissolution of the Soviet Union) in that its colonizing peoples still share the same geography with its colonized indigenous peoples. Such a geopolitical environment surely fuels many of the dichotomies and hypersensitivities inherent in the study of Indian-white relations. But until traditional historians and ethnohistorians can bury their ideological differences, shake hands, and strive toward a complete and meaningful intellectual construction, separate studies of the different participants in the shared history between Indians and non-Indians will continue. Those studies that break the mold in examining the players in this story who are currently out of vogue will likely continue to be looked upon askance, despite the brave efforts of their writers. Such a brave story is *Dog Soldier Justice*, a story that ultimately will illuminate the shared history among Indian Americans and non-Indian Americans in the future.

John H. Monnett

Notes

1. William F. Zarnow, *Kansas: A History of the Jayhawk State* (Norman: University of Oklahoma Press, 1957), 162.

2. Figures tabulated by the Kansas State Historical Society in the *Rooks County Record*, March 29, 1912.

3. One recent study that does finally illuminate western captivity narratives is Gregory Michno and Susan Michno, *A Fate Worse Than Death: Indian Captivities in the West, 1830–1885* (Caldwell ID: Caxton Press, 2007).

4. David Fridtjof Halaas, "America's Blurred Vision: A Review Essay on Indian-White Histories," *Colorado Heritage* 3 (1983): 44.

5. Halaas, "America's Blurred Vision," 46–47.

Preface to the Bison Books Edition

It gives me great pleasure to see *Dog Soldier Justice* available as a Bison Books edition. Now the important story found within these pages will get the distribution it deserves.

It seems that when anyone wants to learn about the first generation of settlers in Kansas, Nebraska, and Colorado Territory, the information comes in the form of reminiscences written many years later. Of course, such reminiscences are usually fraught with factual error. This is because memory is the primary means of reference, and the longer the gap that memory must traverse the greater the chance for error. Historians generally do not like to rely on accounts of events that rest solely on these recollections. Consequently, the voice of the pioneer during the settlement of the West, especially regarding violent encounters with raiding Indians, is today largely ignored.

Where then does one find the pioneer voice if not just in reminiscences? Everybody who lived through this history is long dead. We can't ask someone, "What was it like in 1869?" as we still can today if we wonder about the experience, say, of World War II. Letters and diaries written at the time are key sources, but these seldom present a continuity of events. The researcher is left to seek other ways of getting a more complete picture of the experiences the early pioneers encountered.

If we want to understand what it was like to be on the receiving end of an Indian raid in 1869, our primary sources are few. So much more history was endured than was ever penned, and thus it really becomes a daunting task to gain an appreciable understanding of what the early pioneers faced. To compare events occurring during the Civil War, for instance, we have numerous letters and diaries of the common soldier, and though the amount of what exists is quite small in comparison to the number of persons who participated in that war, we can certainly gain considerable insight into the thoughts and experiences of the common soldier through the materials that survive today. Unfortunately, the number of letters and diaries from pioneers who witnessed firsthand violent Indian raids is too small to give us the information we need to carry us beyond our own imagination into an authentic understanding of the actual thoughts of those who survived such attacks. What are we to do?

As will be seen from reading the original preface to *Dog Soldier Justice*, I was able to solve this problem when I located numerous firsthand accounts housed in the National Archives in Washington DC, in a little-known record group titled "Indian Depredation Claims." From these depredation claims a pioneer voice can now be heard. I was able to cull the claims originating out of Kansas, and from those I began to piece together a more complete picture of what the early settler endured in an Indian raid. I chose to make Susanna Alderdice the centerpiece for this story, for it is her ordeal that best represents the worst of what was feared most in an Indian raid, a fate worse than death—female captivity.

What emerges in *Dog Soldier Justice*, I believe, is a powerful story, a sad story, but hopefully a story that will begin to balance our understanding of one side of the violence perpetrated in the settling of the West. I do not believe this story can be fully understood if one only concentrates on the experiences of the Indian or the military while ignoring the pioneer. The complete picture must also include the pioneer. Only then can the lens of history produce a clear picture of the past. I chose to concentrate on the voice of the pioneer in order to push that voice more prominently into our modern understanding of the settlement of the West. The important task of interpreting history must proceed from the known facts of history, for, as the philosopher David Hume noted, truth "is the basis of history."[1] *Dog Soldier Justice* is narrative history carefully constructed on factual evidence largely ignored today. That evidence has been ignored mostly because it has been unknown. But as one reader said, if the evidence found in the endnotes here were to be presented in a court of law today, the jury would have to conclude the story as true beyond any reasonable doubt. How this story will contribute toward new interpretation and understanding of the frontier West is left for the reader to decide. At the very least it should balance one's comprehension of the nature of the Indian wars in Colorado, Kansas, and Nebraska in the 1860s toward a more compassionate understanding of the sufferings endured by Euro-Americans.

There is an addendum of new information to append to the original story. In appendix 3 I proposed that a monument be erected at the Summit Springs battlefield in honor of Susanna Alderdice. Donations were sought from persons who purchased the first edition of *Dog Soldier Justice*, and within a mere four months enough money was raised to go forward with a monument. The landowner of Summit Springs, Gary Ramey, graciously permitted the erection of a five-foot-tall memorial stone alongside the vehicle roundabout that permits access to the Summit Springs battlefield. In 2004, on the anniversary of the July 11, 1869, battle at Summit Springs (and of the attack upon the Dog Soldier village), more than 150 persons attended ceremonies dedicating this beautiful monument. Six descendants of Susanna traveled from three states to participate. Dozens of people chartered a bus from Lincoln County, Kansas. Everyone endured nearly 100-degree temperatures to honor a fitting memorial tribute to Susanna Alderdice.

Almost immediately, however, visitation at the battlefield grew to such an extent that it interfered with Mr. Ramey's ranch duties. A few insensitive and immature persons committed vandalism at the site to such a degree that Mr. Ramey made the difficult decision to close the roundabout and deny access to anyone wishing to visit the battlefield. Today this marker endures malicious damage that includes bullet marks scarring the inscription honoring Susanna. Someone has even gone to the trouble of toppling the marker, and now the wild prairie growth buries the monument beneath it. It can only be hoped that something can be done to satisfy the property owner with his legitimate concerns while at the same time allowing public access to this important historic site.

In my concluding chapter to the book ("The Rest of the Story"), I tried to identify whether rescued captive Maria Weichel has any living descendants today. Her story had become lost to history. Many people, then and now, speculated on her remarriage, but no one seemed to know who she married and what became of her life. From a typed copy of a letter I discovered in the research collections of the Kansas State Historical Society, written at about the turn of the century, I learned the name of her daughter, "Mrs. Ben Worthman." After genealogical research, I speculated that her real name was Minnie Grace Wurthmann and that she had lived in San Francisco. The 1900 U.S. census says she was born in Omaha in 1870. I conjectured that Minnie was the daughter of Maria and her new husband, whose name remained unknown. I then listed the descendants of Minnie Wurthmann in *Dog Soldier Justice.*

From that information Wichita researcher Mike Day became involved with my project and was able to track down whom Maria Weichel married and where her descendants were presently living. It turns out I was correct in identifying Maria's descendants but incorrect in identifying who Minnie's father was. I had acted on an error in the census that wrongly lists Minnie's birth date. After Maria's rescue she married a man named John Mantz, and the 1880 California census confirms both that marriage and the fact that Maria's daughter was the daughter of her slain first husband, George Weichel. This further confirms General Carr's claim in a letter to Buffalo Bill Cody that Maria was already pregnant when captured. The 1880 California census includes a written note that a stepdaughter to John Mantz was living in the household and names her as ten-year-old "Minnie Weichell." George Weichel, therefore, was her father. Later genealogical research confirmed that Minnie's birth date in Omaha was December 18,

1869, not 1870 as the 1900 census states—the error that misled my speculation on who the father was.

The California Death Index shows that Minnie Wurthmann lived until 1945. The *Oakland Tribune* carried information on Minnie's funeral and where she was buried (Mt. View Cemetery). From this information, which confirms the Wurthmann descendants I had identified in *Dog Soldier Justice*, Mike Day and I were able to locate the daughter and grandchildren of Frances Wurthmann. Jeanette Lyon is the great granddaughter of Minnie and the great-great granddaughter of Maria Weichel/Mantz. Her children are Erik Lyon and Stacey Earles. There are many more descendants to be found.

Maria Weichel/Mantz did not have any other children and, sadly, did not live very long. She died in California on September 20, 1890. A short obituary in the *San Francisco Morning Call*, September 23, 1890, identifies her as the mother of Mrs. Ben Wurthmann, that she was a native of Bavaria, and that she was "45 years, 2 months and 2 days" at her death. This means she was born July 18, 1845, and that she was twenty-three when captured May 30, 1869. Another California record that Mike Day uncovered confirms Maria was born July 18, 1845.

The reader should be aware of one significant historical event relating to the Indian wars that occurred in the area where the 1868–69 Indian raids happened in Kansas, the only Indian war–related event that I failed to cover in *Dog Soldier Justice*. This is what is today known as the Mulberry Creek massacre. A few soldiers and settlers surrounded as many as twenty Pawnee Indians, some recently completing service as Indian scouts for the military and carrying their discharge papers, and then killed them all. Adolph Roenigk devoted several pages of his *Pioneer History of Kansas* (1933) to this, confirming in interviews between 1910 and 1912 with Susanna's husband, Tom Alderdice, her brother Eli Zigler, and her brother-in-law John Alverson that Susanna's family had a

hand in the massacre. Roenigk called it "an awful act, and supposed they [Susanna's relatives] might have looked at it in the
same light. These people were good law abiding citizens and
might have been sorry for their actions in the past."[2]

I did not cover this event in *Dog Soldier Justice* because of
disparities between Roenigk's account and information I
uncovered in the newspapers of the time and the military
reports found in the National Archives. The latter accounts
place this incident in Ellsworth County, just a few miles west
of Fort Harker, on March 13, 1869. Roenigk has the incident
happening more than a month earlier on February 2, 1869, in
Lincoln County, just south of present-day Beverly. The distance between the two is about forty miles. Mulberry Creek
barely runs into northeast Ellsworth County and is nowhere
near the town of Ellsworth, and Roenigk clearly places the incident he describes as happening much farther north in Lincoln
County. It appears, therefore, that the incidents in Lincoln and
Ellsworth counties were two separate events.

The commander of Fort Harker, Capt. Edward H. Leib,
wrote that the "shooting of Pawnee Indians at Ellsworth, from
all the facts, was a most disgraceful transaction and without
provocation, since which time the inhabitants have been much
exercised in regard to threats, and all kind of fabulous reports
are in circulation concerning Indian raids, etc."[3] Newspapers
reported at the time that the Pawnees were going to attack and
burn the town of Ellsworth and avenge the murders.[4] After the
Cheyennes attacked Lincoln County in 1869, killed settlers,
and took Mrs. Alderdice and Mrs. Weichel captive, people
years later still believed that the Pawnees were responsible for
the attack, thinking it was done in retaliation for one or both
of the Pawnee killings earlier in 1869.[5]

If Susanna Alderdice's relatives were involved in the
killings in Lincoln County, the question is worth asking: why
did they do this? The answer is fairly simple to understand.
The settlers in Lincoln County had been devastated by
Cheyenne Indian raids the preceding August, and several of

the men had just survived the harrowing fight at Beecher Island (see chapters 2 and 3). Now Pawnee Indians had returned, according to Roenigk, on the same pretence that had occurred in the deadly August raids—to beg for food.[6] Further, Pawnees had also committed several depredations in Lincoln County and neighboring counties in 1866, 1867, and 1868.[7] Given the above, it is easy to understand why the settlers would act the way they did. When the military was not there to protect them they were, for all intents and purposes, on their own and thus justified in using any means necessary to protect their families and new settlements.[8]

There is another incident connected with the Pawnee killings that arouses indignation today. Warriors' heads would be decapitated, cleaned, and sent to museums for study (some accounts mention the Army Medical Museum while others mention the Smithsonian).[9] This was an order issued in 1868 from the Surgeon General's Office, "a memorandum ordering army field surgeons to collect Indian crania for scientific study."[10] Gen. Eugene Carr was under this order when he attacked the Cheyennes at Summit Springs, but he could not collect any skulls due to their being crushed by his Pawnee scouts during and after the battle. No doubt Darwin's evolutionary theory had influenced policy makers in Washington, and thus the order was made. It had nothing to do with the sentiments any settlers, including Susanna's relatives, might have had at the time.

I would like to make one final note, a note of thanks. It has been my privilege to work with the leaders of the Lincoln County Historical Society during nearly the entire process of researching and writing this book. Their belief in my energies and ability to tell a true story of the experiences of the first pioneers in Lincoln County is what inspired me to write the book. That the University of Nebraska Press has now taken the book is a testament to their faith in my abilities. To all who worked with me in Lincoln County, thank you.

Notes

1. David Hume, *Essays and Treatises on Several Subjects* (London: A. Millar, in the Strand, 1753), 55. See also David Hume, *Essays Moral Political and Literary* (London: Oxford University Press, 1963), 559.

2. Adolph Roenigk, *Pioneer History of Kansas* (n.p., 1933), 128. See also Elizabeth N. Barr, *Souvenir History Lincoln County Kansas* (n.p., 1908), 36–37.

3. Capt. Edward Leib, "Letter, Headquarters, Fort Harker, Kansas, March 16, 1869," Letters Received, Department of the Missouri, Part 1, Entry 2601, 1869, Record Group 393, National Archives Building, Washington DC.

4. See, for example, the *Kansas Daily Tribune*, June 3, 1869, and the *Kansas Daily Record*, June 9, 1869.

5. The Indian depredation claim of James McHenry has testimony from Henry Tucker, one of the wounded survivors of Beecher Island, stating his belief that the Indians who did the May 30, 1869, raid "were Pawnees who were on their way to the Mulberry to revenge the massacre of a large number of their tribe killed by the white settlers in 1868 [sic]." See James McHenry Indian Depredation Claim #7219, p. 6, Indian Depredations Claims Division, Record Group 123, National Archives Building, Washington DC. Of course Tucker was woefully mistaken in his belief, for it was a Cheyenne village that Mrs. Weichel was rescued from, and it was the Pawnee scouts who did the most damage to their lifelong Cheyenne enemy at her rescue at Summit Springs. Nevertheless, Tucker's statement shows what some continued to believe: that the 1869 raid was related to the killing of the Pawnees that Roenigk wrote about.

6. Roenigk, *Pioneer History of Kansas*, 129.

7. *Indian Depredations*, 41st Cong., 2nd sess., 1865, House of Representatives, Mis. Doc. 20, 3–7. See also the following Indian depredation claims: #3572, #3675, #3676, #3677, #3702, #3793 (Record Group 75), #3300 (Record Group 123), Indian Depredations Claims Division, Record Groups 75 and 123, National Archives Building, Washington DC.

8. In 1690 the philosopher John Locke made very clear when deadly force is justified for theft. See #18 in chapter 3 and #182 in chapter 16, *The Second Treatise of Civil Government*, 3rd ed. (Oxford: Basil Blackwell, 1966), 11, 92–93.

9. See, for example, Col. George A. Armes, *Ups and Downs of an Army Officer* (Washington DC, 1900), 273–74; Jerome Greene, *Fort*

Randall on the Missouri, 1856–1892 (Pierre SD: South Dakota State Historical Society Press, 2005), 103; Jerome Greene and Douglas Scott, *Finding Sand Creek: History, Archeology, and the 1864 Massacre Site* (Norman OK: University of Oklahoma Press, 2004), 46. Roenigk wrote that he knew not why the Indians' heads were taken to Fort Harker. See *Pioneer History of Kansas*, 129. See also Charles Martin, "The Pawnee Indian Massacre in Glendale Township, Saline County, Kansas, in 1869" and Adolph Roenigk, "Letter to Kirk Mechem, Sec. Kansas State Historical Society," October 26, 1937, Kansas State Historical Society Archives, Topeka, Kansas.

10. James Riding In, "Six Pawnee Crania: Historical and Contemporary Issues Associated with the Massacre and Decapitation of Pawnee Indians in 1869," *American Indian Culture and Research Journal* 16, no. 2 (1992): 104.

For Christina Jennifer, James David and James Evan.

Memories are what keep alive that which is past.

Table of Contents

List of Illustrations

Eli Zeigler
Willis Daily's family
Willis Daily and granddaughter, Leta Daily
Willis Daily family home with family on the porch
Willis Daily's family
General Eugene Asa Carr and his family
Bogardus—Bell cemetery
Inscription on Bogardus—Bell memorial marker
Grave of David Bogardus
James Alfred Daily headstone
Mr. & Mrs. Willis Daily tombstone
Pioneer monument in Lincoln, Kansas
Close-up view of inscriptions on pioneer monument
Close-up view of inscriptions on pioneer monument
Four-generation picture of Willis Daily family

Preface

Numerous massacres were committed by the redskins, not sparing innocent women and children, and the whites retaliated by treating the Indians in like manner.[1]

Readers of history who have little or no interest in knowing personal details of an author of history are invited to skip this preface, as well as the epilogue, and move to the next chapter. What follows is written for readers who are interested in such matters.

I suppose my interest in western history goes back to childhood. My dear maternal grandmother, as I write this, still alive and going strong after one-hundred-and-two years, had much to do with this. As a young boy, I enjoyed thrilling stories of the Civil War she had heard as a child from relatives who had fought in this greatest of American conflicts. An excellent seamstress, it wasn't long before she began to make me little replica Civil War uniforms. I wore these out imagining myself a soldier of the 19th century. As I grew older, my interest in the Civil War expanded into the Indian wars, especially those conflicts that occurred in the West following the Civil War.

For some time college and work directed me away from my western history interests. Changing career paths after eleven years brought me back to graduate school, pursuing a doctorate in philosophy at the University of Colorado. While immersed in my dissertation I experienced "writer's cramp," and, needing a change of intellectual scenery, I took a month off and diverted my attention back to western history, reading literature for the mere enjoyment of getting away from the intellectual rigors of my dissertation. What happened next came as a complete surprise. I couldn't stop reading books on western history! Hunger for knowledge of the West could not be tamed. Indeed, when returning to my dissertation, it was always with a book on western history in one hand. That was seven years ago (1996) and the interest is unabated and still raging. It wasn't long before my interests focused primarily on the Indian wars of the American West.

With this insatiable interest, and living in Colorado, I shortly thereafter had the opportunity to visit the Summit Springs battlefield. This barren, desolate battleground is privately owned and lies not far from Sterling, in northeastern Colorado. It is a haunting place to visit. The wind nearly always blows, yet there is also a sense of quietness when one walks the battlefield. The wonderment of the unfolding events on July 11, 1869, is easy to conjure when one visits this site.

I remember my first visit. A convenient roundabout allows one to drive to the southwestern edge of the battlefield. Two large markers sit close by just off the dirt road. One was originally erected in 1933. It simply denotes the fact that the Summit Springs battle was fought there in 1869. The other monument was erected in 1970. Put there in honor of the Indians who lost both their lives and their way of life at this battle, it briefly tells the Indian side of the fight. The monument's inscription includes a sad but moving story of a young Indian herder killed in the fight. Instead of escaping, he died trying to alert the village of the surprise soldier attack.

Near this monument, a small brass marker lies flat on the ground. It notes the location of Tall Bull's lodge. If one did not know this marker was there, it would be easy to miss, as it lies out of sight with nothing to attract attention to it. Several yards to the north of these three markers, near the spot where two fences intersect, lies an even more hidden marker. Like the Tall Bull tepee marker, it lies flat on the ground. I did not know it was there on my first visit. Unless they know it is there, most visitors to the battlefield probably miss it. Accidentally finding it during a later visit, I was moved to read its inscription: "This marks the spot where Mrs. Alderdice was found dying by Major Frank North and his brother Captain North. She was buried on the hill above July 11, 1869."

Who was Mrs. Alderdice? What was her story that ended so tragically at Summit Springs? These questions burned in my mind as I walked the battlefield. She was obviously married, but did she have any children? Where did she come from and how did she end up, apparently a captive, in an Indian village? Was she young? I wanted to know the answers to these questions and many more that occupied my thoughts as I wondered about this lonely pioneer woman who had paid the ultimate price in the settlement of the West. I wanted to learn her story.

Armed with this deep desire to know, I turned to published accounts of the Summit Springs fight. What I discovered disappointed me. I could not find anything that all authors agreed on regarding Mrs. Alderdice, including even the spelling of her name.[2] Looking deeper I found major contradictions. She was said to be German and unable to speak English.[3] She was reported as being captured in May 1868, before the battle of Beecher Island.[4] I read many other discrepancies regarding her story. The known facts about this woman seemed lost.

In order to understand her story it was obvious my research needed to delve farther than anyone else had done. I began to learn some facts about her when I consulted three long out-of-print books that dealt with Kansas history, though these books could not agree about much of her story.[5] Elizabeth Barr published her *A Souvenir History of Lincoln County, Kansas* in 1908. Christian Bernhardt's *Indian Raids in Lincoln County, Kansas, 1864 and 1869* followed in 1910. Finally, Adolph Roenigk's *Pioneer History of Kansas* was published in 1933. Each of these tells us, from primary source accounts, a more complete story of Mrs. Alderdice's sad fate, than any book written after them. From them I learned that Mrs. Alderdice was born Susanna Zeigler. She had earlier been married to Mr. Daily and had two young boys, but Daily apparently had died during, or in the Civil War. She then married Tom Alderdice, a Civil War veteran who had been stationed in Kansas during the war. He also fought in the famed Battle of Beecher Island in September 1868. Mrs. Alderdice had two more children with her second husband, Tom.

When Susanna was captured in a violent Indian raid against unprotected settlements along the Saline River and Spillman Creek near present-day Lincoln, Kansas, her four young children became victims of the Kansas Indian War of 1869. Mrs. Alderdice was taken captive on May 30, 1869. Her three young boys left on the prairie, bleeding away life from numerous arrow and gunshot wounds, her daughter living for a short time as a captive with her mother before being brutally killed by their captors, Susanna would remain in captivity along with another young woman, Maria Weichel, for forty-two days. The women were held in Cheyenne Chief Tall Bull's village of Dog Soldier Indians until several companies of the 5th U.S. Cavalry, under the leadership of Brevet Major General Eugene A. Carr, surprised the village at Summit Springs on July 11, 1869. Pawnee scouts had accompanied Carr's troops, commanded by Major Frank North. North's younger brother, Luther, was captain of one Pawnee company. A young Buffalo Bill Cody was also present. Maria Weichel, though gravely wounded by an Indian in the ensuing battle, survived. Susanna, unfortunately, did not. The Indians killed her, rather than allowing her to be rescued.

It is difficult to explain how this unfortunate story of the taming of the prairie moved me. I lost sleep many a night envisioning Susanna's last days. She was buried on the battlefield and her grave's location is now unknown. I can't guess the times I have walked the Summit Springs battleground, wondering about her final minutes of life. Did she know the cavalry was trying to rescue her? Did she unsuccessfully try to escape before she was killed? Did she even know her life was in danger at her moment of rescue? Such questions as these, and many more, were on my mind each time I traversed the lonely battlefield.

I so wished there was something I could do for Mrs. Alderdice. Thus began the research that has led to this book. I soon realized that the information in the writings of Barr, Christensen and Roenigk was incomplete. If there was something I could do for Mrs. Alderdice, perhaps it would be to tell a more complete story of her life, a story that hopefully would endure for the interest of future readers. Her story, of course, must be told in the context of the times in which she lived and thus I immersed myself into a research journey that has cost me an untold amount of money and hours. I have regretted neither. Indeed, my only regret in writing this account today is leaving undiscovered information out of the picture, information that might have been found if I would have persisted in my research efforts instead of putting to print at this point what has so far been discovered. I challenge others to find what is missed.

Research has taken me on two separate, extended visits to the National Archives and Records Administration in Washington, D.C. Numerous trips to Kansas, Nebraska, and the eastern regions of Colorado have followed. Two separate visits were made to the Kansas State Historical Society and the Nebraska State Historical Society. An additional week was spent in the McCracken Research Library at the Buffalo Bill Historical Center in Cody, Wyoming, the fortunate recipient of a generous Garlow Fellowship. Indeed, it is a safe estimate to say that no less than 25,000 miles have been traveled in my automobile to pursue this story. It has, however, been a labor of love.

Though this book tells Susanna's story, it focuses on a history of the violent clash between the white and Indian peoples of the central plains during the latter part of the 1860s. One should be aware that its perspective is primarily that of the pioneers. The military perspective is brought into the story insofar as it relates to understanding the pioneer experience. This is not a book about the Indian perspective of this troubled era in American history. Dee Brown attempted to do this in his panoramic *Bury My Heart at Wounded Knee.* He did it with passion, though he got nearly all the facts wrong about Summit Springs. Brown's book covered the history of the clash between the Indian and White man during the settlement of the West. *Dog Soldier Justice* covers the pioneers' view of two years of that clash. That a book, equally moving, could be written from the Indian perspective of the two years covered in this book, cannot be denied. But that is a book for someone else to write.

A major component in writing *Dog Soldier Justice* comes from numerous individual Indian depredation claims filed by victims of the Indian war of 1868 and 1869. Stored in the vast collections of the National Archives, these stories have remained hidden until now. In addition to additional Record Groups in the National Archives, it was the individual Indian depredation claims that provided much new information for constructing this book. In one Record Group alone (RG 123) are housed nearly ten thousand individual claims for loss of property.[6] The problem for the researcher is to sift and sort from this vast Record Group just those files relevant to one's study.

The purpose for the claims themselves was twofold, viz., to "educate" the settler into not taking revenge for their property losses and to "civilize" the Indian not to steal from the settler. The first act of legislation for this purpose was enacted May 19, 1796. This act enabled the owner of property stolen or destroyed to recover his losses by filing a claim and then presenting it to the superintendent or agent in charge of the guilty tribe.[7] If the claim was approved, the amount of the property loss would be deducted "out of the annual stipend which the United States are bound to pay the tribe."[8] This act was reaffirmed and tweaked several times until 1873, when Congress allowed citizens to re-file on the loss if their claim had been denied in the past.[9]

The requirements for filing a successful claim included several components. First, the raiding Indians had to be in amity with the United States, which usually meant the Indian tribe and the United States had agreed to an existing treaty. Sworn affidavits had to be signed by victims of Indian assaults, including at least two witnesses who could testify to the merits of the losses and the character of the victim. The Indian tribe responsible for the depredation had to be identified, and there had to be an investigation at which time the claim was presented to the tribe and the tribe's response was received. Seldom did the tribe admit to committing any depredations. A special agent with the Department of the Interior investigated the claim as to the validity of the losses and the amounts of the goods stolen or destroyed. Often the agent would not allow the entire dollar amount detailed in the claim to be accepted.

One requirement for a successful claim was that it had to be filed within three years of the depredation, otherwise the claim was barred from compensation. So many claims were denied on this statute of limitation that Congress in 1885 removed the three-year time clause, effective back to 1873. Thus, several thousand claims were refiled in the late 1880s, many of which were consulted for *Dog Soldier Justice.*[10]

With this amended act of 1885, all Indian depredation cases were transferred from the Department of Interior to the United States Court of Claims for final adjudication. But it was the following requirement that today makes such claims useful for study of the history of the conflict between the Indian and the pioneer:

> That all claims shall be presented to the court by petition setting forth in ordinary and concise language, without unnecessary repetition, the facts upon which such claims are based, the persons, classes of persons, tribe or tribes, or band of Indians by whom the alleged illegal acts were committed, as near as may be, the property lost or destroyed, and the value thereof, and any other facts connected with the transactions and material to the proper adjudication of the case involved. The petition shall be verified by the affidavit of the claimant, his agent, administrator, or attorney, and shall be filed

with the clerk of said court. It shall set forth the full name and residence of the claimant, the damages sought to be recovered, praying the court for a judgment upon the facts and the law.[11]

If one wonders just what this might mean to a researcher, simply review the account of the ordeal of Veronica Ulbrich in the "Dog Soldier Captivity" chapter of this book. The depredation files are rich with material such as this. In putting forth an account of the Indian raids in August and October 1868, I relied heavily on the depredation claims to present a more complete picture of what these raids actually did to the newly settled pioneer. I had to pick and choose from the material in order to allow a flow in the narrative. Still, where necessary I freely used the case files, in a few instances listing all property losses. I regret the many depredation claims I could have used had I been able to locate them in the vast records at the National Archives. A book remains to be written which could tell a complete story, but that would require several months of research at the National Archives. I believe, however, a good picture is given in *Dog Soldier Justice* with the numerous accounts I did find.

There are two more things that should be said regarding Indian Depredation claims. First, claims were allowed only for property loss. No remittance was given for emotional or physical injury, or death. In Peter Ulbrich's depredation claim, for instance, no allowance was given for his daughter's sufferings endured during her captivity. Nor was there recompense for the death of Ulbrich's son. Thus, even though Ulbrich claimed $2,000.00 for what he felt were lost wages due to his son's murder, the law permitted no such allowances. Nor could he receive the $5,000.00 sought for the abuse of his daughter during her captivity.[12] Many of the depredation claims sought $5,000.00 for a family member's death. This was apparently a fixed figure that railroads were ordered to pay when causing the unnecessary death of an employee or passenger.[13] But no such recovery was allowed in the laws governing Indian depredations.

The second thing is that in the overwhelming majority of the Indian depredation cases that I drew from for this book, ultimately no compensation was ever given for property losses. The law governing Indian depredation claims was complicated, subject to many revisions. It seems there was no way for Congress to order compensation given from one government agency to citizens, short of appropriating it within Congress itself, which Congress apparently never did.[14] In studying these depredations and noting the various dates in which claims were made, refiled, amended, etc., it was rather contrite to realize that, unknown to the pioneers when making their claims, they were ultimately denied compensation for their losses, almost always on some seemingly trivial filing requirement, or else simply because Congress never made the money available for compensation. This was especially acute when understanding that the settlers also lost the life of one or more members of their family in the initial depredation. In many instances, nearly thirty years later they were still trying to recover the property loss of a horse or a gun, as if such property meant more to the government than did the life of the loved ones lost. Given the modern clamor calling for the government to make reparations for past sins (e.g., slavery) against particular classes of people, it would seem a similar case could be made from the descendants of the many thousands of pioneers who were promised compensation for their losses and yet never received it. But that is another story for another time.

One who is familiar with the battles of Beecher Island or the Washita will discover that I add nothing new to these engagements. There are established works that cover these battles and I have no desire to be in competition with them.[15] The fights of Beecher Island and the Washita relate importantly to the Kansas Indian War of 1868 and 1869, and they are thus included as chapters in *Dog Soldier Justice*. To cover them in depth would encumber the length of this book. My object has been to bring out substantially new information about the

Indian raids in Kansas in 1868 and 1869, and the Republican River Expedition culminating in the battle at Summit Springs. Any reader can choose to ignore the information found in the endnotes, but for the reader that studies them, they will find a deeper story complementary to *Dog Soldier Justice*.

Initially I was going to write two books, a shorter and a longer one. The shorter one was going to be titled *Pioneer Mother: The Ordeal of Susanna Alderdice*. As I began writing that, I kept bringing in the information I wanted to share in my longer book, *Dog Soldier Justice: The Ordeal of Susanna Alderdice in the Kansas Indian War*. I found I couldn't do a shorter book and keep Susanna's story out of the context of the history in which her experiences originated, which might be called the "bigger picture." When I finally realized this, I dropped the shorter book and wrote the longer book. It is my desire, however, that the reader not lose sight of Susanna's story while immersed in the bigger picture.

Acknowledgments

There are many people, groups of people, and organizations, all of whom helped me in my research. Indeed, without their help, this book would have been impossible to create. Oftentimes, what might have seemed a little suggestion, tip, or sharing of information actually turned out to be the discovery of something extremely important.

The following organizations/institutions were cooperative in providing important support and/or information: National Archives and Records Administration, Washington, D.C.; Kansas State Historical Society, Topeka, Kansas; Nebraska State Historical Society, Lincoln, Nebraska; Lincoln County Historical Society, Lincoln, Kansas; Colorado Historical Society, Denver, Colorado; Denver Public Library, Denver, Colorado; Overland Trails Museum, Sterling, Colorado; Carl Albert Center, University of Oklahoma at Norman, Oklahoma; Community Memorial Museum of Sutter County, Yuba City, California; Blue Rapids Public Library, Blue Rapids, Kansas; the Kansas Room of the Salina Public Library, Salina, Kansas; St. John's Military School, Salina, Kansas; Little Bighorn Battlefield National Monument, Crow Agency, Montana; Arapahoe Community College (ACC), ACC Library, ACC Foundation, Littleton, Colorado; Fort Leavenworth National Cemetery, Fort Leavenworth, Kansas; Fort Scott National Monument, Fort Scott, Kansas; posse members of the Denver Westerners, Denver, Colorado; Buffalo Bill Historical Center, Cody, Wyoming; Buffalo Bill Museum, Golden, Colorado; Heritagepac, Little Rock, Arkansas.

In addition to the above organizations, the following people played important roles in my research: Judy Lilly, Jean, North, and West McArthur, Jack Albert, Doug Randolph, and Virgil Loy, Salina, Kansas; Lynne Turner, Don Ubben, and Angeline Bigham, Blue Rapids, Kansas; Jim and Sharon Nelson, Ruby and Lloyd Ahring, Lee and Carol Modrow, Vic and Lola Suelter, Brenda and Richard Peterson, Craig Walker, Alfred Aufdemberge, Virgil Christensen, Loa Page, and Penny Andreson, Lincoln, Kansas; Lowell Larson, Denmark, Kansas; Floy Bowers and Wayne Little, Abilene, Kansas; Mary Allman, Topeka, Kansas; Leo Oliva, Woodston, Kansas; Arnold Schofield, Fort Scott, Kansas; George Ulbrick and Orvel Criqui, Lawrence, Kansas; Mickie Alderdice, Conway Springs, Kansas; Janie Alderdice-Trotter, Wichita, Kansas; Kitty Deernose and John Doerner, Crow Agency, Montana; Larry Finnell, Bob Larzalere, Bill Graepler, and Mike Koury, Fort Collins, Colorado; Bill Conway, Anna Mae Hagemeier, and Cathy Asmus, Sterling, Colorado; Gary Ramey, property owner of the Summit Springs battlefield, Sterling, Colorado; Nell Brown-Propst, Merino, Colorado; Roger Hansen and Delores Young, Aurora, Colorado; Pam and Mitch Milavec, Centennial, Colorado; James Jeffrey Broome, Colorado Springs, Colorado; Jerry Keenan and Greg Michno, Longmont, Colorado; John Monnett, Lafayette, Colorado; Norm Meyer, Conifer, Colorado; Jerry Greene, Arvada, Colorado; Jan Dawson, Brad Edwards and Ray Koernig, Littleton, Colorado; John McDermott, Rapid City, South Dakota; Hank Graepler, Payson, Arizona; Berniece Daily Horton, Phoenix, Arizona; Joeleen Watters Passow, Humboldt, Iowa; Jack Pilk, Aiken, South Carolina; Wayne Sarf and Patricia Luebke, New York City, New York; Jerry Russell, Little Rock, Arkansas; Sharyl Simmons, Yuba City, California; James Williams, Modesto, California; Colonel Ray Sparks, deceased, Kansas City, Missouri; Arlene and Jack Jauken, Peru, Nebraska; George Ulbrick, Hooper, Nebraska; Denise Anderson, Fairbury, Nebraska; Doug Scott, Lincoln, Nebraska; Quito Osuna Carr, Albuquerque, New Mexico; Esther and Ted Van Soelen, Clovis, New Mexico; Jack Manion, Beverly Hills, Florida; Samuel Smith, Longwood, Florida; Sandy Barnard, Terre Haute, Indiana; Elden Davis, Howell, Michigan; Jeanette Suelter, Bob and Betty Lowdermilk, Alexandria, Virginia; Joan Pennington, Fairfax Station, Virginia; Harry H.

Anderson, Milwaukee, Wisconsin; Paul Fees and Juti Winchester, Cody, Wyoming.

For assisting me financially during the course of my research, I would especially like to thank the following people and/or organizations: Lincoln County Historical Society, Lincoln, Kansas; Arapahoe Community College and the Arapahoe Community College Foundation, Littleton, Colorado; Heritagepac and Jerry Russell, Little Rock, Arkansas; The Buffalo Bill Historical Center for their support as a Garlow Research Fellow, Cody, Wyoming; an anonymous Kansas family descendant who appreciated my efforts in uncovering significant information on a great-great aunt.

In writing history it is quite easy to insert claims that are factually untrue, and no doubt such errors might be in this work. It is my desire, however, to minimize these as much as possible. Indeed, the people and organizations listed above are all to be commended for helping me to keep historical errors to a minimum. Errors that might remain are wholly my fault.

Pioneer Monument, 1909, Lincoln, Kansas. C. Bernhardt,
author of Indian Raids in Lincoln County, Kansas 1864 &
1869 *(1910) was instrumental in erecting this monument.*
Author's collection.

Beginnings

Since the Southern plains Indians abducted hundreds of white women and children during the period, 1835-1875, it is quite impossible to follow the fortunes of each captive, or even of the many whose experiences were highly dramatic. This should be done in separate captive sketches.[1]

Susanna Zeigler's life began in the early months of 1840 in Green Township, Ohio.[2] The first of several children born to Michael and Mary Zeigler, Susanna would spend her childhood years there. Her parents came to Ohio from Pennsylvania. They were born between 1814 and 1816, and were about a year apart in age, Mary being the younger.[3] It is not known how or when they met, or if they married back east or in Ohio. In 1840 they were living in northeast Ohio, for this is where Susanna was born. Susanna's exact birth date is unknown, but by the time of the July 1840 U.S. Census she had come into the world. By the early 1850s, the Zeiglers had moved to Missouri where they apparently lived near the Kansas border, not far from Kansas City and Independence, Missouri. The Zeigler family had grown. In addition to Susanna, Michael and Mary Zeigler had the following children: Mary, Sabra, Sophia, Eli, Loretta, William, Ellen (who became disabled in childhood due to scarlet fever and thus lived with Michael and Mary all her life), and Frank.[4]

While living in Missouri, Susanna met James Alfred Daily. They were the same age and soon fell in love. On October 28, 1860, the twenty-year-old lovers married in Clay County, Missouri.[5] Some time after their marriage, Susanna and James moved to Salina, a new town in central Kansas, where they started their family and where James, taking advantage of the Homestead Act of 1862, had staked a claim just north of the city on the Saline River in Elm Creek Township. Their first child, John Daily, was born July 1, 1863.[6] It was frequently the case that families, rather than individuals, moved to new settlements, and this was no different for Susanna. Her family, with all her brothers and sisters, soon moved to Salina and joined Susanna and James on this western edge of civilization. Susanna's sister, Mary, had by this time married John Alverson, and they, too, lived near them.

These were times of great civil unrest in the United States, particularly Kansas. The Civil War began in 1861 and no end was in sight to this devastating conflict. Amid this unrest, particularly in Kansas with the threat of a Confederate invasion, James Daily heeded the call to duty and enlisted on July 16, 1864, in the 17th Kansas Volunteer Infantry. This regiment called for an enlistment of one hundred days and was used to protect Kansas. James's brother-in-law, John Alverson, and John's brother, also enlisted for one hundred days.[7] James was assigned to Company D and sent to Lawrence.[8] Susanna was at this time pregnant with their second child, due early in October, but she was probably not too concerned as James would end his service commitment in November and would soon be home.

The regiment was never filled to capacity, and instead constituted merely a battalion of five companies. The short enlistment requirement made it ineffective for the anticipated Confederate invasion into Kansas by General Sterling Price, though Companies B and E were deployed to the eastern edge of Kansas near Mound City in an attempt to confront invading Rebel forces. Confederates captured two of James's comrades in this pursuit, although no battle was fought and James Daily was not involved. The remaining three companies, including James's, performed garrison duties at Forts Leavenworth and Riley, and at Lawrence, Kansas.[9]

Willis Daily was born October 5, 1864, while James was stationed at Lawrence.[10] Tragedy struck the new family, however, when two days before his enlistment expired, James Daily entered the general hospital at Fort Leavenworth, suffering from fever. He was transferred to quarantine. On November 25, eleven days after entering the hospital, twenty-four-year-old James Daily succumbed to typhoid fever.[11] Suddenly Susanna Daily, called Susan by her family and friends, was left a young widow with two children. She had no choice but to move in with her parents. The 1865 Kansas census shows Susanna living with her two sons in her parents' home. With them were her siblings Sabra, Ellen, Loretta, Eli, William and Frank.[12]

During this time of widowhood, Susanna met her second husband. Tom Alderdice, originally from Pennsylvania, was serving as a drummer in the 2nd U.S. Volunteer Infantry, and had been stationed along the Solomon River not far from Salina. When he met Susanna, Tom had a secret. He was a "galvanized" Yankee, having earlier served in the 44th Mississippi Infantry. Captured at Chickamauga in September 1863, he was sent as a prisoner of war to the Rock Island, Illinois, war camp, where he remained for thirteen months. He took the Oath of Allegiance on October 17, 1864, and enlisted for a year in Union service. Wisely, he was sent to Kansas, away from potential desertion back to Confederate service.[13]

Four days before Tom enlisted in the Union Army, Houstan Anglin also enlisted out of Rock Island and into the 2nd U.S. Volunteer Infantry. Like Tom, Houstan was a "galvanized" Yankee. And like Tom, Houstan also was stationed in the vicinity of Salina. After mustering out at Fort Leavenworth on November 20, 1864, Houstan returned to the Salina area. It was Houstan who first married into the Zeigler family. Sometime during his service enlistment near Salina, he had met them. His eye was on Susanna's sixteen-year-old sister Sabra, whom he married at Salina on June 8, 1865.[14] Tom probably accompanied Houstan to the Zeigler home as Sabra was courted, and thereby met and courted Susanna. Perhaps he met Susanna at Sabra's wedding. He would court Susanna for a year.

On June 28, 1866, Tom married Susanna Zeigler Daily, who now became Mrs. Alderdice.[15] Not long after their marriage, the young family settled on a homestead along the Saline River in Lincoln County, close to Spillman Creek near present-day Lincoln, Kansas. As when James and Susanna lived near Salina, the Zeigler and Alverson households settled in Lincoln County. In 1867, Susanna's third child, Frank Alderdice, was born. In early fall 1868, Susanna's fourth child, a daughter, Alice Alderdice, was born. Susanna's family now included four little children, two by James Daily and two by Tom Alderdice.

Life as a Kansas pioneer in the late 1860s was not an easy task and it took a special person to persevere. For an initial fee of fourteen dollars, an American citizen, under the 1862 Homestead Act, could procure 160 acres of land. After five years of working and living on the land, an additional seven dollars would legally entitle the pioneer to the homesteaded land.[16] Many people who took advantage of the Homestead Act were poor. They might have a cow, several chickens, and perhaps a horse. It took hard work to settle prairie land.

For many settlers, the first dwelling, called a dugout, was usually erected on the side of a small hill near a stream or creek. A living area, measuring about fourteen feet, would be dug out of the hill. A roof would be built over the exposed spot, protected by boards and sod. The front of the dugout would contain a door, possibly a window, and would be built up, usually with stones. These dugouts would be used until a later time when a more permanent log structure could be built, but that might take a few years. In the meantime, the prairie ground needed to be broken and crops planted. This was extremely hard work. The railroads were not yet built through the new homesteads in central Kansas and therefore the furniture and other household goods had to be transported by wagons or made from felled trees that would be found along creeks and riverbanks. Consequently, a typical household would have little furniture and few beds. Kansas at this time had numerous rattlesnakes and even poisonous tarantulas. But game was plentiful, and when Susanna and her family were living along the Saline River buffalo were still present, although one might have to ride a day or so before locating a large herd.

Life was hard for the adventuresome pioneer but also good. Many things could threaten security in these new settlements, not the least of which were droughts, tornados, grasshopper infestations, cholera and prairie fires. But easily the most feared danger would be an Indian raid. Up until 1868, the Indian and the Kansas settler basically held a mutual respect for one another. If an Indian appeared at a settler's house, he expected to be fed. An Indian's business for appearing in the settlements was usually a hunting excursion, although occasionally there would be parties on the warpath against an enemy tribe. In Susanna's neighborhood, usually Cheyenne and Pawnee Indians made appearances. Both tribes could appear in the Saline River valley, and the tribes were enemies to each other. In early August 1868, Cheyenne Dog Soldiers turned their wrath against the new pioneer settlements.

Private James A. Daily, Susanna's first husband, 1864. James died of typhoid fever at Fort Leavenworth, Kansas, November 25, 1864.
Author's collection.

August 1868 Raids

They had to be slain be cause Unkle Sam neglected her duty to protect us.[1]

The year 1868 had been a difficult year for settlers in central Kansas. In addition to the worst drought yet experienced by homesteaders there, Dog Soldier Indians, principally Cheyenne but also Sioux and Arapahoe, began a series of devastating raids in and around Lincoln County. Settlements along the Solomon and Saline River valleys in Cloud, Lincoln, Ottawa and especially Mitchell County were hit the worst. In a series of raids mostly on August 12 and 13, many settlers were killed.[2]

Before these raids along the Solomon and Saline valleys, however, an earlier incident occurred at the beginning of June, alerting settlers of impending trouble. Cheyenne Indians attacked Kaw Indians near Council Grove, Kansas. Their purpose was to strike the Kaw Indians at their reservation, apparently in retaliation for seven Cheyenne killed by Kaws the previous summer.[3] The attack amounted to nothing more than a show of force. One Kaw and three Cheyenne were wounded.

The Council Grove incident involved between two hundred and four hundred Indians. The Cheyenne attack, however, was not just against the Kaws. Pioneers living in the vicinity of the Kaws were also attacked. Settlers in Marion County were especially affected. John Nance lost two cows, a shot pouch and ammunition, and in addition his spinning wheel was damaged. This occurred after Nance fed about twenty of the Indians. Abijah Holloway, Nance's neighbor, hiding in a cornfield to avoid detection by the Indians, observed warriors stealing Nance's stock.[4]

7

David Lucas and James McAlister had to flee their farms, staying away for thirty days before it was deemed safe to return. McAlister noted that during that time "all the white men in the vicinity were under arms and on guard day and night . . . . There were about 400 warriors with said Little Robe, and they covered about 7 miles width of country in their march to Council Grove, but returning, kept more compact."[5] Cheyenne Dog Soldier Tall Bull was also identified as a chief participating in this raid.[6]

Aaron Grigsby and his family, which included five young boys, had a terrifying experience during this raid. The Indians came upon his property, took what they wanted and destroyed the rest. They used their ponies to trample Grigsby's one-acre garden. Said Grigsby: "The Indians came through and destroyed it, they were Cheyenne Indians, and I saw them do it; I know they were Cheyennes because they said they were and I was acquainted with them on the plains."[7] The Indians stayed at his place all night, doing their destruction after Grigsby had fed them. In addition, they killed one hundred chickens, which Grigsby had hauled sixty miles from Junction City. The warriors also carried away a large portion of his household property, including blankets, silverware, knives, cups and saucers, three sacks of flour, thirty-three pounds of bacon, and more than twenty pounds each of coffee and sugar.[8]

The Indians also came upon Patrick O'Bryne's homestead, taking possession of the house and staying for two days. O'Bryne fled for safety. When he finally returned, he found his household goods missing or destroyed. He also lost thirteen turkeys and, like with Grigsby, the Indians turned their horses loose in his five-acre cornfield. The entire crop was destroyed.[9]

The Indians were not finished with their raid. Coming upon the house of Hubert and Elizabeth Pappan around noon, June 3, they continued their destruction. They stole or destroyed nearly everything, including doors, windows, lumber, bedsteads, a wooden cupboard, cooking utensils, crockery, clothing, a looking glass, provisions and groceries. The damage totaled $207.00.[10] The Kansas Adjutant General's Report for 1868 reported the Cheyenne in this raid also "outraged one colored woman and robbed many of the settlers of all their clothing, bedding and provisions and drove off some stock and killed the cows belonging to some poor settlers without using them."[11]

Ten days after this raid Indian Agent Edward Wynkoop submitted Little Robe's version of the events. Little Robe denied any atrocities against whites and said that when the Cheyenne reached the area of the white settlement,

> they found the country entirely devoid of game, and that the consequences were that they were very hungry and it was necessary for them to procure subsistence; therefore they killed seven head of cattle belonging to the whites . . . as they would approach the different farm houses the people would become frightened and run away; that they did not interfere with any person or thing, but simply continued on for the purpose of accomplishing their object; that after their difficulty with the Kaws, while on their return home, they met a large herd of cattle coming from Texas, and the men in charge of the same invited them to kill what they wanted to eat; they killed four, making in all eleven head that they appropriated to their own use.[12]

Special Agent A. G. Boone, however, in an earlier report contradicted Little Robe's version. Boone, accompanied with an escort under the command of Major Elias Stover, arrived at the Kaw Agency the day after the raid. He personally observed the damage and testified as follows: "One Kaw, three Cheyennes, and a few horses wounded; two Indian houses burned and several others robbed, *together with several houses belonging to whites plundered of everything*, was about the amount of damage from the raid."[13]

This incident in Marion County is significant to what happened in the devastating raids along the Solomon and Saline River valleys two months later. First, it alerted the outlying settlements that the Indians, especially the Cheyenne, were aggressive and hostile. It also taught them that attempts to make a treaty had probably failed. Indian anger grew after the military was successful in delaying distribution of arms and ammunition after the Kaw raid. Later, however, Indians at Fort Larned promised General Alfred Sully that they needed arms and ammunition for hunting and would not use them against settlers. General Sully believed them, and Wynkoop sustained the belief that they "were peacefully inclined and that the Indians needed the ammunition for their fall hunt."[14]

As General P. H. Sheridan later recalled, the Indians came to see Sully, "and protested that it was only a few bad young men who had been depredating, and that all would be well and the young men held in check if the agent would but issue the arms and ammunition."[15] On Sully's advice, the agent then disbursed the arms and ammunition that had been promised by treaty. The last of the weapons were distributed at Fort Larned on August 3, the Indians instantly departing.[16] It was the bureaucrats who were being deceived about the necessity of Indians needing guns for hunting purposes. It was understood by those experienced on the plains that "the Indian never kills buffalo with a gun, but always uses his bow and arrow, saving the gun to go to war with."[17]

After the Indians received their weapons and ammunition, the Solomon and Saline River valley raids began. Quickly informed, Governor Samuel Crawford went by special train to Salina and from there toured the devastated settlements near present-day Beloit. He reported to President Andrew Johnson on August 17 in a special dispatch:

> I have just returned from Northwestern Kansas, the scene of a terrible Indian massacre. On the thirteenth and Fourteenth instant, forty of our citizens were killed and wounded by hostile Indians. Men, women and children were murdered indiscriminately. Many of them were scalped, and their bodies mutilated. Women, after receiving mortal wounds, were outraged and otherwise inhumanely

treated in the presence of their dying husbands and children. Two young ladies and two children were carried away by the red-handed assassins, to suffer a fate worse than death.[18]

Crawford was not exaggerating. These were particularly heinous acts. Indians raided homesteads along Spillman Creek in Lincoln County on August 10, and by August 12, had moved to new pioneer settlements in Cloud and Mitchell Counties. The raiding continued the next day in Mitchell County and also involved depredations in Ottawa County. August 14 was again a day of devastating raids in Mitchell County. By August 15, the Indians had departed, due in a large part to the timely arrival of a company of soldiers under the command of Captain Frederick Benteen of the 7th U. S. Cavalry.

The Indians responsible for these acts were primarily Cheyenne, but also some Sioux and Arapahoe. They were of the Dog Soldier Society and numbered at least two hundred warriors, led by Red Nose and The-Man-Who-Breaks-The-Marrow-Bones.[19] Other Indian leaders included Tall Wolf, Porcupine Bear and Bear-That-Goes-Alone.[20] An affidavit dated February 9, 1869, by half-breed scout Edmund Guerrier, stated that the raiding party was "Little Rock's, Black Kettle's, Medicine Arrow's, and Bull Bear's bands" and that the two principal leaders were Red Nose of the Dog Soldier Society and The-Man-Who-Breaks-The-Marrow-Bones of Black Kettle's band.[21] General Sheridan stated that Black Kettle was "with the band on Walnut Creek, where they made their medicine, or held their devilish incantations previous to the party setting out to massacre the settlers."[22]

The question why the Indians perpetrated this violence is not clear. Perhaps it was in vengeance for what earlier happened to them near Fort Larned in 1867. On April 19, 1867, General Winfield S. Hancock ordered a large abandoned Indian village burned and its contents destroyed. He did this after he received misinformation that the Indians who had left

11

the village were the ones responsible for killing several men at a stage station on the Smoky Hill Trail.[23]

General William T. Sherman provides what might be the best explanation of the Indians' decision to commence war. After the government agreed in early March 1868 to abandon three forts in the Powder River territory along what became known as the Bozeman Trail in Wyoming and Montana, returning the land to the Indians for hunting,

> Some of the Sioux, attributing our action to fear, followed up our withdrawal by raids to the line of the Pacific road, and to the south of it into Colorado. Others of them doubtless reached the camps of the Arapahoes on Beaver Creek, and the Cheyenne camps on Pawnee Fork, near Fort Larned, and told them what occurred, and made them believe that by war, or threats of war, they could compel us to abandon the Smoky Hill line, which passes through the very heart of the buffalo region, the best hunting grounds of America.[24]

The Dog Soldier Indians responsible for commencing the war were considered the most dangerous among all Plains Indian tribes. The *Junction City Weekly Union* described the Dog Soldier Society as

> Indians driven out of various tribes for cowardice and other crimes, who having banded themselves together until they have become a dangerous tribe. They are called Dog Soldiers because the vilest word an Indian can use is to call a man a dog, hence these freebooters are thus designated, and by reason of their excellent drill they are called soldiers.[25]

Twenty-seven-year-old Mrs. A. Bacon was captured on Bacon Creek near present-day Ash Grove on August 10 and held in captivity for at least a day. She was repeatedly raped. One account says she had her two-year-old son with her during this ordeal.[26] Mrs. Bacon was hit in the head, causing a deep cut to the skull bone that left her senseless. After her sexual torture, the Indians left her lying on the prairie, only to return to her later that day and recapture her.[27]

Simeon Shaw, Jacob Shafer, George Shafer, John Smith and U. J. Smith all filed depredation claims for property losses during this day, totaling $2043.00.[28] The marauding Indians came to Simeon Shaw's house along Spillman Creek, probably a few miles north of present-day Denmark, Lincoln County, Kansas. They remained on the premises from about ten o'clock in the morning until after dark. With Shaw were his young wife and his wife's sixteen-year-old sister, Miss Foster. Sim Shaw believed the Indians numbered as many as four hundred. A large number of them stayed at the Shaw house all day, pillaging and destroying what they desired. At one point, a neighbor of Shaw's, Ben Smith, who was also at the house, grabbed his rifle and aimed it at one of the Indians. This was in response to the warrior's attempt to steal the rifle. Sim Shaw stopped Smith from firing, instead pleading for peace. For this act, the chief returned three of Sim's horses they were going to take when they were through plundering inside the house.

The Indians remained until dark and it appeared they had every intention to camp in the vicinity of the house. Shaw decided to try to escape with his wife and sister-in-law. It is not known whether Mrs. Shaw and Miss Foster had been raped by this time. If they were, it would have been in the presence of the men living in the house. They would have been helpless to do anything but witness the atrocity. Thinking they could escape in the darkness, Shaw and the women mounted the three horses that earlier had been returned to him. Fleeing in the dark, they didn't get far before a party of about fifty Indians caught them. One warrior swiftly rode alongside Sim, leaned over and with a heavy war club violently knocked him off his horse. Shaw fell to the ground, unconscious and seriously injured. The jubilant Indians quickly pulled both women from their horses, ripped their clothes off, and repeatedly raped them. The Indians again had Mrs. Bacon, whom they had recaptured earlier after abandoning her on the prairie. All three women were "outraged" until about midnight, when Mrs. Bacon was then placed on Sim's horse and the three victimized women released. Mrs. Bacon was unable to stay on the horse, fell to the ground and was left alone on the prairie, to be found by others the next day. Meanwhile, Mrs. Shaw and Miss Foster returned to their home.[29]

While all this was going on, Ben Smith had been hiding in a low place on the prairie. He could hear the women's screams into the night.[30] Before leaving the area the Indians returned to the Shaw house and unsuccessfully tried to set it afire. They failed because the house was recently built using cottonwood trees that were still green and wouldn't burn. But Sim lost everything. What wasn't set on fire was broken up or stolen. Shortly after the raid, Sim and his wife separated. Miss Foster was dead before 1890.

Elizabeth Barr recounted these events in her 1908 *A Souvenir History of Lincoln County, Kansas*:

> . . . about August 8 [August 10], three women, Mrs. Shaw, Mrs. David G. Bacon, and Miss Foster, were captured in a raid on the Spillman. Mrs. Bacon had her baby with her. The women were abused terribly and bound with ropes. Mrs. Bacon became insensible by a blow on the head which cut to the bone, and was left on the prairie for dead. Later in the day she was picked up again by the Indians. At night they placed the women on ponies and told them to go to their wigwams. Mrs. Bacon was so nearly exhausted that she fell off her horse and the other women were obliged to go on without her. Martin Hendrickson, who was the advance guard in the searching party, found her the next morning. She still had her baby but both were suffering intensely.[31]

Roenigk, in *Pioneer History of Kansas*, gave a different account.

> Mrs. Bacon was so terribly unnerved by the frightful circumstances attending her capture, that she was unable to sit on the horse which the savages gave her to ride, and either fell off, or was voluntarily liberated by her captors [she fell off because she had a serious head injury]. The exact details of her horrible experience she could never fully recol-

lect [probably due to her head injury]. Her home
was on the banks of a small stream, which to this
day, is called Bacon Creek. When the Indians made
the attack upon her cabin, she and her husband ran
to some timber nearby. She was overtaken and
carried away [she had her baby with her]; he concealed himself in a hallow log, around which the
Indians vainly searched.[32]

General W. T. Sherman reported that when the Indians first
appeared in the settlement the pioneers received them with
friendly intentions, feeding them and giving them coffee. The
Indians, showing offense because the coffee was given to them
in tin cups, "threw it back in the faces of the women and began
at once to break up furniture and set fire to the houses."[33]
General P. H. Sheridan wrote that the Indians were fed by two
farmers and after throwing the coffee "in the faces of the
women serving it to them, because it was given to them in tin
cups, they then commenced the robbery of the houses, and violated the women until they were insensible."[34] In yet another
report Sheridan said the women were raped forty or fifty times,
"and while insensible from brutality and exhaustion forced
sticks up the persons, and, in one instance, the fortieth or fifti-
eth savage drew his saber and used it on the person of the
woman in the same manner."[35] Mrs. Bacon was so severely
injured that she was not expected to recover. She did recover,
however, and in 1870 she was still living on Bacon Creek with
her husband and two young children.[36] The horrible trauma of
that awful day in August 1868 must have haunted her the rest
of her life.

James and William Wild, nearby neighbors to the Shaws,
fled when the Indians appeared and did not return the rest of
the summer or fall. All of their crops were lost. William Wild's
nine-year-old daughter, Rachel, later recounted those times:

> I have a vivid recollection of the Indian outbreaks
> and how the scouts would come in with their timely
> warnings, and we would have to seek some place of
> safety, usually the town of Salina . . . . In those

three and a half years [living on Spillman Creek, 1866-1870] we left our house a number of times. Once there rode a man up to the gate at one o'clock at night, and at the top of his voice cried out: 'Get for your lives,' and rode away at rapid speed to warn others. Needless to say we did not wait to be told a second time, nor doubt that there was danger at hand. Mother got the grub-box packed and the bedding ready. Father gave his attention to the guns and ammunition, while the two eldest brothers put in readiness the horses and wagons. My oldest sister let the pigs and chickens, cows and calves out. It would not do to go away and leave them shut up to starve, and we had no time to take them with us, for we had to race for our lives.[37]

Both Rachel's father and uncle filed claims for their crop losses for this raid.[38]

While these raids were occurring in Lincoln County, along Spillman Creek, many settlers gathered for mutual protection at the home of William Hendrickson. Susanna was there with Tom and their three boys.[39] She was just entering her last month of pregnancy with her daughter Alice, who would be born in September. The knowledge of what had happened to Mrs. Shaw, Mrs. Bacon, and Miss Foster must have troubled Susanna during this time. She could only imagine how awful it must have been to experience such trauma. The only thing worse would have been to be carried into captivity, never to be rescued back into civilization. Such thoughts must have produced nightmares. What experience could produce a worse terror? Susanna would later know.

The Dog Soldier Indians were not finished with their raiding. They moved several miles northeast into Mitchell County near present-day Beloit. The worst of the atrocities occurred to the Bell and Bogardus families, who were related. Hester Ann Bell had earlier married Civil War veteran David Bogardus and settled in Mitchell County. They had two children, seven- or eight-year-old Matt and nine-month-old

William. They were sharing a house with Hester's brother's family, Braxton Benjamin Bell, wife Elizabeth, and nine-month-old daughter, Ella.

Farther down the Solomon River, near Asher Creek, lived Braxton's and Hester's aged parents, Mary and Benjamin Bell. The parents were living with yet another daughter, Sarah (Bell) Farrow, and her husband, James Farrow. The parents relied on the Farrow clan for their care. Nearby lived yet other relatives, including James's brother, John Farrow, who was married to Leddie Bell. Other children of Ben and Mary living in the Beloit area during this time included sons Seth and Aaron Bell. Aaron had two daughters, eight-year-old Ester and six-year-old Margaret, who were visiting at the Bogardus—Bell home at the time the Indians came to the house.[40]

Living in a dugout next to the Bell—Farrow place was yet another daughter of Mary and Ben Bell, Mrs. Springs, recently relocated from Solomon City, where she had successfully operated a boarding house. Her husband, Samuel, had been killed while serving in the Union Army during the Civil War. The widowed Mrs. Springs had two young daughters living with her, thirteen-year-old Martha and seven-year-old Sarah. Martha had earlier married Charles Smith in Salina. However, she was living with her mother during this raid, while Charles remained in Salina.[41] This was a large family, and nearly all, perhaps, can be entitled as the "founder of Beloit." The Indians devastated nearly all members of this extended family.

On August 11 the Indians stole a mare from elder Ben Bell, but it was on August 12 that this family really suffered. Apparently the Farrow—Bell house was hit first. The Indians approached in an ostensive friendly manner, but soon showed their intentions to pillage and plunder. The families, however, were able to secure their cabin and kept the Indians out. It is not clear if they had weapons for their protection, or if after they closed the door the Indians were unwilling to enter the house, knowing the first one in might be shot. Soon, the Indians left in the direction of the Bogardus—Bell home, about one mile away. At this time, thirteen-year-old Martha Springs (Smith) was walking from the latter house to the Bell—Farrow house when she learned the Indians were there. Before she could return to the Bogardus—Bell home, the Indians had already arrived. She was fortunate to escape without being seen. Meanwhile, the Indians, having left the Bell—Farrow house, allowed the occupants there to hastily escape. The terrified family quickly climbed aboard a hitched wagon and fled in the opposite direction. The Indians returned later, burning and destroying everything in the double household. But all escaped alive.[42] They were lucky.

Events turned much more sinister at the Bogardus—Bell household. About eleven o'clock in the morning, fifty to seventy-five Indians descended upon the house. They would remain for at least three hours. When they were through, David Bogardus was dead, as was Braxton Bell. Elizabeth Bell, twenty-one years old, was mortally wounded. She died several days later from the effects of a bullet wound that pierced both lungs. She was shot because she kept trying to get off a horse the Indians were forcing her to ride.[43] The Indians wanted to keep her as a captive. After shooting her and while lying outside on the ground mortally wounded, several warriors repeatedly raped her.[44] David and Braxton's fatal wounds were also from guns, which the settlers soon learned had been issued days earlier at Fort Larned. As with what happened on August 10 down on Spillman Creek, the events in the Bell—Bogardus home began as a friendly meal. After Elizabeth Bell cooked for the Indians,

> . . . they threw the coffee in her face, whipped her husband with their riding whips then killed him and put her child [eleven months old] on a pony to carry her into a captivity worse than death. She refused to go and was shot through, the ball entering the right of the spine and coming out through the left breast. In this condition she lived two weeks when death came to her relief. They speared the child in the head and back.[45]

As the Indians ransacked the home, young Matt Bogardus quickly darted into a field to try to escape. "I was seven or eight years old when he [Matt's father] was killed. I saw the Indians and ran some distance east of the house. My mother came after me and called me back and I saw my father lying dead on the ground near the house."[46] Matt remembered what happened just before his father was killed. The Indians had forced his father and his uncle, Braxton, to run around the house, the Indians continually whipping them as they ran. When David Bogardus turned to defend himself from the painful whippings, an Indian shot him. Before dying, he warned his wife to escape with the children. After shooting David, the Indians again ordered Braxton to run. As he started to run, an Indian shot him, instantly killing him.[47] Martha Springs (Smith), who would later become Martha Gallup, testified to what she witnessed later in the day when the dead were removed: "The persons who were killed were shot with bullets. The Indians tried to take my Aunt Elizabeth, but she jumped off of the horse and then they shot her. She died about three weeks afterwards."[48]

All of the women were repeatedly raped and otherwise mistreated, but when the Indians finally left, they took only the two children of Aaron Bell as captives. Ester and Margaret Bell had been visiting at the Bogardus—Bell household when the Indians attacked. Ester Bell (Dunlap) later testified:

> David Bogardus was my uncle. I was visiting at his house on the day the Indians came, with my sister. My sister was six years old and I was eight. After they killed my uncle and raided the house, they took me and my little sister and kept us until the next day [August 13] and dropped us on the prairie. We wandered there. We slept out two nights with nothing to eat, until a searching party found us and took us to Fort Harper [Fort Harker] and turned us over to our father . . . . The Indians were Cheyennes and Arapahoes. They took us over on the Saline. There must have been 50 or 60 Indians in the

party, some squaws with them . . . . There were no squaws at first with them but we met some others who joined the party among which were some squaws.[49]

The story of the short captivity of the little Bell girls has endured some misinformed twists in the recorded history of this event. For example, at the time Ester was making her testimony for the property losses of her relatives, General P. H. Sheridan had published his memoirs, in two volumes. Ester might have read what Sheridan remembered. Writing of the Indians' pillage in Mitchell County, he wrote the Indians then "turned back toward the Saline, carrying away as prisoners two little girls named Bell, who have never been heard of since."[50] Sheridan goes on to note that it was the timely arrival of Captain Benteen that saved the rest of the settlers under attack.

Benteen remembered the Bell girls, adding yet another twist to the story. Having surprised the Indians not far from the Schermerhorn Ranch in Lincoln County, his company of troopers gave chase for several miles, until darkness ended the pursuit, crossing the Saline River two times in following the Dog Soldiers to the west. While this was going on, he came to the top of the river bank, where "I found two small white girls, captives, whom the Indians had not been given time to kill, and while awaiting the crossings of my squad I barely had time to impress on their minds to keep moving down the river and they would be all right."[51] J. W. Crandall was with Benteen during this chase of the Dog Soldiers. He remembered chasing the Indians until dark, but they crossed the river back and forth countless times. The next day a settler, seeing something moving on top of a hill, "approached carefully and found two little children the Indians had dropped. He took them to his home and sent word to their father who came after them."[52]

Pioneer reminiscences of the Bell girls seem to support Crandall. Elizabeth Barr wrote the Indians dropped the girls after being surprised by soldiers. They remained alone one night on the prairie before being found by a settler.[53] Roenigk wrote that Martin Hendrickson found the girls "huddled in the grass. They were very much afraid and so starved as to be like ravenous wolves."[54] Bernhardt reaffirms that the girls were found by Hendrickson and taken to his home, where they remained until their father, Aaron Bell, picked them up about a week later. But he adds this disclaimer: "The soldiers did not rescue those girls; in fact the soldiers did not see them, yet the good people over in Mitchell County have it that the soldiers did the rescuing."[55]

Ester's affidavit, noted earlier, should clear up any discrepancies. The girls were captured on August 12, released near the Saline the next day, and remained alone, hungry and scared for two more nights before being found by a search party. The girls were brought to Fort Harker, where their father recovered them. If Benteen did see the girls, his interest in chasing the Indians and not leaving one soldier to take care of them caused the girls to remain two more days alone, hungry, and frightened before being found. This abandonment by Benteen probably inspired pioneers to later claim the military was not involved in their rescue. But it is Ester's memory in her affidavit that should be used when reading these other accounts. Probably, a day or two was spent in the Hendrickson house before the girls were taken to Fort Harker.

After the Bell girls were taken captive, Braxton Ben Bell was found dead in his house, his nine-month-old daughter still held in his arms. He must have been holding her, trying to protect her when he was whipped and then shot dead. She was gravely injured. Little Ella "had its little head and neck hacked up by a lance or sharp instrument . . . and was afterwards taken from the arms of its dead father and recovered and was raised by Mrs. Sarah Farrow."[56] Mrs. Farrow stated that Ella "was horribly injured by the Indians. I took her after the death of her father and mother and raised her and she lived with me until after she was married."[57]

The Indians left the house about two o'clock that afternoon. Neighbors came to the home within a half an hour after the warriors left. Everything in the house was destroyed or missing.[58] A list of all personal items shows this home was better stocked with supplies and household goods than their neighbors. It is also instructive in learning what items comprised a common household in 1868, and their value.

6 new muslin quilts	$30.00
10 muslin sheets	5.00
4 goose feather pillows	8.00
10 muslin pillow cases	3.00
1 muslin straw tick	1.50
1 goose feather bed & tick	25.00
1 heavy feather tick, new	3.70
1 black alpaca dress, 1 gingham dress, and 4 calico dresses	17.00
2 suits canton flannel underwear	4.00
1 heavy all wool overcoat	10.00
1 shawl, all wool, nearly new	9.00
1 suit men's janes	10.00
4 men's cotton shirts	5.50
1 suit men's underwear	3.00
4 pair men's socks	2.00
2 pair ladies woolen hose	2.00
2 lace collars	.50
5 linen handkerchiefs	1.50
7 pr. woolen blankets nearly new	21.00
3 cotton and 2 linen towels	.60
1 linen table cloth	1.50
1 pr. calf shoes nearly new	2.50
1 gold breast-pin and ear drops, good condition	5.00
2 muslin and 2 flannel children's undershirts	2.50
1 white muslin skirt, 4 calico aprons, 2 pair cotton pants, all in good condition	3.00
1 heavy counterpane, good	10.00
1 bed-spread, nearly new	5.00
1 white wood table, 1 year's use	3.00
1 large trunk, fair condition	5.00
1 valise, used some time	2.00
1 rifle, in good shooting order, used some time	15.00

1 large 6 shot Army revolver, fair condition	15.00
coffee, worth	1.00
1 and a half lbs. tea	1.50
3 pounds Soda	.35
1 barrel of meal	5.00
1 barrel of flour	15.00
1 and a half barrels of buffalo meat	10.00
50 head of chickens	20.00
1 small set Queen's ware	2.00
1 china cup, saucer and pitcher	5.00
2 new butcher knives	1.50
1 note of $50 given April, 1868, by Umphrey & Ware drawing 10 per ct. interest, due Sept. 1868	50.00
1 large milk pitcher	1.50
1 silver castor	2.50
2 stewing pans, used years	1.00
2 iron skillets	1.00
1 large stone churn	1.50
1 waist belt	1.00
3 glass jars	1.00
2 gallons vinegar	1.00
salt and spices	1.50
6 lbs. tallow	.75
1 pair buck gloves	1.50
3 wooden chairs, fair	3.00
1 large lamp, used years	1.50
100 ft. rope, used well	2.00
1 heavy wagon sheet, old	2.50
4 new milk pans	2.00
1 large new feed basket	1.50
1 medium sized looking glass	1.50
1 box farming tools, such as files, hammers, hatchets, gimlets, whet-stone, bits and brace, auger, saw, used for some time	6.00
1 coffee mill	1.00
1 cooking stove, fair condition	15.00
1 cup board, wood, well used	3.00
Total	$346.30[59]

The loss of his beloved son Braxton so grieved the elder Benjamin Bell that he died not long after the raid. Mrs. Farrow simply stated that her father "died within a year after the killing of his son. He died of grief." Mary Bell lived about two more years before she too died.[60]

Shortly after the raid on the Bogardus—Bell home, Martha Springs's dugout was raided. She too lost everything, and was so extremely frightened by the terror, abuse, and rape she experienced that she died within three days after the raid. Her family reported her death was caused by fear.[61]

While these depredations and murders were going on in Mitchell County, residents in nearby Cloud County heard of what was happening. Andrew Thompson was living about eight miles west of present-day Concordia when he borrowed a mare from Cornelius Reed. Thompson wanted to scout down into Mitchell County to learn more about the reported Indian raids. It was a fatal mistake. As he got into Mitchell County, the Indians overtook him, killed him, and stole the mare.[62] Times were tough on Cornelius Reed. A few months after losing his mare, in the winter of 1868, Reed was bit by a rabid dog and died. He left his wife Christina and several children. Christina later married William Collins, who died a few years later. In 1866, Collins also had lost two sons, killed by Indians while on a buffalo hunt.[63]

The Indians remained in the area for two more days, where they continued to commit depredations in Mitchell and Cloud Counties. Meanwhile, residents fled for joint protection at present-day Asherville. A summary of some of these depredations shows the state of alarm that residents in the western settled edge of north central Kansas felt at this time. The sentiment was that the Indians were carrying on a prolonged war upon settlers. Many of the affected pioneers were again victimized two months later, when Dog Soldiers again raided the same settlements. One settler was victimized in both raids. John S. Smith lost a mule and five mares on August 13. After being fed, the Indians returned later that night and stole his stock. In October, Smith lost his father and brother in the second raid.[64]

Living about one hundred yards from the Bogardus—Bell house were three brothers named Randall. Earlier, Spencer Randall had left in a wagon to get supplies in Salina and was not at home when the Indians attacked the Bogardus—Bell families. When he returned on August 14, the Indians were still nearby. Not knowing of the earlier raids, he was surprised and killed near the present town of Glasco. Abraham Whitehurst witnessed the attack and saw the Indians "shoot and kill him." The Indians plundered the supplies Spencer had acquired, destroyed the wagon, cut the harnesses to the horses, and "rode the horses off."[65]

Spencer's brothers, Lyman and Marvin, were luckier. When the Indians arrived earlier in the Beloit area on August 12 the brothers were down the Solomon River east of their farm cutting hay. They saw their house on fire and then realized the Indians were raiding. They escaped to Asherville. When they returned later, they found their house and contents in ashes. What hadn't been destroyed and burned had been stolen. Their depredation claim totaled $783.90. Included among their losses were two new Spencer carbines and five hundred rounds of ammunition with a total value of $50.00. These had recently been issued to the Randalls by the state of Kansas, coincidentally for the purpose of protection from anticipated Indian raids. An additional loss of $74.25 was declared for books. Friends of the Randalls testified that they were college educated and had "a great many books."[66] One book, with Marvin Randall's name inscribed in the front, was later found where the Indians had afterward camped on Big Medicine Creek, thus showing that the Indians plundered and burned the contents of the Randall home.[67]

At eleven o'clock on the morning of August 12, another band of Indians raided the farm of William E. Dean. They cut the picket ropes holding one gray horse, one bay gelding, and one "bay mare mule." These all belonged to Abraham Marshall and were together valued at $400.00. Marshall's young daughter, Sarah, had taken the animals to Dean's house, where the Indians "came to where said horses were picketed, cut two of them loose, and took the other from the hands of the affiant [Sarah Marshall]."[68] The Marshall family would have a heavier price to pay on the prairie two days later.

The Dog Soldiers stayed in the area the night of August 12 and continued raiding the next day. The family of John Baertoche resided five miles southwest of present-day Glasco, near the western edge of Cloud County. John had just purchased a land claim from an older settler, having been in Cloud County only since April. He and his wife, Helena ("Lena"), had emigrated from Switzerland in 1864, coming to Kansas from Saint Louis, Missouri. They had also lived in Toledo, Ohio. Their family included two sons, Ernest and Louis. Louis was nine months old, and Ernest was turning three on August 15.

John decided on August 13 to celebrate Ernest's third birthday with buffalo meat, so he left that day on a buffalo hunt. Neighbor Henry Hewitt accompanied John, along with Hewitt's young son, Major. Henry had a large family consisting of three boys and six girls. They didn't get far before the Indians overtook them. Both men were killed. Young Major Hewitt survived with a pistol ball in the leg.[69] Hewitt's daughter, Rosa Hewitt–Burns, later told what happened after her father was killed: "He had just gone away from home that day that the property was taken. He was thrown among the rocks [brush and weeds] and the wolves ate his body and we picked up his bones afterwards."[70]

With both husbands now dead, each family was without protection. The Indians soon descended upon the households. Somehow Lena escaped detection, and with her two young boys, hid in the creek bank about one hundred yards from the house. She "ruptured" herself escaping, from which she never fully recovered. The Indians came around noon and remained at the house about an hour. From her hiding place, Lena could see the Indians "when they cut the [three] feather beds open and heard them shout as they scattered the feathers. They did not carry the ticks away but put them in the molasses. There were linen covers over the bed ticks. Those were used by the Indians to take the tea and coffee away on their ponies."[71]

Lena, terrorized and unwilling to leave her hiding place, stayed with her children for two nights in the creek bank. Finally, two settlers found them and took them to Minneapolis, Kansas, where neighbors had earlier fled for safety. She returned about a week later and recovered some clothes that were not taken. Everything else, with the exception of her stove and some little things, was either destroyed or stolen. All the hogs and chickens were killed. She had hid three hundred dollars in gold coin and currency behind the tea-box on the mantle. It was gone, along with a lot of German silverware.

Lena eventually moved to Fort Harker where she was employed for about two years by the fort sutler. After 1870, she hired a teamster to haul her possessions back to her home near the Solomon. After the teamster left, but before she could move everything into her old house, a man appeared and ordered her to get off the property. He said it was now his. She could not haul her things with her so she only took what she and her children could carry. She gradually made her way back to Salina where she remained another three years before going to El Mora, Colorado. There she met a Mr. Thompson, whom she married in 1877. However, he died nine months later and she was again widowed. By 1890, she was still unmarried. What started as an American dream was tragically cut to pieces in August 1868. She never did receive any compensation for her losses, though she was still trying to get compensation as late as 1890.[72]

Mrs. Nancy Hewitt didn't fare much better. Almost immediately after her husband was killed, the Indians descended upon her house. Though she survived the raid, she and her young son, Major, were wounded. It is unknown whether Major was wounded when his father was killed or when he later was with his mother. At any rate the Indians shot Nancy in the hip with an arrow. Her other children were able to run to a neighbor's home for protection. Nancy's home was then pillaged. Nothing is said regarding the depredations committed inside the house, and the records do not say if Nancy was raped and otherwise mistreated. But it is likely that she was. Since no compensation would be awarded for any mistreatment she might have incurred during her encounter with the Dog Soldiers, there was no need for her to report this fact in her affidavit for compensation. Following the raid, it was reported that her reputation was not good. Given the difficulty for an abused woman to integrate back into society, it seems likely she was gang raped.[73]

The August 13 raid also affected other settlers. Farther to the north, near present-day Concordia, Bazil Saunders was forced to abandon his lumber mill, which caused the fresh lumber he was milling to be ruined.[74] Back in Mitchell County, Thomas Allingham and James Duff lost two yoke of oxen, and everything in their sod house was stolen or destroyed. Aaron Humphrey was escaping to Asherville upon Nathaniel Brook's mare when the Indians saw him and gave chase. He hid in a creek but lost the mare to the Indians. Nathaniel Brooks lived farther down the Solomon on a farm adjoining the farm of James Morgan, who was soon to marry Anna Brewster. The Morgans would suffer greatly in the October raid.[75]

The better-known event in the August raid, which occurred on August 13, was the capture of Sarah Catherine White. She would remain in captivity until rescued by Brevet Major General George Armstrong Custer March 18, 1869.[76] About eight miles west of present-day Concordia and four miles southwest of the Republican River, along what was later named White's Creek, Ben White had settled a homestead in Cloud County. There were seven children in the family, Sarah being the oldest at eighteen. About ten o'clock in the morning, six Indians came upon the home. Ben White, along with his three sons, had earlier gone up to the Republican River to cut hay.

Seeing no men in the house, the warriors entered and immediately began to destroy everything they did not want to steal. Screaming and resisting, Sarah was forced upon a pony. During this commotion Mary, Ben's wife, escaped with her three younger daughters, hiding in the heavy brush along the creek several yards to the east of the house. After leaving with their captive, the raiding Indians took Sarah about five miles north, across Buffalo Creek, where they joined about fifteen other Indians. Here several Indians raped her, while the other warriors continued to hunt for unsuspecting settlers.[77] The Dog Soldiers descended on Benjamin White and his sons cutting hay. There they killed Ben, but the three boys escaped on two horses.[78] Pioneer Milton Spencer was also working a hay camp at this time, but on the north side of the Republican River. Ben White was on the south side when killed. Milton noted that he "saw him [Ben White] a short time after he was killed."[79]

The Indians remained in Cloud County that night and continued raiding the next day. Alfred Schull was forced to flee his house. Warriors then set fire to the prairie around his home, destroying the hay he had harvested. They entered his home "and destroyed much valuable property."[80] Farther south in Ottawa County, George Shafer was living with his family about three miles from James Morgan. On August 14 the Indians forced Shafer's family to flee and then burned the house down. Morgan testified later that a "short time afterwards, I went to his place and found that his house, a lot of lumber, doors, windows, household furniture, clothing, wheat, and mare and colt . . . had all been burned or carried away by said Indians."[81] Shafer's family was a large one, consisting of his wife and ten children. Together with the neighboring Hay family, they were able to escape in a wagon. Anna Hay, a daughter of the Hay family, said the Indians came in sight of the wagon and followed it until some soldiers appeared and the Indians withdrew. The Shafer house was a combination of log and sod. Everything was lost, including five feather beds. Thomas Stewart witnessed four Indians set Shafer's house afire. In addition to losing his house, Shafer also lost a mare and colt valued at $275.00.[82]

One of George Shafer's daughters, Olive, later wrote of her experiences during this raid.[83] She remembered her neighbors as the Fowlers and not the Hays. "Our dugout was destroyed and the addition burned. The lumber which father had hauled from Junction City and piled in a neat pile by the dugout was also burned."[84] Mr. Fowler [Hay] was working away from his place at the time of the raid. Mr. Shafer, knowing he couldn't place both families together in one wagon, sent Mrs. Fowler [Hay] along with his own older daughter, Mary, on two horses to where Fowler [Hay] was working, in order to warn him of the Indian attack. Meanwhile, Shafer collected the children of both families into the wagon. Mrs. Fowler [Hay] and Mary had barely gotten out of sight when the Indians spotted them and gave chase. "They pursued the women for perhaps five miles, where a small number of United States soldiers were encountered."[85] This timely arrival of the soldiers saved their lives.

The Marshall family in Mitchell County was hit both on August 12 and 14. James McConnell, who was married to Nancy J. Marshall, was breaking prairie on August 12 near present-day Beloit. He had three horses with him when the Indians suddenly appeared where he was working. He fought them off and at the same time kept his horses with him. He was trying to make it back to a camp of dugouts about a half a mile from Asherville on Asher Creek, about seven miles southeast of present-day Beloit. These dugouts had been constructed for mutual protection during the Indian raids. The dugouts were near the house of McConnell's in-laws, Abraham Marshall, Senior, and his wife, Julia. Next to this residence was the home of William Dean, who was married to Levina Marshall. Abraham and Julia also had two sons, both Union veterans of the Civil War. John, thirty-two at the time, lived with his parents and was unmarried. Abraham, Junior, was twenty-eight and lived nearby with his wife.

As McConnell fought his way back to the family settlement, he was wounded in his heel. He succeeded in getting to his destination, but along the way he came upon six-year-old Sarah Marshall, who had been asked by her father, Abraham, Senior, to watch two horses and a mule, which were at the house of her sister, Levina Dean. This house sat about one hundred yards east of the dugouts. There the Indians appeared about eleven o'clock in the morning, cut two of the horses loose, and took the mule from the hands of young Sarah.[86] Here the Dog Soldiers also captured one of McConnell's horses.

This was just the beginning of the tragedy that befell the Marshall family. Two days later, on August 14, the Indians returned and caught sons John and Abraham on horses just west of the fortified settlement, along Asher Creek, near the home of their parents. Little Sarah "was in camp about one mile away and was watching her brothers with a field glass; saw them fall off their horses and saw the Indians take and drive off said horses."[87] In addition to stealing the horses, the warriors also took four revolvers the men carried, and cut up their saddles and bridles.[88]

Hiram Bickerdyke, brother of famed charity worker Mother Mary Bickerdyke, arrived in the vicinity with the party accompanying Governor Samuel Crawford. Hiram vividly remembered the dead Marshal men:

> I assisted Dr. Crowley in covering the dead bodies of Marshall and Thompson [sic] with blankets to screen them from the view of the women and children of the Asher Creek Block House (near where Beloit Mitchell Co. stands) or the first R.R. station east of Beloit, as they lay only a short distance from the building (1/2 to 3/4 miles) where they had fallen; and no one had made the attempt to go near them until our relief party reached there.[89]

Abraham Marshall, Senior, lived until 1882, leaving his widow Julia to make do on her own. By 1891 she was destitute and wrote to the government, begging for payment on her losses during this 1868 raid. She earlier had been denied her claim due to technicalities in filing. In her appeal it is obvious she was bitter. "To the honorable Secretary of the Interior," she wrote,

> . . . now I want Unkle Sam for to not disapoint us any longer for we want our money for our property those savages ran off from us and shot my two boys in cold blood for to rot on the prairie like dogs and Unkle Sam was to blame for all those Indian out brakes for they went and gave them arms and ammunition for to come and kill us poor settlers when us settlers was trying to open up a farm stead that Unkle Sam gave to the soldiers at the close of the war. They had to be slain be cause Unkle Sam neglected her duty to protect us. How can they deny us from year to year we haft to pay taxes for to feed these reptiles of the forrist and it makes my blood boile for me to see how congress will turn these blames a side from one session to session and not have to settle. Sir my boys fought for to help save our union and had to be slashed up like dogs by the hands of these reptile snakes of the forrist and it sets pretty hard on me and be sides all the boys I had in the world for my support. Sir I am old and feble and cant part my husband are all so dead and I am left a lone beat hog or die now. I want pay for my horses that those red skins took from my boys . . . .[90]

Julia was denied payment a final time, due to the technicality of filing too late for reimbursement. With the death of her boys and the timely arrival of a company of the 7th Cavalry under the command of Captain F. W. Benteen, the Dog Soldiers finally withdrew from the settlements.

The federal government did order a commission to investigate the August and later October raids in these outlying Kansas settlements. This special Kansas Indian Raid Commission noted a total of forty-six families who filed for their losses, just for the raids in August.[91] Tom and Susanna Alderdice escaped unharmed in this devastating raid into Lincoln County and adjoining counties. Their thoughts, of course, must have been on the government and the protection of the settler and his family. What the settlers wanted was for the government to organize a military expedition to chastise the Indians responsible for causing such havoc in these new pioneer settlements.

Homestead site where Sarah White was taken captive August 13, 1868. She, along with Mrs. Morgan, remained captive for seven months until they were rescued by General G.A. Custer. Author's collection.

*Lieutenant Colonel George Armstrong Custer, holding his
Spencer carbine, Fort Dodge, Kansas, 1868.*
Courtesy of Little Bighorn Battlefield National Monument.

Beecher Island Battle

*No man among this band of heroes displayed a
higher order of courage and fortitude than the boy
Eli Zigler.*[1]

As a result of these devastating raids, a call to arms was
made along the affected settlements. General Sheridan soon
authorized fifty civilian scouts to serve under Brevet Colonel
George A. ("Sandy") Forsyth. Sheridan's orders, dated August
24, 1868 stated:

> The general commanding directs that you, without
> delay, employ fifty first-class hardy frontiersmen to
> be used as scouts against the hostile Indians, to be
> commanded by yourself, with Lieutenant Beecher,
> Third Infantry, as your subordinate. You can enter
> into such articles of agreement with these men as
> will compel obedience.[2]

At least twenty-three of Forsyth's men were from the Saline
valley; several signed up at the Schermerhorn Ranch in
Lincoln County.[3] One scout was Susanna's younger brother,
sixteen-year-old Eli Zeigler, the youngest of the scouts by
almost a year.[4] Tom Alderdice, Susanna's husband, also
enlisted. It is no wonder that so many men from the Saline and
Solomon valleys responded, given the devastation in the settlements that they just witnessed. These men became known
as Forsyth's scouts, but they had referred to themselves then
as the Solomon Avengers. Their enlistment was for four
months. For Susanna, this meant she was again going to have
her husband away when she gave birth to her second child
with Tom.

In what later went down in Indian wars history as one of the
most desperate fights ever against overwhelming odds,

Forsyth's scouts were hotly engaged by Cheyenne war leader Roman Nose and perhaps as many as 700 Dog Soldier Indians, including Tall Bull, from September 17-25, 1868. This fight occurred along the Arikaree River, a tributary of the Republican River, just past the Kansas border into northeast Colorado Territory. In three days of numerous Indian charges, Forsyth's scouts staved off every attempt to overwhelm them. They quickly made their stand on a small island on the mostly dry creek bed at the beginning of the fight. It would be nine long days before relief came. On the evening following the first day's fighting, two men volunteered to escape the island to get relief. Again on the third night two more men were able to escape from the island. Unknown to the besieged scouts, both groups of men succeeded in getting military aid. Finally, after nine days of siege, living on the putrid meat of the dead horses and mules killed at the beginning of the fight, and with no medical attention for the more than twenty-five wounded men, some desperately hurt, Forsyth's scouts were rescued.[5]

Lieutenant Frederick Beecher was among the five who died, and the battle was named after him. The Battle of Beecher Island entered American history as an amazing story of frontier heroics against overwhelming numbers of Indian warriors. The mighty Roman Nose was killed leading a charge against the scouts. In 1898, the site was rediscovered by some of the surviving scouts and to this day the Beecher Island Memorial Association celebrates with annual activities at the battle site on the weekend closest to the anniversary of the September fight. The large obelisk erected at the site nearly one hundred years ago bears the names of each of the scouts.[6] Coincidentally, Susanna's husband, Tom, is the first name and her brother, Eli Zeigler, is the last name noted on the monument.

Manifest Destiny has been a controversial concept used to explain the settling of the West. In an address given at the 1905 reunion of the surviving veterans of Beecher Island, Manifest Destiny was explained this way:

I have not – I cannot have any degree of sympathy with the maudlin sentimentality which possesses some, and which prates as of an evil, of the passing of the Indian and the buffalo. God's law of progress is upon our race, and His inflexible law dooms the people who will not advance. He never intended that this vast country, with all its unsurpassed possibilities, should remain a mere roaming place for the buffalo, or the hunting ground for a few savages. Our beautiful towns and cities, the fertile farms, our schools of which we are so justly proud, the thousands of our people who have made this desert bloom as the rose, declare to some extent the Divine purpose.[7]

Roenigk, in *Pioneer History of Kansas*, gave it a secular twist: "Right or wrong, nature takes its course and proves the contention of the scientists that the fittest will survive."[8] Regardless how this concept might be interpreted today, Susanna's family was right in the center of the process.

Eli Zeigler would later write an account of his experiences at the Beecher Island fight and siege. His account gives insight into how it developed. It is simply amazing to realize that Susanna's brother Eli at the time of the fight was the equivalent of a second semester sophomore in high school.[9]

After Forsyth's expedition was organized, the scouts went from Fort Harker to Fort Hays and finally to Fort Wallace in western Kansas, arriving on the evening of September 5. Lieutenant F. Beecher was a nephew to the well-known Reverend Henry Ward Beecher.[10] Each scout had been given a new Colt revolver and Spencer carbine, which could fire seven shots before being reloaded. The men also carried 140 Spencer rounds and 30 rounds for their revolver. Surgeon J. H. Mooers and Post Sergeant William McCall were also with the command. Four mules accompanied the expedition, carrying supplies and an additional four thousand rounds of ammunition.[11]

The morning after the column arrived at Fort Wallace they learned of an attack at Sheridan, a new town a few miles east of the fort. Two teamsters had been killed in this raid. Forsyth immediately ordered his command to Sheridan to follow the trail of the raiding Indians. The warriors, as was customary, had scattered, thus leaving no trail. The scouts, however, went toward the Republican River to the north, hoping they could pick up a trail. Luck was with them. Finding the trail, they followed it up the Arikaree River. As they followed it, the trail became bigger and fresher. Forsyth recalled that as it grew bigger a group of men approached him and asked about the wisdom of the small command encountering what would obviously be an overwhelming number of Indians. Forsyth replied that they had come to find Indians and fight them, he was taking no more risks than were his men, and the Indians they were following were some of the same Indians who had committed all the depredations in the Saline and Solomon valleys the month before. Forsyth: "The men quietly fell back, and as, fortunately, there were many old soldiers in the command, nothing more was said regarding the matter."[12] Soon the men went into camp on the afternoon of September 16.

According to Eli, about dusk that night the scouts observed "a signal light [flaming arrow] go up south of us and a little east and then we saw more go up in different directions, so we were pretty certain we would have more for breakfast than we had had for supper."[13] Eli and fellow Lincoln County resident George Culver, who would be killed during the battle, decided to sleep nearer their horses, close to the Arikaree's mostly dry streambed. The rest of the scouts had camped in a flat area some distance to the north of the Arikaree banks. The Indians attacked before dawn the next morning, which surprised Eli. The first war whoop quickly awoke him. "I gave a jump and said to Culver, 'They are here.' As we were all dressed and our revolvers and cartridge boxes all buckled on and our carbines [Spencer] lying by our sides we were ready for action as soon as we raised up."[14]

This first attack was nothing more than an attempt to stampede the horses. Only a few young and impatient warriors were involved but they did succeed in stealing a few of the horses. This impetuous act alerted the scouts to the presence of Indians and eliminated the element of a coordinated surprise attack. Had the warriors been able to make such an attack, none of Forsyth's small command would have likely survived. As it began to get light, the Indians had not yet mounted a coordinated attack. During this lull, the scouts began to prepare breakfast. Indians were seen in small groups, scattered in all directions. Occasionally a scout would fire toward an Indian, but the distance was too great to cause any damage. Eli remembered what happened next: "There soon was quite a stir. It seemed as if the whole valley kind of raised and then they commenced riding and whooping around there and in a movement they all started down the river."[15]

Some of the men began to take shelter on the north bank across from the river channel, and Eli started to join them, thinking that would be safer. As it turned out, those men were the most exposed. Colonel Forsyth stopped Eli from joining the men across the river, telling Eli to remain with him near the east side of the little island separating the two branches of the Arikaree, where Forsyth had directed the men to go when the fight first began. Eli obeyed his commander and shortly thereafter, while kneeling near Forsyth, he "heard something strike and the Colonel said 'I'm shot,' and put his hand on his leg and said 'They hit me in the leg.' He turned over a time or two and said, 'I am shot again'."[16] Forsyth recounted that first wound,

> Scarcely had I lain down when I received a shot in the fore part of the right thigh, the bullet ranging upward; and notwithstanding it remained imbedded in the flesh, it was by far the most painful wound I have ever received. For a moment I could not speak, so intense was the agony.[17]

With the help of some other scouts, Forsyth was quickly removed to the center of the island. Soon the men were alternately shooting at the Indians or digging small holes for protection. As Eli dug his hole, he heard Lincoln County neighbor,

Henry Tucker, announce that he had been shot in the arm and needed help in stopping the bleeding. Neighbor John Haley was helping Tucker when Haley was also hit. Eli then told Tucker to crawl over to his hole and he would help him. Tucker crawled over and just about when Eli finished tying up Tucker's arm, an arrow glanced off of his leg and imbedded itself into Tucker's leg. "As our legs were close together, I felt the arrow strike me on the upper part of my right leg. Looking down, I saw the arrow had passed down and through Tucker's left leg above the knee."[18]

The metal point of the arrow had protruded to the other side of Tucker's leg. Eli attempted to pull the arrow back through the leg, but it would not pull. The effort to withdraw it caused Tucker immense pain. Despite his young age, Eli showed his quick thinking. "I then took hold of the point of the arrow-head that was sticking through his leg, and with the other hand hit the feather end of the arrow and drove it through."[19] Tucker would survive this battle and would still be nursing his arm wound the following May when the Indians returned to Lincoln County in the raid that would so devastate the life of Eli's older sister, Susanna.

After helping Tucker, then giving Tucker the hole he had dug for himself, Eli again thought he would join his friends across the dry riverbed. This time Jack Donovan stopped him, inviting Eli instead to dig Donovan's hole larger so that both could fit in it together. Eli wrote: "I have always been glad that I stopped there because I believe that Jack was as good and brave a boy as we had on the island. He was very cheerful and cool and certainly did good work, but made me do most of the digging."[20]

Donovan and Eli had dug their rifle pit at the northwest corner of the island. It afforded them an ideal location to defend themselves against the ensuing attacks. The Dog Soldiers continued to charge at the island for most of the day. It was a hot day and Eli had no water to quench his thirst. The horses were all killed by noon, and when the last one went down, Eli heard a man among the Indians shout, "There goes their last damned horse."[21] This alerted the beleaguered scouts to the belief that white men were included among the Indians.

By dark the Indians withdrew, allowing the men to prepare their dinner, care for the gravely wounded, and better fortify their positions for more attacks the next day. Trenches were dug connecting the individual pits. Water was found by digging some of the trenches deeper. The wounded were all put together, but Surgeon Mooers had earlier been mortally wounded, leaving the care of the hurt to the inexperienced scouts. Lieutenant Beecher was among the dead, as was Roman Nose. The only food for the scouts was meat cut from the dead animals. This meat, soon quite putrid, became the scouts' sustenance for nine days. Eli: "We first cared for the wounded the best we could and then prepared our supper. We had plenty of it, such as it was. We built small fires in the rifle pits and then went to the horses and cut off small pieces and roasted them; we had to eat it without salt."[22]

According to Eli, no one slept that first night. Late in the night, young Jack Stillwell and the older Pierre Trudeau agreed to try to slip out from the island and seek help at Fort Wallace, nearly one hundred miles distant. Eli remembered Jack as a great imitator of an Indian. Fixing their feet in rags and pieces of blankets, "so that if the Indians saw their tracks next day they would think it some of their own party," the men left in the middle of the night in a bold and daring attempt to get to Fort Wallace.[23] A. J. Pliley and Jack Donovan left on the third night, and beat Stillwell and Trudeau in bringing relief to the suffering scouts on September 25. They made it to the Cheyenne Wells stage stop, west of Fort Wallace and closer to where the scouts were hunkered down. At Cheyenne Wells was a column of buffalo soldiers under the command of Brevet Colonel Louis Carpenter. Stillwell and Trudeau, meanwhile, made it all the way to Fort Wallace. Both pairs of scouts brought relief to Beecher Island, arriving hours apart on the same day.

41

After Stillwell and Trudeau left the island, Eli and the other men expanded the rifle pits. By morning, "we got all connected together and enlarged our hospital, as we called it, where we kept the worst wounded."[24] The warriors again attacked just before daylight on the morning of the second day. "It seemed to me that the Indians were more determined than ever to get us out, as they charged in from every direction and it seemed to take more than one volley to stop them."[25] Indian women and children were on the hills to the north just out of rifle range, where they watched the battle, screaming and yelling encouragement to the warriors. Indian chiefs and medicine men also shouted encouragements as charge after charge was made upon the island. When it became necessary for a scout to raise his head to see to fire back, Indian "sharpshooters in the grass would pour in a deadly fire upon us, but we always succeeded in turning them around. . . ."[26]

Before long the Indians realized the scouts were well fortified. They then tried the trick of the white flag, "but most of us were too old to be scalped alive that way and we showed no signs of a white flag so that did not last long with them."[27]

The fighting continued strong until sundown when the warriors again retreated for the night. The scouts cut more meat from the dead animals. Fearing that the scouts who left the first night might not have succeeded in getting away, Jack Donovan and another scout tried to leave the second night. They returned after a few hours, unable to get past the Indians. The rest of the evening was uneventful. As Eli recalled, "We had not had any sleep and very little rest for the last two days so we took turns at sleeping and watching, so we fared better that night than we had the night before."[28]

The next morning commenced the third day of fighting, and as Eli remembered it, the Indians "continued their fight all day, but not as strong, I did not think, as it had been the other two days. The fight continued until sundown and again they fell back as they had the previous days and quit fighting."[29] On this night Pliley and Donovan made their escape from the

E. S. Godfrey, F. M. Gibson, and Edward Law, 1867. Lt. Law was in charge of Company G, 7th Cavalry when they arrived at the Saline River settlement, just as the Dog Soldiers were ending their deadly raid.
Courtesy of Little Bighorn Battlefield National Monument

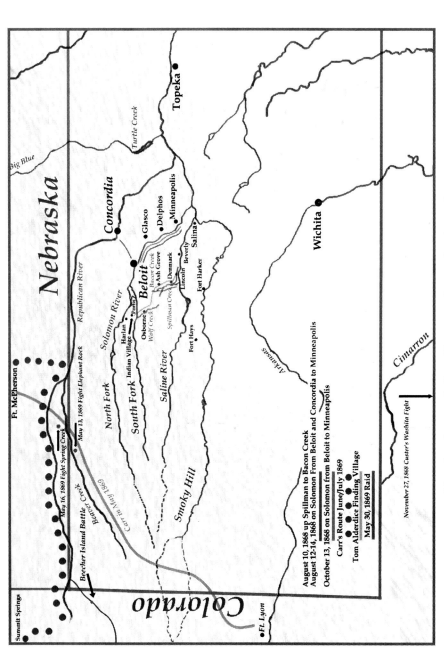

Map by James Jeffrey Broome, the author's nephew.

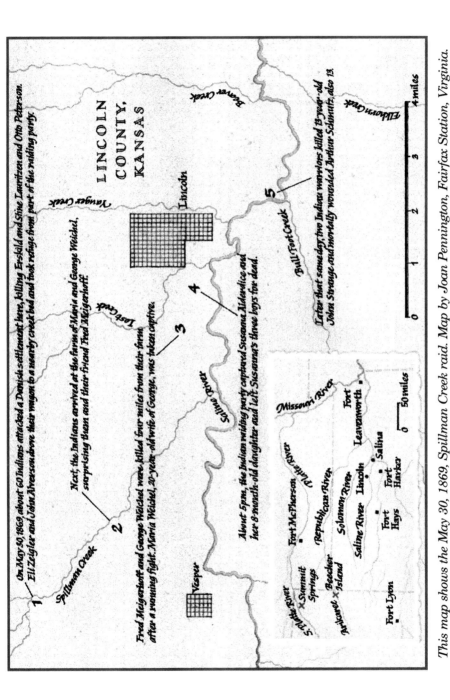

This map shows the May 30, 1869, Spillman Creek raid. Map by Joan Pennington, Fairfax Station, Virginia.

LINCOLN COUNTY, KANSAS

1 — On May 30, 1869, about 60 Indians attacked a Danish settlement here, killing Erskild and Stine Lauritzen and Otto Peterson. Eli Ziegler and John Alverson drove their wagon to a nearby creek bed and took refuge from part of the raiding party.

2 — Next, the Indians arrived at the farm of Maria and George Weichel, surprising them and their friend Fred Meigerhoff.

3 — Fred Meigerhoff and George Weichel were killed four miles from their farm after a running fight. Maria Weichel, 20-year-old wife of George, was taken captive.

4 — About 5 p.m., the Indian raiding party captured Susanna Alderdice and her 8-month-old daughter and left Susanna's three boys for dead.

5 — Later that same day, two Indian warriors killed 13-year-old John Strange and mortally wounded Arthur Schmutz, also 13.

Spillman Creek

Lost Creek

Yauger Creek

Beaver Creek

Lincoln

Saline River

Vesper

Bull Fort Creek

Elkhorn Creek

0   1   2   3   4 miles

Missouri River

S. Platte River

X Summit Springs

Arkansas X Beecher Island

Fort McPherson

Republican River

Solomon River

Saline River

Lincoln

Salina

Fort Harker

Fort Hays

Fort Leavenworth

Fort Lyon

Fort

0   50 miles

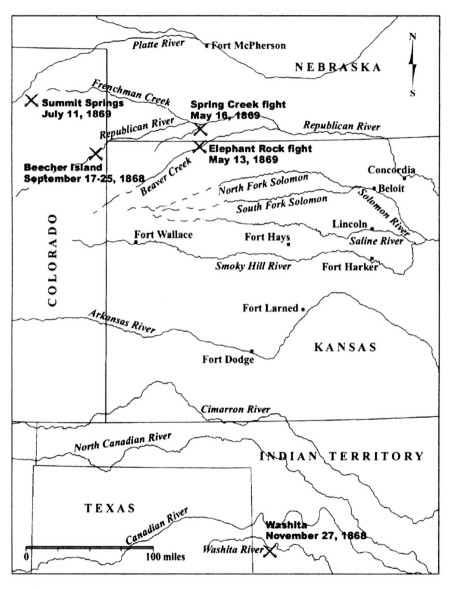

Susanna Alderdice was captured one mile west of present-day Lincoln, Kansas. Map by Joan Pennington, Fairfax Station, Virginia.

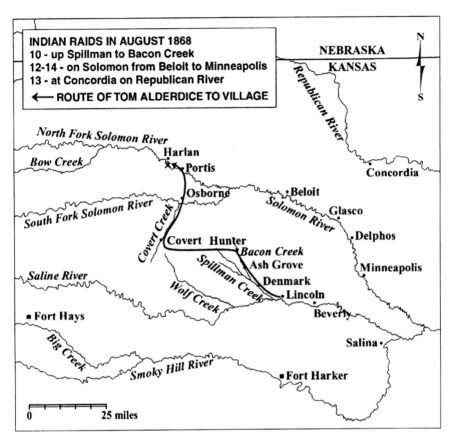

This map shows the area of the Indian raids in 1868 - 1869. Map by Joan Pennington, Fairfax Station, Virginia.

General Eugene A. Carr (colonel in picture), seated wearing a campaign hat. John J. "Black Jack" Pershing is standing in the back row, ninth from the right. Courtesy of Quito Osuna Carr, M.D., Albuquerque, New Mexico.

Buffalo Bill leads the charge at the battle of Summit Springs.
Sketch courtesy of Buffalo Bill Historical Center, Cody, Wyoming.

Portrait of Buffalo Bill in 7th Cavalry uniform, c. 1888. Early in Cody's career, General P. H. Sheridan offered him a commission in the 5th Cavalry.
Courtesy of Buffalo Bill Historical Center, Cody, Wyoming.

Buffalo Bill and three unidentified men.
Only known photo of Lucretia Borgia, Cody's famous rifle, c. 1869.
This photo of Cody is how he appeared when serving under General
E. A. Carr during the Republican River Expedition.
Courtesy of Buffalo Bill Historical Center, Cody, Wyoming.

Luther North in officer's uniform, c. 1860s. North was the
officer who found Susanna's body at Summit Springs.
This recently discovered photo of North is courtesy of Jean,
West and North McArthur, Salina, Kansas,

beleaguered scouts. Fighting the fourth day, September 20, was nothing more than skirmishing and by night the Indians had withdrawn from the fight. On the fifth morning Eli observed that "the Indian camp fires were all out, everything was quiet, and no Indians were in sight."[30]

The scouts were in a real predicament. The fight was over but they had no means to do anything but remain where they were. All their horses and mules were dead, they had no supplies, nothing to eat but the rotten meat from the dead animals, and no ability to transport the wounded to safety. They could only wait and hope that one of the escaping parties of scouts had been able to summon aid. Eli remembered the sixth day as quiet, "except the howling of the wolves and our horse meat was so rotten and alive with maggots we thought we would try to find some game or something to live on so we rustled out a little and found nothing much but prickly pears."[31]

Things remained uneventful until on the ninth morning when Eli strolled out of camp with Fletcher Vilott. While the two walked together, Fletcher told Eli of a dream he had the night before. He dreamt that this day they were either all going to be killed or else rescued by soldiers. As they were talking about such prospects, Eli observed movement in the hills to the south. It was obviously a large party of men but they were unable to recognize whether they were Indians or a rescue party. "We could not make it out so we hurried back to camp to make ready in case it was Indians."[32]

After entering the camp, Eli remembered that two other scouts earlier had ventured in the direction of the approaching column of men. Eli left camp to try to warn them. "In a short while I saw a man at full gallop. When he got a little closer to my great surprise it was my old friend Jack Peate."[33] Jack had been responsible for organizing the twenty-three men from the Saline valley as Forsyth Scouts, but had missed being with the men at Beecher Island when he returned to Lincoln County from Fort Harker to get additional men to join the command.

When he brought back the additional men, Forsyth's command had already departed. Peate and the other men followed them but were delayed at Fort Hays and missed rejoining the scouts when the command left Fort Wallace shortly before the Beecher Island battle. Those additional scouts were with Peate now with the relief column. They were a part of Colonel Carpenter's 10th Cavalry, the Buffalo Soldiers.

Eli remembered Peate giving him a "little piece of bacon about an inch thick and about two inches long. . . . I suppose you people think you have had something good to eat in your life, but you never had anything as good as that was."[34] With relief at hand, the wounded were finally able to be properly cared. "There were plenty of doctors and they encouraged them and went right to work dressing their wounds."[35] The whole command was moved away from the island to high ground on the south, where they remained for several days before returning to Fort Wallace. "During that time Jack Stillwell led in his command, so that made quite a large command and when the wounded were strong enough we started for the fort."[36] Thus ended the fight and siege at Beecher Island.

October 1868 Raids

I hunted around and found that father had crawled into an out house that had been built for a chicken coop. He had been shot through the right lung and they had thrust a lance and it had gone through his mouth and come out on the left side of his neck. He gave me to understand that he wanted some water . . . he lived about an hour.[1]

Susanna's husband, Tom, was a participant in the Beecher Island fight, but no account of his experiences there is known to exist, nor did anyone else mention anything particular about his involvement during the fight and siege. Though Beecher Island was over, the scouts were not finished with their four-month enlistment. Most of those uninjured at Beecher Island were soon placed under the command of Lieutenant Silas Pepoon of the 10th Cavalry. Shortly thereafter, they were part of a larger military escort that included seven companies of the 5th Cavalry under Brevet Major General Eugene A. Carr. With Carr, these scouts would be engaged in two more Indian fights.

They fought nearly 400 Indians in Kansas along Beaver Creek on October 18, the same band of Indians who had fought at Beecher Island. Nine warriors were killed and an unknown number wounded.[2] One of the wounded warriors was captured and told General Carr where the Indian village was camped on Chalk Bluffs.[3] This led to another skirmish on October 25 at Chalk Bluffs. In this fight, Pepoon's scouts were ordered to the front. Warriors were trying to delay Carr's advance so their families could escape with their lodges. Much abandoned property was captured. Ten braves and seventy ponies were killed. The soldiers suffered several wounded, but no dead.[4] Carr would later remember Pepoon's scouts at this fight. "If he [Tom

Alderdice] was with the Scouts who were with Forsyth when he was surprised on Frenchmen's Fork (or rather on the Arickaree) in '68 he was most likely with me: as I had those scouts in my campaign & fight at Chalk Bluffs October 25th, 1868."[5] Of the thirty uninjured scouts at Beecher Island, only seventeen continued on with Lieutenant Pepoon. Both Eli Zeigler and Tom Alderdice apparently were not with Pepoon and thus missed these fights with Carr.[6] Who were the Dog Soldiers Carr fought? They were Cheyenne under Tall Bull and Ogallala-Sioux under Whistler.[7]

Beecher Island and these subsequent fights, however, did little to stop or even slow the Indian raids against outlying pioneer settlements along the Solomon and Saline Rivers. Within a month after Beecher Island, frontier families along the Solomon River in Mitchell, Cloud, and Ottawa Counties were hit again just as hard, if not harder, than in August.[8] In addition to numerous murders of settlers, recently wed Anna Morgan was captured. Her husband, James, was able to escape, though gravely wounded in his hip.[9] About a month after her capture, she would join Sarah White in Cheyenne Chief Stone Forehead's village.

The first sighting of raiding Indians occurred on October 5, coincidentally, Willis Daily-Alderdice's fourth birthday. Robert Smith, as with most of the men who remained near their home-steads after the August raids, was in camp on West Asher Creek about six miles southeast of present-day Beloit. He was serving with a company of militia under the command of J. A. Potts, which had been formed September 20 to protect the set-tlements. About eight or nine o'clock in the morning, aided by a heavy fog, a band of Indians suddenly descended upon some horses grazing about seventy-five yards from this militia camp. Screaming their war whoops, the Indians swiftly charged through the horse herd, stealing several horses, Smith's among them.[10]

This was just the beginning. Like the extended Bogardus–Bell and Marshall families so severely affected in the August raids, the Smith family was also an extended family. They, too, would feel tragic losses in the October raids.

This family included the elder father, Alexander Smith, Senior, and his wife. There were five male Smith children, all grown men, two of whom were married. Robert Smith was married, but had no children. John Smith was unmarried and lived with Samuel Boyd about five-and-a-half miles west of Beloit along Brown's Creek, near where the father, Alexander Smith, Senior, lived. During the August raid John had helped bury John Baertoche and Henry Hewitt. While away on that task, the Indians plundered his and Boyd's home, destroying everything in it.[11] James Smith was unmarried and apparently lived with his parents. He suffered from some disability and was called a cripple. Richard Smith lived near his parents and was in the cattle business with his brother, John. Alexander Smith, Junior, lived with his wife, Mary, and two young daughters, Mary and Maggie. His home was nestled along the Solomon River nearly twenty miles southeast, in Ottawa County, about four miles southwest of present-day Delphos, Kansas.

After the August raids, the Smith families near present-day Beloit thought it would be safer to live at the home of Alexander, Junior, down in Ottawa County. Robert, Richard, and John joined the militia and camped along Asher Creek about half way between the Beloit and the Delphos home sites. That October, Alexander Smith Junior's home included the elder Alexander Smith and wife, Robert's wife, his brother James, plus his own wife and two children. On October 13, both father and son were working about two hundred yards from the house, building a fire line in order to protect the place in case the Indians again raided and kindled prairie fires, as had been done the previous August.

Suddenly, about eleven o'clock in the morning, seventeen warriors dashed in front of the house and began firing on the two men working in the field. Mary saw both men as they were shot and fell from their horses. While the Indians captured the horses, the three women and two children quickly fled from their home toward the river, which to their luck was in the opposite direction of the threatening Indians. They were able to hide in the brush and from there see the killers enter their home. Everything inside was either taken or destroyed. As Mary remembered, "we saw them destroy our household goods, empty the feather beds, cut up the harness and lead off my two horses."[12]

During this time, brother John Smith was on a scout with the state militia and had gone down the valley to check on his family. John later remembered:

> I took two of my friends with me and as I was going down I met a band of about 17 Indians and they had Mrs. Morgan with them (a white woman whom they had captured) and a lot of loose stock. I was on the opposite side of the river from them. They saw us and five of them started toward the river as though they were going to cross and I fired on them and they turned back. When I [finally] got down to the home ranch there was no one to be found. It was dark. I found the ranch vacant and no one there and things all mixed up. They had taken the feather beds, cut the ticks and emptied the feathers out, took the flour that was in the house, cut the sacks open and emptied the flour into the dug out. And took the sorgum [sic], I think that there was two or three barrels, and emptied them among the flour and feathers and made a general mix up. They took all of the blankets and bed clothing that was around the house. My sister-in-law, Mary E. Smith [whom Robert would marry two years later], had a trunk which contained the clothing of herself and children and that had been broken open and the contents taken away. The sugar and coffee that was in the house when I left there two days before that was gone and I suppose they took that with them. I called and hunted around the place to see if there was anyone around there. I got no reply from anyone. I went down the river about a mile and a half or two miles to another ranch to see whether any of the folks had passed that way or gone down there. They told me they had seen none of the folks

and I went back to the ranch. I got there just before daylight [Oct. 14]. I hunted around and found father had crawled into an out house that had been built for a chicken coop. He had been shot through the right lung and they had thrust a lance and it had gone through his mouth and come out on the left side of his neck. He gave me to understand that he wanted some water. We took him into the house. The women folks with the children [Mary and Maggie, both whom later married and carried the name of Mrs. Rowe and lived in Solomon Rapids] who were in the thicket on the other side of the river, answered my call. They came across the river and between us we got father into the house. After we got him into the house he lived about an hour. It was two days after that before we discovered my brother, Alex, in the river. It seemed he had attempted to cross the river at that place and had failed. He had got his arm hooked around a limb that was sticking out of the water and sand and that was how we came to discover him. We saw his arm over the limb. He had been shot in the small of the back. The bullet did not come through.[13]

Milton Kellor would place himself in these scenes of destruction. He was hauling hay for John Virtue when the Indians came upon them. Surprising the men at work, the screaming warriors quickly charged them. The frightened men immediately darted in the direction of Alexander Smith's home, where they hoped to find protection. The Dog Soldiers followed as the men fled toward Smith's home. As the fleeing settlers approached the home, the warriors spotted the Smiths working their fire line not far from the home. The raiders then "turned their attention to them and commenced firing on them, he [Kellor] saw the Smiths fall and then concluded he could not save his horses and took the women and escaped in the timber . . . ."[14]

About this time, seven miles east of present-day Beloit in Mitchell County, another party of Indians captured two teams of horses from Peter Hansen and a Mr. Nelson. Several men found shelter in Hansen's dugout where they held the Indians

49

off. The raiders fired through the windows but missed everyone inside.[15] Thirteen miles farther east in Cloud County, William McDowell was driving a wagon, filled with buffalo hides, to Junction City. The Indians attacked him. He escaped but lost his team of mules and the contents of his wagon, including all his provisions.[16]

It was obvious the Indians involved in these multiple attacks had divided into several groups, usually in bands of five or more.[17] Many settlers were attacked near the Solomon River between the present-day towns of Glasco and Delphos. One pioneer, David Mortimer, escaped, but everything in his house was destroyed.[18] West of Glasco, near the military camp, brothers William and Edward Abbot were attacked in their home. They, too, escaped to the camp. When the militia arrived at the Abbot home they discovered that the Indians had "cut the bed tick and pillows open and scattered the straw and feathers on the floor and took the ticks and pillow slips, the blankets and clothing with them." The warriors also scattered "the flour, meal, molasses, eggs and other provisions on the floor all mixed with the straw and feathers, leaving nothing in said cabin but what was destroyed."[19] The Abbot losses included

cash	$10.00
bedding	10.00
clothing	15.00
cooking utensils	3.00
provisions	8.00
Masonic pin	2.50
one window	1.50
ammunition	.50
looking glass	.75[20]

Nearby a party of five Dog Soldiers surprised three children of Thomas Misell, who were living in a dugout about one and three-quarters of a mile northeast of Glasco. Tom was working in nearby Solomon City, trying to provide for his children, the oldest of whom was only thirteen. Apparently they had earlier lost their mother, as she is not mentioned as living with them.

As the Indians descended upon the crude dugout, the children spotted them, knew their danger, and immediately fled. Tom's seven-year-old son, Benjamin, and the two older boys ran toward neighbor Feasley's house on the adjoining farm. As he scrambled for safety, young Benjamin's fright must have been exacerbated upon hearing the screaming Indians as they raced closer toward him on their ponies. It would be the last sounds this little boy would hear. The Indians shot him as he was running and he fell to the ground, dead.[21] The two older children made it to the Feasley house. Once inside, they were no longer molested. Tom later recovered his surviving boys at Minneapolis, Kansas, where everyone in the vicinity fled.

Tom's claim for losses, after the Dog Soldiers took or destroyed everything in his small dugout, reveals how meager were the household possessions of many first-generation homesteaders in western Kansas. His total claim amounted to only $52.55. This included bed and bed clothing for $15.00, 260 lbs. of meal for $11.05, furniture for $14.00, and 25 chickens valued at $12.50. The agent for the Bureau of Indian Affairs investigating the claim wrote that Tom

> . . . had one bed consisting of a straw tick blankets and comforts worth $25 or $30. He had no stove but used camp cooking utensils. He had a Dutch oven some frying pans coffee pots and kettles and a few dishes knives forks and spoons and tin cups worth $10. The furniture did not amount to much simply stools and benches worth $5.[22]

John Andrews was killed within thirty minutes after young Benjamin Misell. The manner of his scalping helped to identify some of the Indians responsible for the October raid. James Hendershot testified that he lived in the vicinity of Thomas Misell and visited the destroyed dugout after the Indians left. He also saw the body of John Andrews. He knew the raiding Indians included Sioux "from the manner in which they scalped John Andrews, they took a long scalp while the Cheyennes took generally an oval scalp."[23]

The best-known incident connected with this raid, however, was the capture of recently wed Anna Belle Brewster Morgan. When the August raids occurred, Anna was twenty-three years old and living with her brother, Daniel. Said to be remarkably beautiful, Anna was born December 10, 1844, in New Brunswick, New Jersey. Her father was John W. Brewster. Her mother's maiden name was Prudence Nau. Anna's childhood was not a good one. Her father died four months before she was born and she was raised in poverty. The youngest of five children, two of whom did not survive childhood, Anna was making her own way by 1857. In 1861 her brother, Daniel, volunteered for the Civil War, joining the 1st Volunteers of New Jersey. Her other brother joined the 7th New Jersey Regiment in 1862 and died the next year at Chancellorsville.[24] Shortly after the war, Anna's mother "lost her mind and died in a hospital for insane patients."[25] After she died, Daniel and Anna moved to Illinois. In 1867, Daniel left Illinois and homesteaded near present-day Delphos, Kansas. Anna soon followed, "to keep house for him."[26] When the August raids occurred, Anna had a harrowing experience and was almost captured, but escaped safely to Minneapolis. She was no doubt extremely grateful to avoid being captured in August. But now mother luck eluded her.

She met her future husband, James S. Morgan, shortly after she had moved in with her brother. After a brief courtship, they were married on September 13, 1868, exactly one month after the August raid when Sarah White was captured.[27] Now, one month after her marriage, she was captured. Shortly before snaring Mrs. Morgan, the warriors killed Peter Karnes nearby. Karnes was out working in his field when he was surprised and killed.[28]

James Morgan was twenty-nine in 1868, and had come to the Solomon valley in 1866, after serving for the Union during the Civil War. Nestled along the Solomon River, his homestead was about two miles south of present-day Delphos. On the morning of October 13, James was working on the farm of his neighbor, David Mortimer. About eight o'clock the Indians surprised him. James:

> I was gathering corn upon a farm about two miles from the farm of Milton Kellor . . . when a band of several Indians suddenly came upon me and shot at me several times hitting me once in the hip. They then took my horses with which I was gathering corn and started down upon the river in the direction of Milton Keller's. After being shot I crawled to a Mr. (Daniel) Yockey's near by then Mr. Hillhouse another neighbor who was at Mr. Yockey's took me with others in his wagon and we went to Milton Keller's . . . and went with us in to Minneapolis for protection.[29]

James' hip wound was nearly fatal. He "was for several months so helpless from his wounds as to be scarcely able to hold his head up . . . ."[30] James testified how Anna was captured. When the Indians went to take his horses from his wagon after he was shot, "one of the horses made its escape and went to his house. His wife supposing he had run away got on the horse and took a revolver with her and started to where he [James] was working and was met by said Indians and captured."[31] James lost his army Colt revolver, two horses, his harness, and his wagon was damaged. Additionally, the Indians found his house and took several blankets. When Mrs. Morgan first saw the Indians, she kicked her heels into the horse in an attempt to escape, but the Indians soon caught up with her. A warrior struck her with a war club, which caused her to fall off the horse.[32] Anna later recounted her capture:

> About nine or ten o'clock a.m., one of the horses he [James] had driven came running home with the harness on. I knew there had been an accident. Stripping the harness from the horse, I mounted him, and rode as fast as the horse could go in the direction my husband had taken [two miles]. I followed the river . . . . In going around a bend of the river I ran right into a band of Indians, not fifty yards from me. I turned and started back, but my

horse was tired. On looking back I saw one of them right behind me. Then a blow,—a fall,—and nothing more. When I recovered I was on one of the Indian ponies with an Indian on each side of me.[33]

In a letter by Morgan's attorney years later, in which James was still seeking compensation for his losses, the attorney claimed the Indians burned his house, stable and wagon.[34] His attorney was none other than former Kansas Governor Samuel J. Crawford, who, after these October raids, had resigned his office to lead the newly formed 19th Regiment of Kansas Volunteer Cavalry. He would have been on hand with General G. A. Custer later in March 1869, when Mrs. Morgan and Sarah White were rescued in the Texas Panhandle along the Sweetwater Creek, except he had resigned his commission February 14, one month before the rescue.[35]

James later learned that the Indians who wounded him, captured his wife and stole or destroyed his property were Sioux Indians, not Cheyenne. Wrote James:

> The reason I believe the Indians who committed the depredations at this time were Sioux is, that my wife Anna B. Morgan was captured by these same Indians at that time and subsequently upon her return she said they were Sioux. My wife was rescued by Genl Custer in the following spring.[36]

This supports the claim noted earlier that said John Andrews was scalped in the manner of the Sioux.

Lieutenant General W. T. Sherman, in his report to the Fortieth Congress in the fall of 1867, wrote that "General Hancock learned that certain Ogalalla [sic] and Brule Sioux had come down from the far north, and were in treaty with the Cheyennes and Dog-Soldiers, arranging for general hostilities and a concert of action on their part."[37] Two Ogallala Sioux, leaders of small bands known to have been in Kansas during this time, included Whistler and Pawnee Killer. They were later fortunate when they left Tall Bull's camp at Summit Springs in 1869, one day before General E. A. Carr attacked that village. Pawnee Killer was also linked with the killing of Lieutenant Lyman S. Kidder and his detail of eleven men in western Kansas in 1867.[38] Captain David C. Poole gave a graphic description of Pawnee Killer shortly after the Summit Springs battle, when Pawnee Killer appeared on a northern Sioux reservation "for rest and recreation for the winter:"

> So far as villainy can be depicted in the human countenance, it was to be found in Pawnee Killer's. His face had a lean and hungry look; he was long and lank, and reminded one of a prowling wolf. He seldom smiled while talking with his companions, but stalked about with his blanket closely wrapped around him, as if expecting at each turn to pounce upon an enemy, or be himself attacked. He had a murderous looking set of followers.[39]

Anna Morgan was captured by Sioux and taken up north to Sioux country, but was later traded to Cheyenne and ended up in the camp of Southern Cheyenne Chief Stone Forehead, where she joined Sarah White. Trading white captives was a common practice at this time.[40] This is also evidence that the intermingling between southern and northern tribes during summer months was common. At any rate, James Morgan understood his wife was captured by Sioux and taken north immediately after her capture. A reporter with the *Kansas City Star* interviewed Sarah White, who later married E. O. Brooks, late in life. There she stated that Mrs. Morgan joined her band of Cheyenne three months after Sarah's capture, having been traded for some ponies.[41] If Sarah's memory was correct, Mrs. Morgan was traded by Sioux one month after her capture.

Lieutenant Colonel George Armstrong Custer, 1868.
Courtesy of Little Bighorn Battlefield National Monument.

The Washita Battle and Custer's Rescue

Sherman to Sheridan:
I can well understand that you feel the injustice of attacks in newspapers against General Custer, yourself and myself . . . . I feel certain that the great mass of our people sustain us fully, but we cannot silence those who have an interest in keeping up an eternal war on the plains, for "none are so blind as those who will not see." Those who profess to be peace men are really they who work to keep up an eternal state of war whilst we who profess war have most interest in producing a state of peace.[1]

Both Colonel George Forsyth and General Eugene Carr failed to subdue the Indians, and the Dog Soldiers continued raiding into the fall. General Sheridan now changed his tactics and began an aggressive, radical winter campaign. Brevet Major General George Armstrong Custer, now a lieutenant colonel after the Civil War, but, as with all officers who received brevet ranks earlier, was still addressed by his brevet rank, assumed command of eleven companies of the 7th Cavalry. General Custer had just ended a year's suspension, having been court-martialed and suspended from service for a series of charges incurred during the failed Hancock Expedition. This 1867 summer expedition in Kansas had been a sorry military attempt to subdue the Indians. It failed in every way conceivable.[2] Further, it contributed to Indian animosity fueling the raids of 1868 and 1869.

General Sheridan, commander of the Department of the Missouri, which included the state of Kansas, fully expected the Indians to stop their hostile activity, retreat south of Kansas "when the inclemency of the weather would give them ample security, and they could live on their plunder, glory in the scalps taken and the debasement of the poor unfortunate women whom they held as prisoners."[3] He authorized this winter campaign October 9, 1868. A small column under General George W. Getty was sent from Fort Bascom, New Mexico, to enter Indian Territory to the east. At the same time Brevet General Eugene A. Carr left Fort Lyon in southeastern Colorado. Custer was reinstated and ordered to command the largest column and to travel more than one hundred miles to the south of Fort Dodge, Kansas, to the junction of Beaver Creek with the North Canadian River in present northwest Oklahoma. His command included eleven companies of his own 7th Cavalry, twelve companies of the specially organized 19th Kansas Volunteer Cavalry under the command of recently resigned Kansas Governor Samuel Crawford, three companies of the 3rd Infantry, and one company of the 28th Infantry.[4] The 19th Kansas Cavalry left Topeka on November 5, while the 7th Cavalry and 3rd Infantry left Fort Dodge on November 11. The Fort Bascom column had already moved, while Carr's column would not leave until November 12. The destination for all was the newly formed Camp Supply, located 110 miles south of Fort Dodge. As Sheridan would note, the purpose of this winter campaign was to

> . . . strike the Indians a hard blow and force them on the reservations set apart for them, and if this could not be accomplished to show to the Indian that the winter season would not give him rest, and that he and his villages and stock could be destroyed; and that he would have no security, winter or summer, except in obeying the laws of peace and humanity.[5]

The columns of troops under Getty and Carr were not expected to attack the Indian encampments or accomplish very much, other than to prevent the Indians escaping from their winter quarters. Custer's column was expected to find and strike the Indian village. Sheridan himself did not arrive at

Camp Supply until November 21, at which time a severe snow-storm began. The 19th Kansas Cavalry was expected to already be at Camp Supply when Sheridan arrived, but they were not there. Traveling from Topeka in country unknown to the scouts, they had become lost. The snowstorm that struck the region on November 21 caused further delays for the Kansas regiment. Sheridan had wanted them united with Custer's command before sending Custer in search of the Indians' winter quarters. He changed his mind when he learned Indians had been observed on hills surrounding Camp Supply. Further, tracks of a fresh war party were discovered by another column of soldiers. Fearing the Indians might be alerted to the amassing of troops at Camp Supply and escape their winter rendezvous, Sheridan decided not to wait and ordered Custer "to move his regiment, storm or no storm, on the morning of November 23d."[6]

When the command left on November 23, the weather was still stormy and cold. Nevertheless, the soldiers slowly trudged on. On November 26 Custer got the break he wanted. A war party trail was discovered that was less than twenty-four hours old.[7] It was a war party because no dog or moccasin prints appeared in the snow, which would have been the case if it were a hunting party.[8] This trail was followed directly to the village. At the crack of dawn, November 27, 1868, on the banks of the Washita River in Indian Territory (present-day Oklahoma), Custer achieved what would be his greatest success as an Indian fighter. Completely surprising the Cheyenne village of Black Kettle, Custer's men quickly took possession of the village. The night before the attack Custer divided his command into four columns and positioned them around the village. Once the fight started, at the first break of the light of dawn, it was only ten minutes before Black Kettle's village was occupied by Custer's command. Heavy fighting continued outside the village.[9] By the end of the fight, Black Kettle and one of his wives lay dead in the shallow icy waters of the Washita, and more than one hundred warriors, as well as a few

women and children, were killed. There was no evidence of any
women or children being indiscriminately killed. Rather, those
killed were either alongside warriors or in the line of fire. Fifty-
three women and children were taken captive.[10] They were
eventually taken to Fort Hays, Kansas, where they remained
several weeks before being returned to their reservation at
Darlington Agency in present-day Oklahoma.[11]

Custer reported capturing the following property:

> We captured in good condition 875 horses, ponies
> and mules, 241 saddles, some of very fine and costly
> workmanship; 573 buffalo robes, 390 buffalo skins
> for lodges, 160 un-tanned robes, 210 axes, 140
> hatchets, 35 revolvers, 47 rifles, 535 pounds of
> powder, 1,050 pounds of lead, 4,000 arrows and
> arrow-heads, 75 spears, 90 bullet moulds, 35 bows
> and quivers, 12 shields, 300 pounds of bullets, 775
> lariats, 940 buckskin saddle bags, 470 blankets, 93
> coats, 700 pounds of tobacco. In addition we cap-
> tured all their winter supply of buffalo meat, all
> their meal, flour, and other provisions, and, in fact,
> everything they possessed, even driving the war-
> riors from the village with little or no clothing.[12]

Custer ordered all the captured animals shot and all the
property burned. The village he attacked was at the end of an
extremely large, multi-tribal encampment. He had struck
where the returning war party had led him. As the day
unfolded, more and more warriors began to appear near Black
Kettle's camp. They wouldn't attack, however, apparently
fearing that the soldiers would kill the captured women and
children. Custer withdrew after dark and returned to Camp
Supply.

Sheridan would later report on Custer's success:

> The blow that Custer struck was a hard one, and
> fell on the guiltiest of all the bands – that of Black
> Kettle. It was this band that, without provocation,
> had massacred the settlers on the Saline and
> Solomon, and perpetrated cruelties too fiendish for
> recital. Black Kettle, its nominal chief – a worn out

and worthless old cipher – was said to be friendly; but when I sent him word to come into Dodge before any of the troops had commenced operations, saying that I would feed and protect himself and family, he refused, and was killed in the fight. He was also with the band on Walnut Creek, where they made their medicine, or held their devilish incantations previous to the party setting out to massacre the settlers.[13]

Custer's victory did not come without a cost. Two officers and nineteen enlisted men died in the battle. One officer, Captain Louis McLane Hamilton, was killed instantly in the opening charge into the village. The twenty-four-year-old Hamilton was the grandson of the eminent Alexander Hamilton. The pedigree on his mother's side of the family was equally impressive. Her father was twice minister to England and served as both secretary of the treasury and secretary of state in President Andrew Jackson's cabinet.[14]

The other officer killed was Custer's second in command, Major Joel Elliott. Sometime in the opening phases of the fight he led a party of sixteen men, including Custer's sergeant major, outside of the village in pursuit of fleeing Indians. He was not seen again, and he and his small command were presumed dead when Custer withdrew from the village later that night.[15]

When Custer returned to Camp Supply, the 19th Kansas Cavalry had arrived in camp and were rested. Many men were without mounts, having lost them in the harrowing winter storm during their march from Topeka. On December 7, each trooper supplied with thirty days of rations, Custer again led his forces back to the vicinity of the Washita battleground. This time the 19th Kansas Cavalry joined with Custer's command. Mrs. Morgan's brother, Daniel Brewster, also accompanied Custer's expedition. He had come to Custer before this second expedition and asked if he could go with the command. At first Custer refused, but then Brewster told him Mrs. Morgan was his sister. Realizing his motives were not money or the thrill of a campaign, Custer immediately set him up with arms, a horse, and even put him on the payroll.[16]

The command arrived at the Washita battleground on December 10. The next day they discovered the bodies of Elliott's small detachment of soldiers, missing since the Washita fight. All seventeen men were stripped naked and horribly mutilated.[17] General Sheridan, who accompanied Custer on this second expedition, noted that in the abandoned and burned village of Black Kettle were found "photographs and daguerreotypes, clothing, and bedding, from the houses of the persons massacred on the Solomon and Saline."[18]

About six miles down the river from where Black Kettle was killed, soldiers found two more bodies, a young pioneer mother and son. Clara Blinn and her two-year-old son, Willie, had been captured on October 9, 1868, east of Fort Lyon in the southeastern part of Colorado Territory.[19]

Like Susanna Alderdice would endure less than a year later, Clara suffered several weeks of captivity before being killed at her moment of rescue. And like Susanna, Clara's story was especially sad. She, too, was born in Ohio, seven years after Susanna, on October 21, 1847. She would turn twenty-one on her twelfth day of captivity. Her parents had eventually settled in Ottawa, Kansas, not far from the Missouri border.[20] Clara married Richard Foote Blinn on August 12, 1865. Her son, Willie, was born sometime in 1866. In 1867 she moved to Colorado Territory with her new family, settling near Fort Lyon, where her husband engaged in a trading business with his brother, Hubble Blinn, and brother-in-law, John Buttles. Richard Blinn was a Civil War veteran and had suffered a serious arm wound that still affected him while they were living in Colorado. After nearly a year of hard work, the young family decided to return to the States, leaving from near Fort Lyon on October 5, 1868.[21]

On October 9, a party of about 200 Cheyenne attacked the small wagon train along the Santa Fe Trail, about fifty miles east of Fort Lyon. The whooping warriors quickly succeeded in separating Clara and Willie, who were riding in the supply wagon, from the rest of the small party of men. A fight ensued, but the Indians had what they wanted, prisoners and property. They jubilantly burned and destroyed what they did not want, and near sundown departed with their captives, leaving the men uninjured.[22]

In addition to losing his wife and son as captives, Richard Blinn lost $500.00 in cash, a man's silver watch and woman's gold watch, valued together at $150.00, all the family apparel, jewelry, beds and bedding valued at $800.00, all household provisions and furniture worth $800.00, and one sorrel gelding horse valued at $150.00.[23]

On November 7, Clara, now four weeks into her ordeal, was able to sneak a note out of the Cheyenne camp by way of a half-breed Indian trader who was visiting the Indians. It is a pitiful plea for rescue. Little did Clara know that she had but twenty more days to live:

> Kind Friends, whoever you may be: I thank you for your kindness to me and my child. You want me to let you know my wishes. If you could only buy us of the Indians with ponies or anything and let me come and stay with you until I could get word to my friends, they would pay you, and I would work and do all I could for you. If it is not too far from their camp, and you are not afraid to come, I pray that you will try. They tell me, as near as I can understand, they expect traders to come, and they will sell us to them. Can you find out by this man and let me know if it is white men? If it is Mexicans I am afraid they would sell us into slavery in Mexico. If you can do nothing for me, write to W. T. Harrington, Ottawa, Franklin County, Kansas, my father; tell him we are with the Cheyennes, and they say when the white men make peace we can go home. Tell him to write to the governor of Kansas about it, and for them to make peace. Send this to him. We were taken on the 9th of October, on the Arkansas, below Fort Lyon. I cannot tell whether they killed my husband or not.

My name is Mrs. Clara Blinn; my little boy, Willie Blinn, is two years old. Do all you can for me. Write to the peace commissioners to make peace this fall. For our sakes do all you can and God will bless you. If you can, let me hear from you again; let me know what you think about it. Write to my father. Send him this.

Good Bye.

Mrs. R. F. Blinn

I am as well as can be expected, but my baby is very weak.[24]

Clara's powerfully moving plea for rescue died in the harsh cold along the Washita River, where the frozen bodies of her and her son were discovered near the creek in an abandoned Indian encampment on December 11, two weeks after being brutally murdered sometime during the Washita battle at Black Kettle's camp. Clara was shot through the forehead, her scalp completely removed, and her skull horribly crushed. Two-year-old Willie "bore numerous marks of violence" and had his "head crushed by a blow against a tree."[25]

It was not just Clara who sought her rescue. Her own family was also trying to save her. Her mother, Mrs. Harrington, had written to Indian Agent A. G. Boone on December 15, seeking his assistance in Clara's rescue. She did not know that her daughter had been killed. Coincidently, Boone received this letter from Mrs. Harrington while at Fort Cobb, the same day that Clara's husband arrived there in his own effort to rescue his family. It was Boone's forlorn duty to write Clara's mother and tell her the disheartening news of her daughter's death. He would also inform her that Clara and Willie's bodies had been buried in the cemetery at Fort Arbuckle.[26] After graphically describing Clara and Willie's murder, Boone wrote that Clara was probably hoping to escape, "as she had her bosom full of meat and bread when found, and there was a dead squaw close to her."[27] He mentioned the dead squaw in an attempt to alleviate Mrs. Harrington's concerns that troopers might have accidentally killed Clara during the fight. He told her also that Clara "was in a party some ten or twelve miles from the main fight, and from the fact of her being scalped shows it was done by the infernal savages."[28]

After finding the bodies of Clara, Willie, and Major Elliott and his men, Custer's combined force of nearly 1,700 men picked up and followed an Indian trail near the Washita battlefield. After four days of marching, on the evening of December 16, they came upon an Indian camp, composed mostly of Kiowa. The soldiers went into camp, but that night the Indians discovered them because of the numerous soldier campfires. Alarmed at the large number of fires, the Indians sought sanctuary with General W. B. Hazen at Fort Cobb, only twenty miles away. By quick means of relays, the Indians secured a letter from General Hazen declaring that they were friendly Indians and that they had not been on the warpath the past season. A scout from the fort arrived at Custer's camp on the morning of December 17 and delivered the letter that had been hastily prepared by Hazen. About the same time Custer received this dispatch, Indians approached his front with a flag of truce.[29]

Among the chiefs accompanying the peace mission were Lone Wolf and Satanta. Sheridan reported that he did not order an attack on the village because of Hazen's letter and "because I did not at that time know the extent of their guilt."[30] Custer, however, soon learned of their guilt. One of the captured women from the Washita fight accompanied this expedition, acting as a go-between should the army encounter Indians, as it had done now. Mah-wis-sa, Black Kettle's sister, reported to Custer where Satanta's village was at the time of the Washita fight, and confirmed to him that Satanta's warriors participated in the Kansas raids and also at the Washita battle.[31] She also said that Clara Blinn was held captive in Satanta's camp, and thus was killed by someone associated with the very Indians Custer now encountered.[32]

Custer was stuck between the proverbial rock and hard place. Sheridan ordered the chiefs held under guard, then used their arrest as a means to force the Indians to report to Fort Cobb. From there they would be sent to their reservation. But on reaching Fort Cobb that evening with the prisoners, Sheridan and Custer learned that the rest of the Indians were actually following the Washita away from Fort Cobb. Sheridan then took desperate measures. "I immediately ordered the execution of Lone Wolf and Satanta unless the villages came back in two days, and delivered themselves up at Fort Cobb."[33] This threat had its desired effect. Before the deadline had passed, the band reported to Fort Cobb and surrendered.

As this was going on, a column under Col. A. W. Evans corralled hostile Comanche Indians near the north fork of the Red River in Indian Territory close to present-day Blair, Oklahoma. General E. A. Carr, operating to the southwest, inspired the Arapahoe and Cheyenne in his area to promise to come in to Fort Cobb. The Arapahoe, under Little Raven, kept their promise, but the Cheyenne did not. Custer was then ordered on yet a third expedition, this time to get the remaining Cheyenne who had not come into Fort Cobb.[34]

On March 2, Custer, again with ten companies of the 19th Kansas Cavalry and eleven companies of the 7th Cavalry, left to find the remaining Cheyenne village that had not reported to Fort Cobb. He soon divided his column into two regiments, kept about 800 of the best outfitted soldiers from both commands, and sent the remainder to establish a camp near the Washita battlefield to await further instructions.[35] Custer's consolidated command went south, searching for the recalcitrant Cheyenne village. He soon found the trail of a lone tepee, following it, and surprised about nine Cheyenne, who promptly scattered.

No other trail was discovered until March 11, 1869, when another trail was discovered, this one nearly a month old. The column followed the trail and before long it grew larger and fresher, eventually including more than 100 lodges.[36] On March 15, Custer reached an Indian camp that had been abandoned only two days before.[37]

Proceeding on, Custer was soon informed that some Indian horse herders had noticed the soldiers and rushed toward heavy timber two or three miles away. Using a handful of soldiers as an escort, Custer started in that direction. Many Indians were observed in the timber. Custer motioned for a parlay and a party of about fifty warriors came out and slowly approached him. From them he learned the make up of the village. It consisted of several bands of Cheyenne. Chief Medicine Arrow informed Custer that more than 200 lodges were directly to his front. Little Robe, with an additional sixty lodges, was several miles farther away. Custer: "Included in the two hundred lodges were nearly all the lodges belonging to the Dog Soldiers: the most mischievous, blood-thirsty and barbarous band of Indians that infest the plains."[38]

Learning of the presence of the Dog Soldiers, Custer at once saw his opportunity "to administer a well merited punishment to the worst of all Indians."[39] He soon changed his plans, however, when he learned that the camp included Miss Sarah White and Mrs. Morgan. He adjusted his strategy:

> It was then out of the question to assume a hostile attitude, at least until the captives were in our possession, or until every peaceable means for their recovery had been exhausted. The opening of our attack would have been the signal for their murder by their captors as is very well known.[40]

Rather than immediately attack the large village to his front, Custer instead accompanied Medicine Arrow to his lodge at the center of the village. Once he was in the village, Custer observed that the women were obviously making for a quick disassembly of the camp. Still, the village at this time was vulnerable to attack, but he knew that the "recovery of the captive white women was now my first object."[41]

Meanwhile, Custer's troops came closer to the village. The Indian women and children were by now sitting on ponies, anticipating fleeing. As the soldiers approached the village, the women's

> . . . fears, coupled with the remembrance of the
> crimes of the tribe and their deserved punishment
> got the better of them and like a herd of frightened
> sheep old and young squaws, papooses, ponies, and
> mules, started in the direction of Little Robe's
> village: abandoning to us all their lodges and poles,
> and innumerable numbers of camp kettles, robes,
> shields, and ponies.[42]

At this instant, Custer ordered his men to arrest what chiefs
they could. Four were caught, including two principal Dog
Soldier chiefs – Big Head and Dull Knife. Custer had learned
well from Sheridan's earlier action. Having these chiefs as captives gave him bargaining power which he used to the fullest.
He promised not to destroy the captured village if those
Indians who had just fled, agreed to come to Little Robe's
village. He then sent a runner, one of his four captive chiefs, to
Little Robe, inviting him to enter a discussion with Custer:

> I was determined to secure their release and that
> unconditionally and thereby discourage the custom
> of ransoming captives from Indians which in reality
> is nothing more nor less than offering the latter a
> premium upon every captive.[43]

Little Robe met with Custer and promised to use his influence and secure the release of the female captives. Nothing
happened the rest of that day. Another day went by and still no
deliverance of the women. Late that second day, a sub-chief
entered Custer's camp, seeking the release of Custer's prisoners. Custer shared the fact that he had waited three days and
still the captives were not released. Therefore, "if by sunset the
following day the white women were not delivered up, I would
hang to a tree there designated – three of the men held captive
by me . . . and that the following day I would follow and attack
the village."[44]

This final threat did the trick. Custer's report on March 21
notes what happened next:

The ropes were ready and the limb selected [for hanging the chiefs] when about three P.M. a small party of Indian warriors were seen approaching Camp. They halted on a knoll about one mile distant while one of their number came forward with the welcome intelligence that the women were with them and would be given up, but this was coupled with the proposition that I should exchange the three men, or two of them, for the women. This was refused, and the return of the women demanded at once, and unconditionally. A reluctant assent to this proposition was given. The Indians however, feared to come inside our lines. Lt. Col. Moore and Majors Jones and Jenkins of the 19th Kansas were therefore detailed to go out and receive them.

Officers and men were assembled near the outpost to welcome two of their own people to freedom from a bondage more horrible than death.

More than one voice faltered with emotion, and many eyes deceived [?] with tears as all crowded around the released captives and tendered heart-felt congratulations upon their release. Both the latter belong to highly respectable families. Both are young – Miss White being about eighteen, Mrs. Morgan about twenty-four. The story of their captivity and their treatment by their captors is a recital of such harboring cruelties, and enormous indignities that it is surprising that civilized beings could endure it and still survive. After conferring with the released captives I was confirmed in my opinion regarding the propriety of not attacking the village. The Indians had expressed their determination to kill them had the attack been made. Many interesting facts are elicited from Mrs. Morgan and Miss White. It seems that prior to the Battle of the Washita where we captured so many of their women and children, the Indians subjected their two captives to the most cruel treatment frequently beating them in the most savage manner. Since that battle they have never given them a blow.[45]

Both women were reported pregnant as a result of their captivity.[46] Custer's orders were to deliver the Cheyenne to Camp Supply, subsequent to their removal to their reservation. Custer used his three captive chiefs as a bargaining tool to get the tribe to come in, promising their release when the Indians were at their reservation. He was simply repeating what he observed Sheridan do with the Kiowa a few weeks earlier. It was a sound move and involved no deceit upon Custer's part, as some might want to argue today. Further, Custer had with him several hundred men of the 19th Kansas Cavalry, whose motive for enlistment was to punish the Indians for the devastating August and October raids in Kansas the previous fall. These men, along with the soldiers of the 7th Cavalry, were there to fight. Private Samuel Blauser, in Company H of the 19th Kansas Cavalry, later recalled that when Custer issued the order not to fire on the Indians, for a bit "there was mutiny in the ranks. The men begged, argued, swore, and some even shed tears in their disappointment."[47] That Custer was able to prevent a fight, successfully rescue the two captives, and then get the recalcitrant warriors to Camp Supply validates the contention that Custer was not an Indian killer who was bloodthirsty for the glory of battle, a view unjustly taken after his unfortunate demise at the Little Bighorn a little more than seven years later.

Carr's First Fight With Tall Bull

A figure with apparently a red cap rose slowly up on the hill. For an instant it puzzled me, as it wore the buckskin and had long hair, but on seeing the horse I recognized it as Cody's 'Powder face' and saw that it was Buffalo Bill without his broad brimmed sombrero. On closer inspection I saw his head was swathed in a bloody handkerchief, which served not only as a temporary bandage – but as a chapeau – his hat having been shot off, the bullet plowing his scalp badly for about five inches. It had ridged along the bone, and he was bleeding profusely – a very 'close call', but a lucky one.[1]

After the rescue of Sarah White and Mrs. Morgan, many believed that Custer had finally succeeded in bringing peace to the Kansas frontier. Indeed, Custer himself in the conclusion of his report detailing his operations wrote, "This I consider as the termination of the Indian war."[2] However, this was far from the truth, for less than a month later Dog Soldier Indians, this time under the leadership of Tall Bull, made murderous raids against the same settlements in and along the Solomon and Saline valleys that were victimized in 1868. Sheridan reported that Tall Bull's tribe was a part of the Cheyenne village Custer confronted on the Sweetwater, but Tall Bull's followers did not go to Camp Supply as promised. Sheridan wrote: "Tall Bull's band again violated the promise made, and went north to the Republican, where he joined a party of Sioux."[3]

Custer's men were in no condition to go after Tall Bull. Following the release of the women captives, the cavalrymen were tired, ragged, and nearing starvation. It was really all they could do to return to Camp Supply. In addition, the 19th

Kansas Cavalry was mustered out and those men returned to their homesteads.

With Tall Bull's band escaping north and connecting with the Dog Soldiers under Sioux chiefs Pawnee Killer and Whistler, there was once again a formidable band of hostiles threatening the pioneer settlements in Kansas. The motivation for the May 1869 raid into the Saline and Solomon valley had occurred earlier in a clash with the military in northwestern Kansas. After the Washita campaign, General E. A. Carr traveled with seven companies of the 5th Cavalry from Fort Lyon to Fort McPherson, east of present-day North Platte, Nebraska. He was to take his command out of the Department of the Missouri and place it under the authority of General Christopher C. Augur in the Department of the Platte.[4] This was because General Sherman expected trouble from the Northern Sioux and Cheyenne later that summer and he wanted Carr's command there to protect the railroad. All thought there would be no more trouble in Kansas.

On his way from Fort Lyon, while traveling through northwest Kansas, not far from Nebraska's southern border, Carr's command accidentally encountered Tall Bull's warriors. Neither group expected to run into the other. A sharp fight occurred on May 13 near the rock formation known as Elephant Rock along Beaver Creek, in Decatur County, Kansas. It resulted in at least twenty-five dead Dog Soldiers and four dead cavalrymen.[5] Twenty-five lodges, complete with all their furnishings, were captured and destroyed.

Carr, writing from camp on May 22, gave an account of this fight. Crossing Beaver Creek near Elephant Rock, about five miles south of the Nebraska border and near present-day Traer, Kansas, Carr's scouts encountered an Indian trail that was more than a week old. Carr ordered 1st Lieutenant Edward Ward to take ten men and a scout, and follow the trail to see where it went. About eight miles out of Carr's camp, Ward observed smoke from an Indian village. While observing from a nearby hill, "he was discovered by a hunting party. He immediately sent a messenger and returned himself towards camp, pursued by Indians in increasing numbers. On the way he met another hunting party of twenty five, and charged through it."[6]

Carr, receiving the report from Ward's messenger, immediately ordered two-thirds of each company to charge, while the others remained as escort for the wagons, which were ordered to follow the command. While preparing to advance, Carr received a second report from Lieutenant Ward, informing him the Indians were pressing him hard. Carr ordered Company F, under command of its first sergeant, to immediately report to Ward. Close on their heels, Captain Gustavus Urban was ordered to take Companies I and A and follow Company F. Carr:

> Following with the rest of the command at a gallop, I soon saw the three companies in front hotly engaged. A party of about thirty five Indians were trying to outflank their left, and I sent Company B under 1st Lieut. J. C. A. Schenofsky to charge them. He pursued for seven miles, and did not rejoin the command until the next day. He lost one sergeant and two privates killed, and three horses, and reports ten Indians as falling from their horses and requiring assistance to get off.[7]

Meanwhile, Carr, with the other companies, pursued the remaining warriors downstream until darkness ended the fight. He then retreated back to the wagons and camped for the night. The village was estimated at 150 lodges. About 300 Dog Soldiers showed themselves during the fight, a number consistent with that size village. The next morning, Lieutenant Jules Schenofsky returned and reported that three Company B men had been killed the day before. A fourth soldier was missing and presumed dead. Carr ordered a detail of six soldiers to go out and bury the dead, "but they were met by a stronger party of Indians, and abandoned the enterprise."[8] Thus ended the fight with Tall Bull at Elephant Rock.

The next day, May 15, Carr ordered three days cooked rations prepared and placed in each soldier's haversack. He then set out with 188 troopers in pursuit of Tall Bull's band. These were all the men he could muster for service who had horses fit for a forced march. The remaining men were ordered to accompany the wagons to Fort McPherson. On May 16 another fight with Tall Bull occurred a few miles to the north, not far inside Nebraska, near Spring Creek. This fight resulted in an unknown number of Indians killed. At least twenty Indians were wounded. No soldiers were killed, but several were wounded.[9] Though Spring Creek was not far from Elephant Rock, the terrain was quite rough, with many ravines and steep hills, requiring the cavalry to dismount on several occasions.

It was during this part of Carr's pursuit that William F. (Buffalo Bill) Cody distinguished himself as Carr's chief of scouts. Carr wrote:

> Our Scout William Cody, who has been with the Detachment since last September displayed great skill in following it [the Indians' trail], and also deserves great credit for his fighting in both engagements, his marksmanship being very conspicuous. He deserves honorable mention for this and other services, and I hope to be able to retain him as long as I am engaged in this duty.[10]

Cody had been assigned to Carr's regiment after General Sheridan used his services earlier in the fall of 1868 to carry dispatches between Kansas Forts Larned, Dodge, and Hays. This was especially dangerous country at the time, with many couriers being killed performing their duty. Sheridan recalled the time Cody rode about 350 miles in less than sixty hours, noting that "such an exhibition of endurance and courage was more than enough to convince me that his services would be extremely valuable in the [forthcoming] campaign, so I retained him at Fort Hays till the battalion of the Fifth Cavalry arrived, and then made him chief of scouts for that regiment."[11] Indeed, Carr had been equally impressed with Cody's service. In a letter to General George D. Ruggles, Carr requested "authority be given me to pay my scout William Cody, one hundred dollars extra for extra-ordinarily good service as trailer and fighter in my pursuit of hostile Indians. . . ."[12]

Like Elephant Rock, the Spring Creek fight involved about 200 Indians. It began when a party of five warriors appeared on distant hills. Lieutenant William J. Volkmar and his topographical crew of ten soldiers were in the vicinity where the Indians had been spotted, so Carr ordered Brevet Major John B. Babcock with Company M to support Volkmar's crew. After going two miles, about 200 screaming warriors suddenly emerged from where they had been concealed in deep ravines. Quickly they descended upon Babcock's small command. The soldiers scrambled to nearby high ground where they dismounted and formed into a circle. A desperate fight ensued, lasting about thirty minutes. Carr, hearing the heavy firing, sent a company to investigate. When the company came into sight of the Dog Soldiers, the warriors withdrew. They apparently thought the whole regiment had come to the rescue of Company M. When the Indians took flight, the advancing company chased them for about twelve miles. By that time the Indians had scattered in all directions and vanished.[13]

John Babcock gave a stellar performance in holding his men together. When he advanced them to the high ground, he ordered his men to dismount, while he remained on horseback, encouraging them. His horse was wounded but Babcock remained mounted. For his action at Spring Creek he was awarded the Congressional Medal of Honor, issued in 1897.[14]

After the fight at Spring Creek, Carr went to Fort Kearny, Nebraska, and then to Fort McPherson. Rations were exhausted and the men were without food for two days. They were also precariously short on ammunition, having used nearly all of it in their two fights with Tall Bull's Dog Soldiers.[15]

With Carr's men out of the picture, no other command was available to pursue Tall Bull. The Dog Soldier Indians were free to exact revenge for the deaths of their people in the fights of May 13 and 16. The retaliatory raids began within a week. The decision to go on a raid was an elaborate process. An announcement would be made in the village that a raid was planned. Women, children, and warriors would converge to hear the details. When would the raid start? Who would be chosen to go? Carl C. Rister, in his book, *Border Captives: The Traffic in Prisoners by Southern Plains Indians*, noted what would happen next: ". . . the chiefs would announce their selections, and through long hours they would explain to the chosen braves the details of the journey – the exact route of travel, where watering places were to be found, identification of land marks, and other important matters."[16] When raiding frontier settlements, the raiders would divide into smaller parties, "in order to project simultaneous forays along an extended line. The plan was now to move silently and quickly in the work of pillage, theft, and death."[17]

On Sunday, May 23, a party of seventy to eighty Indians fell on a settlement along White Rock Creek in Jewell County, Kansas, about four-and-a-half miles west of present-day Lovewell. Most of the men in the surrounding settlements were away on a burial detail for four buffalo hunters, part of a group of seven that the Indians had surprised and killed earlier near the Nebraska border in the northwest corner of Jewell County.[18]

In the home of settlers Peter Tanner and Charles Hogan were three young sons of Gustavus Norlin. Norlin had just emigrated from Sweden with his large family of thirteen children. Fortunately, he had left his ten youngest with his wife at Junction City, Kansas. Only two weeks earlier he had come to this Jewell County settlement with his three oldest boys, to locate a claim before bringing the rest of his family west. Kansas at this time welcomed about 1,500 such immigrant families from Sweden, which was then in the throes of a severe famine, and Kansas sought her share of these immigrants.[19]

76

Gustavus and his boys were staying at Tanner—Hogan's two-room log house until they could get their own place built. At least two other men also lived in the Tanner—Hogan house. As fate would have it, the three Norlin boys along with a hired man were at the home when they saw the Indians raiding the nearby Dahl house. In the Dahl home brothers Martin and Paul lived, along with their sixteen-year-old nephew, Thomas Voarness.

Earlier in the day, the Dahl brothers had gone for a long exploratory walk while their nephew stayed home to prepare dinner. Like the Norlins, the Dahls had been in Kansas only two weeks. While the Dahls were out walking, the Indians came upon young Thomas. Returning about four hours later by way of the Tanner—Hogan home, the Dahls saw that this house was ransacked, and virtually everything in it scattered about the yard and destroyed. Concerned for their nephew, they rushed to their house. Their worst fears were realized. Amid the ransacked and destroyed household items, their nephew was lying near the fireplace. Voarness had been shot through the bowels. He suffered several hours before dying. He told his Uncle Martin that a

> . . . short time after we left the house and he was preparing dinner for Paul and me, that he heard a noise at the door of the house and turned around to see what it was, and the door was filled with Indians; he reached for his carbine, which was near him, and before he could get his gun, the Indians shot him clear through the body, he fell down, and lay there he told us that the Indians paid no more attention to him, although he was conscious all the time, he said the Indians went about the house broke open our trunks the same as they had done at Hogan's place, and ransacked everywhere and into everything, and we found as our Nephew said what they did not take away with them they destroyed, breaking it up into pieces or cutting it up, and from what he told us there was about a hundred Indians

there at the time, in and around the house, from what he saw and according to his judgement.[20]

The Dahls used a door from their home as a stretcher and carried their nephew seven miles to White Rock City, hoping to find a doctor who could treat him. No doctor was found and by nightfall young Thomas's sufferings had ended. He was dead.

While the Indians attacked the Dahl house, fourteen-year-old Charles Norlin saw a warrior for the first time. Charles's brothers, Chris and John, were with him, along with the hired man, Bergland, who was there to help Gustavus build his new home. They, along with several other men, were staying at the Tanner—Hogan home, visible about 100 feet from the Dahl house, but on the opposite side of a small creek.[21]

Charles heard a noise, causing him to look in the direction of the Dahl home. To his surprise he saw about sixty men. Because they were all wearing blue overcoats, at first he thought they were cavalrymen. He proceeded outside to greet them. The Dog Soldiers saw him coming and brandished their spears in the air. One can imagine his fright as he realized his mistake. Shouting loud war whoops, the warriors advanced toward him and his brothers, who had followed him outside, but for an unknown reason they stopped and turned toward the Dahl house. It was only a momentary diversion. When Charles realized his awful mistake, he "was paralyzed and unable to move from fright."[22]

Fortunately for Charles and his young brothers, this diversion toward the Dahl home gave them time to flee to the creek, which was close by in the opposite direction. The boys, now joined by Bergland, scrambled into the high brush along the creek where they found a hole left by a fallen tree. It was big enough to conceal all of them, and from there they soon saw the Indians leaving the Dahl home and approaching the home they had just fled:

> The Indians destroyed and carried off everything in the Tanner and Dahl houses; they scattered the flour and provisions which they left behind on the

floor [cattle later entered the unprotected Dahl home and further destroyed it. The Tanner—Hogan home was a few days later burned as the Indians made another jaunt back into the area]. They cut feather beds open and scattered the feathers and took the ticks with them.[23]

At the same time, about twenty miles to the west, four men were out on a buffalo hunt. Brothers William and Joseph Newlon, along with John McFarlane and Joseph Myers, on their third morning out noticed that one of Myers's horses had gotten loose during the night. Myers followed the tracks of his horse all the way back to his home near White Rock City. Meanwhile, his companions rode west in the direction of the Republican River. About four o'clock that afternoon, William observed something crossing the valley about two miles distant. Curious, he used his field glass and saw an Indian pony with warrior "lying flat on its back, I had not long to look before it disappeared over the ridge out of sight."[24]

Cautiously moving toward the hill where the Indian had been spotted, William, now hiding behind his own horse, slowly peered over the ridge. His suspicions were confirmed. Down on the other side of the hill was a band of about seventy warriors. A large grove of trees lay farther to the west on the hunters' side of the hill, opposite from where the Indians were. The Indians apparently surmised the party would head to the grove of trees. They looked to be waiting until the hunters had time to settle in the timber. Instead, the hunters noticed a "blow out" just below the spot where William had seen the hiding Indians. It was big enough to fit both them and their wagon. Quickly they drove their wagon into their concealed spot.

While the wagon was being concealed, William remained at the ridge to keep an eye on the Indians. Finally, the Indians, thinking the men had had enough time to nestle in the timber, came out of their hiding place, slowly approached and then charged toward the grove of trees. William had made it to the "blow out" just before the Indians announced their charge with their piercing cries of battle. The warriors seemed confused when the buffalo hunters were not where they expected them. But it wasn't long before the Indians discovered and quickly surrounded them. No warrior, however, was willing to approach the hole, fully respecting the marksmanship of the hunters. They were safe, for the time, and that night they were able to escape. William remembered seeing Indian pickets on duty, both to the right and left, as the men slowly crawled past them under cover of darkness. The men had to abandon their wagon and provisions in making their escape. They safely reached the settlements the next day.[25]

Back on May 10, farther east in Washington County, near the town of Waterville, across the line from Marshall County, four men and three boys went west on an extended buffalo hunt. The party included Union veterans Philip Burke and Reuben Winklepleck, Reuben's son, Alonzo, and nephew, Edward Winklepleck, Mr. Cole and his young son, and John McChesney. It had been a grand time for the men and boys. The hunters had been successful, having secured several buffalo hides and a wagonload of meat. On the evening of May 25, returning to Waterville, they decided to camp on the Republican River near the mouth of White Rock Creek just west of present-day Republic, Kansas. Unfortunately, they chose a campsite in the very area where the Dog Soldiers had been raiding the Swedish settlements.

Early in the evening, one of the hunters found signs of Indians. Knowing their danger, they put out their campfire and went to bed without eating. Their hope was to leave quietly the next morning. They should have considered abandoning their wagon and fleeing the area in the dark of night. Rising early in the morning, they followed the course of the river east, hoping they could escape detection. This was not to be. When they got down near the river, about 75-100 Indians came charging at them. "They [the hunting party] all made a rush to the river and got across and were making their way for the underbrush, but before they could get to it, they were surrounded and killed."[26] All swam across the river except John McChesney. When the men came to the Republican, John, knowing he could not swim, had no choice but to drop low into a thicket of young willows along the riverbank. Everyone else, including the boys, hastily swam across. The Indians in their rush of the hunt did not notice that one man stayed back. John hid while he heard the futile fight of his friends.

The next day, May 27, McChesney arrived at the town of Scandia, Kansas, where he reported the killings. A party of four or five men accompanied him back to the Republican River to bury the dead men and boys. When the victims were found, it was obvious that Rueben Winklepleck had put up a hard fight. "He was a big strong man and he was shot with arrows and gunshot wounds and was badly mutilated." All the victims were stripped of their clothing and one was scalped, the scalp lying beside his body. Winklepleck's rifle was on the ground nearby, broken and bent.[27]

These depredations in Jewell and Republic County merely marked the beginning of Tall Bull's murderous foray upon the Kansas settlements. Not satisfied with his early success, Tall Bull decided to risk driving farther into central Kansas, which brought him closer to the forts. The Dog Soldiers soon appeared in Russell County.

Railroad workers were the next victims. About two o'clock on the afternoon of May 28, about thirty Indians surprised seven railroad men working on the line west of Fossil Creek Station in present-day Russell, Kansas.[28] Only three of the seven were armed, but their rifles were back at the handcar several yards away. When the Dog Soldiers appeared out of a nearby ravine, all the men ran to the handcar. They got on the car. The men with the weapons fired at the Indians, while the others frantically pushed the handcar toward the station more than a mile and a half away. One of the workers, Adolph Roenigk, vividly recalled his experiences. "On that well remembered, fatal day we were working on the railroad track about one and three-fourths miles west of the station, at a point about three hundred yards east of a large ravine running northeast to the Saline River."[29]

From this deep ravine the Indians were able to get close to the crew without being detected. Roenigk's gun was near the handcar and not where he was working. When the screaming Indians came riding out of the ravine, Roenigk quickly ran to the handcar, retrieved and loaded his Spencer carbine. In his haste, he inadvertently overloaded it and was unable to fire it until he extracted the extra cartridge. "By this time the savages were almost upon us. They were firing rapidly and the bullets made the dust fly on every side."[30]

Fortunately for the men, the whooping warriors were equally excited and bad shots. The chase went on for almost half a mile before the first man was hit. Then more Indians emerged from a smaller ravine from the workers' front. In quick order, the men were surrounded, but continued pumping the handcar toward the station. Soon those Indians in the front opened up, which permitted the handcar to pass through. Had the Indians not allowed this they would have endangered their own safety, as any missed shot could potentially hit an Indian on the other side. Roenigk:

> As we raised our guns to our shoulders the Indians would glide to the other side of their ponies, but we continued to fire as best our position would allow. About half way to the station Alexander McKeever and John Lynch were killed and fell from the car. Both fell within a distance of two hundred yards. Each time a man fell a crowd of Indians sprung from their poines [sic] and gathered around the victim. The last one when struck exclaimed, "Oh, God." I turned to look at him and saw he was shot and while I turned to face the Indians, he tumbled from the car. Again the Indians gathered around the fallen man, and I fired a shot into their midst, with what effect I do not know. When the savages had emptied their gune [sic] we received a shower of arrows, most of which went wild. George Seely was struck in the thigh by one but he jerked it out

the next moment. I saw the boys bleeding, but so far I had not received a scratch, but just as the last three shots rang out I felt a sting in my breast, spurts of blood came from my mouth and nose, and I felt my time to live was short. We were now within a half a mile of the station and the Indians turned and left us. While near the station we met John Cook coming toward us carrying his rifle.[31]

Cook covered them while the wounded men were able to get into the station. Though this ended the fight, the Indians did not leave. They remained in the vicinity well into the night, destroying much of the track about two miles east of the station. The driver of the train coming from the west later that night observed a bale of hay burning near the station, earlier put there by Cook as a warning. It stopped and did not enter the station until morning, when the engineer could see the track. This train also brought in the two dead men, crewmen having picked them up near where the train had stopped to avoid derailment. About midnight a train coming from the east approached the station. The engineer did not understand the fire warning to stop and the train derailed. Fortunately, no one was injured, and the dozen passengers on the derailed train were able to walk safely to the station the next morning.

Roenigk's injury was a serious one and he would spend some time recovering at the Fort Harker hospital. Shot through the lungs with a heavy caliber lead ball, he was fortunate in that "the bullet that entered my breast had passed out at my back, thus leaving me literally shot through."[32]

The two dead men in Roenigk's party were horribly mutilated. Stripped of their clothing and scalped, their bodies were "stuck full of arrows and rings of telegraph wire pierced through the calves of their legs and other parts of their bodies."[33] A newspaper noted that one of the men "had three large gashes cut the entire length of his back, and leather strings made from his shoes drawn through them."[34] These mutilations produced an interesting commentary in the

Leavenworth Times and Conservative. Quoting from Major John Parks, the paper noted that the men had their ears, scalps, heads all cut off, but further, their tongues and hearts were also removed, boiled, and eaten by the warriors.[35] The *Leavenworth Daily Commercial* added that such practices were notable as a Cheyenne act in accordance with their beliefs regarding the afterlife. Specifically referring to the two men killed at Fossil Creek, the story continued:

> Aside from the cutting of the flesh from the calf of the leg, and likewise a strip from each shoulder, they cut out also the heart and tongue, roasting the former to be used eventually in a medicinal way. Some of the bodies were further mutilated by the cutting open of the flesh of the upper portion of the thighs, pulling the same out and backward, and affixing thereto by means of telegraph wires the boots or shoes of the man thus mutilated. This the Indians do in accordance with a belief which prevails with them, that no one scalped can enter the happy hunting grounds – and in the event such white man gets there, after this maltreatment, he must go upon his "haunches" rather than upon his feet.[36]

Fort Hays was twenty-five miles to the west of Fossil Creek. The officers there soon learned of the attack. Custer's command was camped on Big Creek nearby. He led a detachment of about twenty-five men in pursuit of the Indians. They scouted the country for twenty-five miles but found no sign of the warriors. Darkness ended the search.[37] The reason the Dog Soldiers were not found was probably because of confusion in knowing from which direction the Indians had come. Some thought the war party came from the south, which indeed it had, but much earlier than when they made their attack. About a week before the raid at Fossil Creek, a scout had warned the workers that Indians had broken away from their reservation in the south and were coming north, and to be on the lookout for them.[38]

Though they had come from the south, they had come earlier and had circled far to the north, where they joined up with renegade Sioux from the Spotted Tail Agency. These included Dog Soldier Sioux from the bands of Pawnee Killer, Whistler, Little Wound, and others.[39] They had joined with Tall Bull, who with his band had escaped from Custer earlier in the spring when Custer used the captured Cheyenne chiefs as a means to get the various Cheyenne bands onto their reservation. It was this combined band of Indians that Carr twice fought earlier in May in northwest Kansas and southern Nebraska. It is doubtful that Custer believed the Indians would go east toward the settlements, which is precisely where they went.

Indian raiding continued the next day, Saturday, May 29. This time the warriors surprised a party of four buffalo hunters who had been out hunting for about three weeks. Henry Trask, William Earle, Napoleon Alley and Solomon Humbarger had loaded two wagons with provisions and left Lincoln County to hunt buffalo to the northwest. Their hunt had been successful, the men killing more than eighty buffalo. They made a temporary camp in Osborne County, to the north and a little east of where the Fossil Creek attack had taken place. It was on what was then called Pond Creek, a tributary of the south fork of the Solomon River.[40]

On the day of the raid it had been raining. Alley left the camp to climb a hill and see if buffalo were still in the area. As he left the timber, he heard sounds of an owl and then a wolf. He immediately grew suspicious, as they didn't quite sound authentic. His thoughts then turned to the possibility of Indians making signals to draw attention to him. He proceeded farther up the hill when suddenly many screaming Indians charged out of the timber. He darted up the hill, hoping to be able to descend on the other side and hide in the timber along the creek. However, when he got to the top of the hill, he discovered a "rocky bluff, too steep to climb down and so high that to leap off seemed certain death."[41]

With the Indians quickly closing the gap, he seemed to have two choices, probable death by jumping or certain death by the Dog Soldiers. He preferred the former, and spotting where the shallow water appeared deepest, he jumped off the cliff. He landed safely, but the force of the fall caused him to sink deep into the mud at the bottom of the water. By the time he began to pull himself out, the Indians were on the edge of the cliff, firing guns and arrows down at him. Fortunately, he wasn't struck and soon was able to make his escape to the thick timber on the other side of the creek. The Indians now diverted their attention to the remaining men back at the camp. From his hiding place in the timber, Alley heard firing, and not long after it was silent. He waited for what seemed a long time and then cautiously followed the creek back to the camp. There he found the rest of the party alive. Sol Humbarger was wounded with an arrow in his lower hip.[42] One Indian had been killed. Though the men survived by running into the timber along the creek, they lost everything in their two wagons, which included camp equipage, food, and buffalo.[43]

The hunters slowly began following the creek beds back to Lincoln County. After the first night, Humbarger's leg had become so swollen and infected he was unable to continue walking. His wound was a desperate one and it was thought he would not recover.[44] Alley remained with him, while Trask and Earle continued on to Lincoln County. They would eventually return with a rescue party.[45] When they came to Lincoln County, they followed Spillman Creek to the Saline and then went east on the Saline all the way to Beverly before they found other settlers, where most had fled because of the May 30 raid. Trask and Earle were aware that they were following behind the murderous Dog Soldiers.[46]

In 1926, Alley's version of his harrowing experience in 1869 was published in the *Beverly Tribune*. It is very similar to the account in the depredation claim made decades earlier. It's a lively story:

Along in the afternoon Dick Alley decided to go upon a hill near their camp and see whether the buffalo were still there. They had no thought of danger. So Alley did not take his gun with him. Alley ... said that he had just got out of the timber when he heard an owl hoot over on the other side of the camp. And, he said, 'that didn't sound like a "rale" honest wolf neither.'

He stopped and studied about going back to camp but there had been no Indian raids for some time and they had seen no signs of Indians. He said he was afraid the boys would laugh at him if he went back to camp and told them why he changed his mind. So he went on. When he got a little way up the hill he heard Indians yelling behind him and when he looked back he saw them coming.

They came out of the woods on their ponies in a semi-circle between him and the camp. The only direction he could go was straight ahead up the hill. So Alley started with the Indians yelling behind him. In telling the story he said, 'I was a good deal younger than I am now, and I was pretty peart on my feet, and I don't think I ever ran faster in my life.' His only hope was to get into the timber again. The creek made a bend so that by running over the hill and down the other side he could keep ahead of the Indians. To his surprise they didn't seem to try very hard to catch him. Soon he reached the top of the hill, ran down the other side and reached the creek bank. Then he understood why the Indians let him get away so easily.

The Indians possessed a sort of grim humor and they were playing with him somewhat as a cat plays with a mouse. They had spread out behind him so as to force him to the creek bank at a point where the bank was a rocky bluff, too steep to climb down, and so high that to leap off seemed certain death. Here they came yelling like fiends. Dick looked back at the Indians and down at the creek below. Capture by the Indians meant certain death, and to jump seemed to mean the same thing. But death was preferable to torture by the Indians. So he picked out the place where the water looked deepest and leaped for it.

Fortune favored him. He landed in a hole in the creek where ... had washed in some mud, and it was deep enough to break his fall. He said it seemed to him that he would never stop going down. He landed on his feet, and sunk in the mud to his knees before his feet hit the hard bottom. Then his back gave way and he went down till his face was down in the mud before he stopped. He got his face out of the mud and lay there getting his breath back.

The Indians gathered on the bank above him but didn't shoot, evidently thinking he had been killed. When he got his breath back so that he felt he was able to make another effort he worked his arms loose from the mud so that he could raise up. The timber came down to the bank of the creek on the other side, and if he could get into the timber he stood a chance of escape; but he knew that as soon as the Indians saw him move they would begin to shoot at him. Finally he concluded to make the effort. So he raised up and threw himself over on the other bank and tried to get his legs out of the mud. The Indians began to yell and shoot at him, and arrows struck all around him, but as they were shooting almost straight down most of them passed over him. He said it seemed to him that he would never get his legs out of the mud, but finally got them loose and scrambled up the bank and out of the timber. The Indians sat on their horses for awhile upon the top of the bluff watching for a chance to shoot at him. Finally they turned and started off down the creek toward the camp.[47]

The raiding Indians were drawing closer to the settlements along the Saline River in Lincoln County. By the early afternoon of the next day they would be there.

Captured!

*The Primary object [of an Indian raid] was to steal
horses and mules, but if homes could be burned, settlers killed and scalped, and women and children
carried away as captives, the raid was considered
all the more successful.*[1]

Unlike the rain of the day before, Sunday, May 30, 1869,
began as a pleasant, beautiful Kansas spring day. It ended in
fear, destruction and death for the settlers living along
Spillman Creek and the Saline River. The raid began about
two o'clock in the afternoon, when sixty to seventy-five Dog
Soldiers descended upon a new Danish colony nestled along
the banks of Spillman Creek, about ten miles above its junction
with the Saline River, and three miles west of present-day
Lincoln, Kansas. The town of Denmark now marks where the
raid began.

Susanna Alderdice's brother, Eli Zeigler, and brother-in-
law, John Alverson, were on their way to stake a homestead
claim near the juncture of Bacon and Spillman creeks, about
ten miles from where Susanna was living. Eli had learned that
a settler abandoned a claim up there as a result of the 1868
raids. Seventeen-year-old Eli intended to work the previously
tilled but now abandoned land in order to file on it for himself.

Before parting on their journey, Eli and John had loaded
John's wagon with two weeks' supply of provisions to cover
their needs while they worked the land. On their way out, they
first stopped at Michael Haley's home along the Saline, about
two miles west of what would later become Lincoln. Their
purpose for stopping was to have lunch ("dinner") with
Susanna and her four children. Susanna was about five

months pregnant with her fifth child. Eli at this time was still living at his father's house, which was along the Saline east of present Lincoln and just south of what would later become the town of Beverly. Tom Alderdice built his house just west of present Lincoln, along the Saline River, not too far east of the Michael Haley home. Michael Haley's brother, John, was one of Forsyth's scouts wounded at Beecher Island.[2]

Susanna and her children were staying at Michael's house, while her husband, Tom, was away with several other men dealing with legal issues at the Land Office in Junction City, two days' trip each way. The men were due back on Monday, May 31. Others accompanying Tom included Timothy Kine, brothers Mart and William Hendrickson, and the Hendricksons' brother-in-law, John Strange.[3] Just before Tom and the other men left for Junction City, several people in the settlement had heard rumors that Indians were again raiding Kansas settlements. There was mounting concern the Indians might return to this area.[4] Indeed, Michael Haley, when hearing the rumors, chose to take his family, which included several children, to Ellsworth, where nearby Fort Harker provided a sanctuary against raiding Indians. Haley had taken his family there the previous August when the Cheyenne raided the area. In fact, Haley had suffered a loss on May 10, 1868, when Pawnee Indians forcefully entered his home and robbed him and his family of $190.00 worth of household goods.[5] He had "seen the elephant," so to speak, and wisely, he was not interested in seeing it again.

The Haley house was a larger house than most houses in the neighborhood, and he graciously allowed it to be used by other families for general protection in case the Indians did raid the valley again. Several families were staying at Haley's house. Susanna and her children were to stay there until Tom returned. The same was true with Bridget Kine and her two-month-old daughter, Katherine.[6] Thomas Noon and his wife were also staying at the Haley house, as was Nicholas Whalen. It was understood that Whalen and Noon would protect the vulnerable women and children should the Indians appear while Tom and Tim were away.[7] When the Indians did appear at the house, however, this was not to be, and Bridget and Susanna were left alone to fend for themselves.

During the Sunday noon meal Susanna shared with Eli Zeigler and John Alverson that fateful day, she warned them of the rumors that Indians were nearby, urging them to be careful.[8] After leaving the Haley place, Eli and John directed their wagon north, following Lost Creek to its head, where they turned west toward Bacon Creek. While heading up Lost Creek, Eli saw a man on horseback "riding fast toward the west."[9] The rider was too far away to tell whether he was an Indian or a settler, but it was obvious he was in a hurry, and he was going in the same direction they were heading.

Eli was driving the wagon. As they turned west from Lost Creek, both men were studying the rider as he galloped west. They continued to watch the rider for about four miles until they came to Trail Creek where the rider disappeared over a hill. About two o'clock they crossed Trail Creek a little north of present-day Denmark. From a knoll west of Trail Creek and north of Spillman Creek, they could see across the Spillman, and there, just north of the new Danish settlement, they saw what appeared to be soldiers, as many as sixty of them. Eli remembered: "The sun glistened on their guns so plain that I still thought they were soldiers, but John would not have it that way, and I had about made up my mind that they were."[10]

All doubt was quickly erased, however, when the contingent of Dog Soldiers, minus about a dozen warriors, bolted across the Spillman, charging at Eli and John about half a mile away. Quickly Eli turned the wagon around and headed back to Trail Creek. The hope was that they might save themselves if they could make it to the high banks of the creek before the Indians caught up with them. Eli's story now turns dramatic:

> When we got to the creek the Indians were close behind us. I looked across the creek and thought there was a little bank on the other side that would

protect us some. So I drove across, but John misunderstood me and jumped out into the creek and I drove up the bank. John ran along under the bank on the side I was on; the Indians were coming across the creek within a few yards of us, shooting and yelling. John was calling for me to get out of the wagon, when I got to that little bank, I stopped the horses, seeing nothing more could be done to save the team and that we must defend ourselves, I dropped the lines, grabbed my gun and jumped out on the off side of the wagon. Reaching in the box for my cartridges, I could only get the box, about 20 rounds. While I was getting the cartridges the Indians were close all around. One of them rode up and picked up the lines just as I had laid them down and he held the horses. I thought sure I'll put a hole through you, but before I could get my gun around he jumped off his pony down beside the wagon, and still held the horses. The Indians were shooting all this time. John was calling for me to get under the bank. Just then another Indian darted up right close to the wagon and I thought I would get him, but before I could cover him with my gun he jumped his pony on the opposite side of the wagon, so I could not get him.

John was still begging me to jump over the bank and I had about made up my mind to. As I stepped out from the wagon I looked toward the rear and behind the wagon and saw three Indians standing about four rods away, having me covered with their guns. I had no time for a shot, so made a spring for the creek bank; my foot slipped and I fell just as they fired. I think they over shot me. I also think that the slip is what saved me. I kept going on my hands and feet over the bank. As they were pouring their shots right at us at short range we saw a log lying up the bank a little below us, we ran to that, thinking that would protect us on the side.[11]

When the Indians realized it would take a fight to kill Eli and John, they turned their attention to the abandoned wagon and its contents. Both men would later file claims for their loss.

Eli's claim was for $100.00, covering what he described as household furniture. John's losses included his wagon, team of horses, provisions, and camp equipage.[12] It is no surprise the Indians chose to ignore the men after they had secured themselves along the bank of Trail Creek. Their purpose for raiding settlements was not to engage in a fight that might get some of them killed, but to plunder, raid, and murder only when there was little risk to them. A newspaper noted after the raid, "wherever a gun was fired the savages made no fight."[13]

Eli and John remained hidden in the creek bank until dark, and during the night they slowly made their way back to the Saline, hiding inside the tall banks of Trail Creek and Spillman Creek down to the Saline River. From there they followed the banks of the Saline east. At sunrise they arrived at Ferdinand Erhardt's place near the junction of Bullfoot Creek and the Saline River. Erhardt's place was a little more than a mile northwest of the Schermerhorn Ranch on Elkhorn Creek.

Just before the Dog Soldiers charged Eli and John near Trail Creek, Eli saw between ten and fifteen of them separate from the main body and head in the direction of the Danish settlement near where Trail Creek joins Spillman Creek. This is where the raid turned deadly. Earlier in the day Danes Erskild and Stine Lauritzen allowed their twelve-year-old son to play with Hans Christensen at the nearby Christensen home.[14] This house included the families of two brothers, Petr and Lorentz Christensen. Lorentz's wife, Marie, had a baby daughter, Mary. Petr's wife was Nicoline. Their three children, much older than brother Lorentz's family, were Christian, Helena, and Hans.[15] Christian was working at the Schermerhorn Ranch and was not present this fateful Sunday. The Christensen house amounted to little more than a combination log and sod dugout, built near the banks of Spillman Creek.

The settlement was new; Danes began building crude homes there in February 1869. Nearby, but on the other side of Spillman Creek, was the home of the Lauritzen family. They, too, had been at their site for only a few months. About the time they made their home along Spillman Creek, a German-speaking family arrived in the Saline valley. George and Maria Weichel, along with family friend, Fred Meigerhoff, had recently arrived from Luneburg, Hanover, Germany.[16] Maria Weichel was about twenty years old, and described simply as a well-built and beautiful woman. She was about three months pregnant that May.[17] Her husband, George, was about thirty years old. Together with Fred Meigerhoff, they had been temporarily living at the Ferdinand Erhardt house, about seven miles southeast near the Saline River. While staying at the Erhardt place and during one of their visits to the store at the Schermerhorn Ranch, they met the German-speaking Lauritzens. The Lauritzens encouraged them to stay at their house on Spillman Creek until they could make their own homestead claim near this new Danish settlement. They did this against the advice of Erhardt, who had tried to get them to settle farther up Bullfoot Creek, south of the Saline which was safer from Indian attack.[18] Erhardt said, "But they did not take my advice but took claims on the Spillman. Not more than a week later the Indians appeared on Sunday, May 30th, 1869."[19]

Another adult lived at the Lauritzen home. Otto Peterson, a jeweler, had emigrated with the Lauritzens from northern Germany a few years earlier, to avoid service in the German army.[20] It seems that when the Indians commenced their raid, no one was at the Lauritzen home. Of the seven living there, five would be killed and one taken captive. The first victims killed were Erskild and his wife, Stine Lauritzen. About the time that they went in the direction of the Christensen home to retrieve their son, the Weichels and Fred Meigerhoff took a stroll down Spillman Creek, perhaps to view their newly-claimed land. It is not known if Erskild Lauritzen had a weapon, but George Weichel and Fred Meigerhoff were armed. Otto Peterson was probably not armed. He was likely out investigating his land. It is possible he might have been accompanying the Lauritzens, but this is not known. When found a couple days after the raid, his body was on the opposite side of the creek from the Lauritzens.[21]

The Lauritzens were no doubt quickly surprised and murdered. Why Stine was not taken captive is unknown. Perhaps Erskild carried a pistol and shot her to prevent her capture. Perhaps she was ravished where she was found, and then killed. When discovered the next day, Erskild had been shot in the head and Stine shot in the abdomen.[22] Stine had been scalped and stripped naked except for her stockings and hoop skirt.[23] Her scalp was said to be on display for many years in Pawnee Bill's museum in Oklahoma City. It had been found in the Indian village after the fight at Summit Springs.

Not far from the Lauritzen home, about a dozen Dog Soldiers surprised the Weichels and Meigerhoff. As the men were armed, the Indians were not immediately able to overtake them. Probably, if the group had only included the two men, the Indians might well have ignored them as was earlier done with Zeigler and Alverson. But Maria Weichel was with them, and capturing her would be worth the effort and risk of an armed engagement. The trio made a running fight for almost four miles, going south along Spillman Creek, before running out of ammunition. They were probably trying to escape to the Schermerhorn Ranch, where they knew there would be protection.[24] One can only imagine their state of mind as they tried to elude their pursuers. That they didn't simply succumb to terror at the first shot is a tribute to their courage during this time.

They got roughly half way to the Schermerhorn ranch when the men fired their last bullets. At that moment, the yelling warriors quickly descended upon the men and killed them. Maria was now a captive. She saw the Indians cut her husband's finger off, believing it was to retrieve his ring. However, it was not unusual for Cheyenne Dog Soldiers to cut off a finger from their victim, to make into a human finger necklace. Such an ornament gave power to their beliefs regarding the mutilation of their victims. The Dog Soldiers that captured Maria were now apparently done with their raiding for the day, for she later reported that immediately after she was taken captive, the Indians "put her on a horse and made her ride till they thought they were beyond immediate pursuit where they laid her on the ground and with four holding her arms and legs they all ravished her. She was then gone about three months in pregnancy."[25]

The chase and capture of Maria took about two hours. At about the time that she was captured, another group of Dog Soldiers came upon the Haley home where Susanna and her children, Bridget Kine and her infant daughter, Thomas Noon and his wife, and Nicholas Whalen were all then at the house. Susanna's two older boys might have been playing outside. The house was on the north side of the Saline, about a quarter mile from the banks of the river and two miles west of present-day Lincoln. If Susanna's boys were outside playing, they probably were the first to alert everyone that Indians were approaching. Bridget Kine later recalled that horrifying moment:

> She well remembers the raid of said Indians and saw them when they captured the black mare and colt near her house and was so excited about the loss that she forgot her own danger and came near to falling into the hands of the Indians. Michael Healy [Haley] had taken his family to Ellsworth for protection and left Mrs. Alderdice with her family in his house on the next farm to affiants. Thomas Noon and his wife also Nicholas Whalen were there and the affiant went there for safety during the absence of the claimant [Timothy Kine] at Junction City Kansas. It was Sunday and she could see her own house from Healy's. Affiant stood watching them take said mare until she noticed that all the rest had left her making their escape and then took her two month old baby and followed and took nothing with her but the clothes she had on.[26]

Bridget's husband Timothy also testified about this moment:

> That at the time of said depredation he was on the way to [i.e., returning from] Junction City Kansas

to prove up on his claim before the Land Office and left his wife Bridget Kine at home and she was on the place when the Indians came and he believes saw them there when they captured the black mare. He believes that Nicholas Whalen and Thomas Noon saw them. If Mrs. Kine was not on said farm she was on the one next to it as she was to remain there for safety at night – while he was at Junction City. Michael Healy [Haley] owned the adjoining farm and was at the time in Ellsworth or Ft. Harker but Nicholas Whalen was at his house and so was Thomas Noon and wife and Mrs. Alderdice and her children. Affiant's wife made her escape and with a number of settlers met him at Frank A. Schermerhorn's store on Elkhorn Creek about five miles southeast of where affiant lived. The Indians captured Mrs. Alderdice and her children whom they shamefully abused and murdered.[27]

When Bridget recovered from her initial fright, she quickly grabbed her daughter Katherine, left the Haley home, and ran toward the Saline River, hoping the Indians might not spot her. As her testimony noted, Susanna was already hurrying away with her own children. Bridget at some point helped Susanna by grabbing one of her children, perhaps two-year-old Frank, and then ran "in a wild race for shelter."[28] Her hope was for everyone to run and hide in the grass along the banks of the Saline. But the blue stem grew high and it was difficult to run into it and not leave a trail. Two Dog Soldiers spotted them.[29] Susanna was having trouble bringing the rest of her children, but she would not desert them. When Bridget came close to the river she looked back and saw several of the warriors rushing in her direction. She had been seen!

Being already exhausted from her long flight and carrying the children in her arms she saw that she could not hold out unless she disposed of part of her burden. With great presence of mind she concealed, as she thought, the Alderdice child in the tall grass, at a time when the Indians were not in sight, and then made another rush to the river. She reached the river bank and upon looking back she saw the Indians driving a spear into the defenseless body of the child. They had carried the child a short distance in the direction in which she had gone. During the time that the killing of the Alderdice child was taking place the Indians were yelling and riding round and round in the tall grass looking for Mrs. Kyne but in a few minutes they made straight for the river at a point near where Mrs. Kyne had disappeared.[30]

Bridget then slid down the muddy banks and into the river. Fortunately, there was a large tree that had fallen away from the river. Some of the roots were still in the water, causing a wash out under where the tree once stood:

Into the water Mrs. Kyne plunged to her waist and crawled beneath the bank. It is difficult to imagine how she managed to prevent the infant child from making some outcry but as Mrs. Kyne often stated afterward there 'was never a whimper.' A few feet above her stood the Indians, shouting and screaming, one of them in plain view of Mrs. Kyne. In one arm clasped to her breast she held the child and with the other she took up her apron and was prepared in case the child should attempt to cry, to thrust the end of the apron in the mouth of the child. But for this she had no occasion. After some parlaying among themselves the Indians went east along the north bank of the river.[31]

There she quietly hid, holding her daughter Katherine above her shoulders outside the clear water. Her daughter did not make a sound, and they were not discovered. The Indians came so close to where she was hiding that "she could have put out her hand and touched them."[32] They walked around her hiding spot several times, coming so close she "could see their moccasins, but fortunately they did not see her."[33] Years later, it was reported that she heard one Indian say in English to the other that there had been two women seen running, and thus the other woman must be near in the high grass.[34]

Just before Bridget fled, the Noons and Nicholas Whalen, seeing the Indians at the Kine home nearby, and apparently thinking only of their own safety, mounted their horses and escaped to the west. Three or four Indians chased after them for a short distance but soon gave up, returning to the small band that had captured Susanna and her children. The Noons and Whalen survived uninjured except for the psychological trauma of their own flight and the abandonment of the young mothers and their children. Supposedly, Thomas Noon was a good marksman with his rifle.[35] That he and Whalen did not defend the women led some settlers later to consider killing them for cowardice. Bridget Kine, however, successfully pleaded with the angry settlers not to exact such revenge.[36] It should not be surprising that the Kines went to their defense, as they were all cousins.

When Susanna discovered Indians in the vicinity of the Haley home, the dread of that moment must have been simply awful. There had to be an especially strong sense of angst when she saw the Noons and Whalen mount their horses and flee. Certainly her two oldest sons, John and Willis, were old enough to realize their danger and they, too, must have been overwhelmed with fear. The frantic flight toward the river could not have been done quickly. Susanna was probably carrying Alice under one arm, while perhaps holding Willis's hand as she ran, and being five months pregnant made it more difficult for her. When she could go no farther she "was overcome with terror and sank to the ground incapable of further flight."[37]

What happened next had to be a living nightmare. Timothy Kine said Susanna's children were shamefully abused *and* murdered. This would imply some sort of mistreatment before their murder. Such actions were not uncommon among Dog Soldiers, as noted earlier in the account of the murders of the Bogardus–Bell families in 1868, and as will be shown in the chapter that includes the captivity account of Veronica Ulbrich. Terrible things were probably done to Susanna's children before they were finally murdered in an orgy of violence. Bridget would have heard this.

In 1896, because of her trauma in the 1869 raid, Bridget was institutionalized at the Kansas Insane Asylum in Topeka.[38] She was released and readmitted in 1900 and again in 1906. Her first episode lasted six months, the second one eighteen months. The duration of her third stay is unknown.[39] In 1896, she lost a child and this, along with her Indian terror in 1869, was identified as a contributing cause of the first legal ruling of her insanity. She suffered spiritual delusions of a permanent nature. At times she needed restraint. She would remove her shoes, "dance on the streets and goes all over town barefoot."[40] It is pretty clear that the trauma of her Indian scare was problematic for her for the rest of her life. Bridget died in 1913, about one month after being severely burned in an accident in her home.[41]

When the Indians finally left after killing the children, Susanna was now their captive. Somehow, as her boys were being "abused and murdered," she was able to hold on to her only daughter, her youngest child, little Alice. Together they were tied to a pony. The first newspaper account of this Indian raid reported that Susanna's dead boys were "stripped, but not scalped or mutilated."[42] However, another account reported the children as having their "brains beaten out and their teeth driven into their mouths."[43] Yet a third account noted that Tom Alderdice, upon returning to his home the next day, found "his three children dead; with bullets and arrows yet in their tender bodies, while his wife and babe were carried away captive by the Indian murderers."[44]

When Susanna's family was being killed and she and Alice captured, another band of Dog Soldiers raided two miles further east along the Saline River. There, a mounted warrior and a mounted young teenage Indian boy approached thirteen-year-olds John Strange and Arthur Schmutz. Speaking in broken English, the older warrior said that they were good Pawnee Indians. The older warrior then touched them gently upon their shoulders with a spear.[45] This was done evidently to count coup and to fool the boys into thinking that they would not be harmed. The older Indian nonchalantly rode beyond the boys. The Indian boy, riding his pony, then approached the boys. Without warning, the younger warrior rose up from his pony and violently struck John Strange in the head with his war club. The force of the blow was so fierce that it broke the club and instantly killed young Strange. All John had time to do before he was struck was to utter the words "Oh Lord."[46] The young Indian then turned to Arthur and shot an arrow into his left breast.[47] Although badly wounded, Arthur ran as fast as he could to try to escape from the murderous Indian boy. While running he was able to pull the shaft of the arrow from his breast, but the metal arrowhead remained imbedded in his lung. Young Arthur was taken to the hospital at Fort Harker but the doctors were unable to extract the arrowhead from inside him. He would suffer in the hospital until August 10, nearly eleven weeks after being wounded, when he finally died. The arrowhead had made Arthur the eleventh victim of the deadly Saline River massacre.[48]

C. C. Hendrickson, a cousin to John Strange and about the same age, was a witness to this attack and later wrote an account of what happened. His father and two uncles, including John Strange's father, were the other men accompanying Tom Alderdice and Timothy Kine to Junction City and were all away this Sunday. C. C. Hendrickson's father's house was along the Saline about three-fourths of a mile west from the Strange home. That day Mrs. Strange came to the Hendrickson home to visit, leaving her boys at their house. Later that afternoon, Mrs. George Green also stopped by to visit. Her husband had been in the Beecher Island fight in 1868. She had brought along her two daughters, Lizzie and Bell. Little Lizzie had the distinction of being the first white child born in Lincoln County, back in 1866.[49] Suffering from a headache, Mrs. Green decided to rest at the Hendrickson home. Meanwhile, her two daughters, along with C. C. Hendrickson, joined Arthur Schmutz and John Strange, on a hike to a nearby hill to dig Indian dolios, a vegetable similar to turnips. Fortunately, just before the Dog Soldiers came upon Strange and Schmutz, the two girls and Hendrickson returned to the Hendrickson house.

After Strange was clubbed to death, he was also shot in the head. Everyone in the house heard the shots. Looking out the window, Hendrickson recalled observing

> . . . the Schmutz boy running around the point of the bluff west of our house, and an Indian after him. From the Strange house they [Strange boys in the house] could see them [the Indians] before we could and two of the Strange boys, Riley and Marion [ages twelve and nine][50], took their guns and went to meet the Schmutz boy. He had been shot with an arrow in the back. He pulled the arrow out as he ran but the arrowhead pulled out and was left in his back. When the Indian saw the Strange boys coming, they gave up the chase and started for the house. There were two Indians in sight by this time and in less time than it takes to tell it there was another one or two of them coming toward the house. One was driving off our work horses. They were shot at from the house so they turned back and went to drive the horses off.
>
> About that time one of the women looked south and saw a band of men on horses coming and said, "My God, look at the Indians coming from the south. We are gone." But it proved to be a company of soldiers that had come from Fort Harker.[51]

Newspaper accounts noted Mrs. Green's heroism in saving the women and children from capture and death. The *Manhattan Standard* reported that upon seeing the Indians coming, she retired to a dugout, "- a place dug in the side of a hill or high bank, with port holes looking out – and there with her carbine successfully kept at bay some two dozen Indians or more."[52] Another newspaper reported Mrs. Hendrickson's contribution: "The house of Wm. Hendrickson was saved by the heroism of two women – Mrs. Hendrickson and Mrs. Green – who fired on the savages several times, and finally drove them away."[53]

This act of bravery by two women, done roughly at the same time the Noons and Whalen ignobly fled farther west along the Saline, thus leaving Susanna Alderdice and Bridget Kine alone with their children, no doubt contributed much to the animosity of the local citizens toward Thomas Noon and Nicholas Whalen. It is a strong tribute to the character of the early pioneers in Lincoln County that Noon and Whalen weren't executed for what they had done. It was certainly shameful at best, and cowardly at worst, to have fled as they did, contrary to the claim later made by Mrs. Kine that they could not protect the women and children "against so many Indians."[54] Mrs. Green and Mrs. Hendrickson did it. Why would it have been any different with Noon and Whalen?

It is significant that C. C. Hendrickson recalled the presence of military aid, because later accounts accused the military of doing nothing to assist. Susanna's own brother Eli Zeigler was the first to make this accusation. He noted that the day after the attack, he discovered a company of cavalry camped near Bullfoot Creek near the Erhardt farm, just south of the Saline River from the Hendrickson house. When he informed the officer of the Indian raid of the day before, the officer declined to pursue the Indians, saying instead he would await further orders from Fort Harker. Eli recalled: "We were disgusted with his reply, ate a hard tack and started on home, keeping on the south side of the river. . . ."[55] J. J. Peate also said the military did not aid the pioneer victims, claiming that the cavalry commander said "he knew that the Indians attacked the settlement, but without orders he would not go to their relief."[56] Because of these accounts, some historians have repeated this damaging claim.[57]

Contemporary newspapers at that time contradict such allegations, as do military records. The *Leavenworth Times and Conservative* on June 1, just two days after the raid, reported a dispatch dated from Ellsworth May 31:

T. J. March, Second Lieut. of Troop G, 7th Cavalry, reports that yesterday the Indians attacked the settlements within one mile of his camp on the north side of the Saline River, near the mouth of Bull Foot Creek. He pursued them with thirty men, the Indians taking a southwest course. After a pursuit of several miles he found a small party grazing their horses. He fired on them, and they immediately fled. He followed them fifteen miles after dark, their only loss being ponies, mules and horses abandoned.[58]

The *Junction City Weekly Union* for June 5 noted the Indians "were chased for fifteen miles by a company of the 7th Cavalry, who were in the vicinity but they were unable to get close enough to do them injury."[59] Even the *New York Times* on June 2 said of March's effort to find the Indians: "Lieutenant March and a scouting party, a day or two ago, came up with a small war party of Indians . . . and pursued them fifteen miles, until darkness compelled him to desist."[60] By June 5 General John Schofield, writing from his headquarters at Fort Leavenworth, would comment on this Indian attack in the Saline valley: "They [the Dog Soldiers] have shown no disposition to fight, when they have met with even a slight show of resistance. In every case I have heard of the people killed have either been unarmed, or have attempted to run away without making a fight."[61] In two short weeks General Schofield would accommodate a distraught Tom Alderdice in his office at Fort Leavenworth.

It is a remarkable coincidence that Company G, 7th Cavalry, was actually at the scene of the depredations just as the Indians were finishing up their murderous sortie. Lieutenant Thomas J. March filed an official report of his actions on May 30. It shows the accuracy of the newspaper accounts noted above. Dated May 31, he reported:

Soon after going into camp it was reported to me that the Indians were attacking the settlers not more than a mile from us [Strange and Schmutz killings]. I immediately ordered a detail of fifteen men to remain at the encampment with that portion of the train then in camp, this detail with the one belonging to the remainder of the train coming in, made a force I supposed of about twenty men to remain behind. This was more than one third of the troop, the remainder of about thirty men I took with me and commenced pursuit; after passing the place of attack we could see nothing of Indians for more than two & a half miles. Could only follow the general direction of the course they were reported to have taken viz. (southwest) at the time it was reported that some of the horses were giving out, as they had already made a hard march before coming into camp. I ordered five of the best to move forward to accompany me & took the advance ordering the remainder to act as a reserve and to move up as fast as the horses would allow. After moving about a mile further & while ascending a gentle slope we saw a small party – grazing their ponies near some ravines beyond. I dismounted the men with me and fired into the party – but with no effect. I immediately commenced pursuit and continued it at a rapid pace but our new horses soon commenced faging out & appeared to be gaining but little upon them, night coming on we finally lost sight of them after scouting the different ravines and satisfying ourselves that further pursuit would be useless. I ordered a return march after having pursued them for more than fifteen miles after dark. Returning to camp after midnight, on my return I ascertained the following facts from the settlers, that this was a war party (of about 9 warriors); that we were pursuing but a detached portion of about four or five; that the settlers report one woman and three children missing & are supposed to have been taken by the remaining portion of this band.[62]

The end of March's report helps to understand what was known the day after the raid. He notes that the Dog Soldiers that came upon the Strange and Schmutz boys were an offshoot from the Indians who attacked Susanna, which was a larger party of about nine warriors. He also at this time believed that Susanna and her children were taken captive. It would soon be learned that only Susanna and her daughter were carried off.

Some settlers joined the soldiers to pursue the Indians. Jacob Shafer, a neighbor of the Strange family, who was a few miles away from his home at the time of the raid but quickly learned of it, was one of the pioneers who immediately informed the military about the raiding Indians. He notified the soldiers within half an hour after the killing of John Strange.[63] In an affidavit supporting Timothy Kine's claim for his losses, Shafer reported being with the soldiers when they chased the Indians. He recognized Timothy Kine's black mare in the Indian's possession, plus four horses belonging to Frank Schermerhorn. "The Indians saw the soldiers and escaped with said horses."[64] The soldiers camped across Bullfoot Creek on the evening of May 30, on Shafer's property. A portion of the command remained there for some time.

Shafer also reported on the Kine losses. In addition to stealing the mare and colt, the Indians destroyed everything in the Kine house that they did not take with them. They ripped open the feather mattresses, scattering the contents about the yard. The feather bed had been purchased in Washington, D. C., where Bridget Kine worked as a servant before coming to Kansas. Their cook stove was destroyed. Utensils, silverware, dishes, etc., were all taken. All furniture was destroyed, a rifle stolen, twenty-four chickens lost, quilts, blankets, pillows, etc., all stolen. The Kine's property losses, including the mare, totaled $396.40.[65]

Aftermath of May 30 Raid

The Price of the Prairie[1]

The next day the settlers and soldiers discovered the many murdered victims scattered along Spillman Creek and the Saline River. Tom Alderdice, returning from Junction City with the other men, had been told earlier that morning by one of the Hendrickson brothers of an evil foreboding that something terrible had happened in the settlement while they were gone. This sense of doom caused anxiety in all of the men. Soon a messenger was seen approaching. Mart Hendrickson then turned to everyone and said,

> "Strange, your boy is killed. Alderdice, your family is all killed or captured." Such proved to be the melancholy tidings borne by the courier. This new[s] redoubled their haste, although their horses were almost exhausted. Those who had lost their loved ones at the hands of the murderous fiends were beside themselves with grief and despair and urged their horses to still greater exertions. Hendrickson begged them to spare their teams or they would fail entirely.[2]

At the Schermerhorn Ranch, Timothy Kine found Bridget and his daughter, Katherine. Shortly after sunset on the evening of the raid, Bridget carefully emerged from her hiding place in the Saline River and went east on the south side of the river until she came to the Erhardt place about four miles away.[3] From there she gathered with other settlers at the Schermerhorn Ranch another mile further east. Bridget told Tim of her terrifying ordeal.

Tom Alderdice went to the Hendrickson home where his dead boys had been taken. Young John Strange was also lying dead there. The dead boy had been brought to the house about five o'clock that morning. Susanna and Tom's dead children were brought over later that morning. C. C. Hendrickson recalled the scene when both fathers saw their dead children: "I can never forget the sad look of my uncle J. S. Strange, when he looked on the lifeless form of his boy. I also cannot forget the heart rending cry of Alderdice when he came into the house. . . ."[4]

After the Dog Soldier raid the military remained in the area and surrounding neighborhoods for the rest of the summer. Henry Tucker was still carrying his arm in a sling from the effects of his wound at Beecher Island. Nevertheless, he helped form a command of about sixty men from the area. They would remain on the Hendrickson and Shafer farms until fall.[5] A. J. Pliley, both a veteran of Beecher Island and the 19th Kansas Volunteer Cavalry at the Sweetwater where Sarah White and Mrs. Morgan were rescued, commanded another company of men near where the raid began along Spillman Creek just outside present-day Denmark. There a blockhouse was constructed and named Camp Pliley.

Times were rough for the settlers. The month after the Indian raid, a man named Pat Clary got into a gunfight at the Schermerhorn Ranch. He wounded four men before escaping on horseback to the west. Schermerhorn was shot through the hand. George Green, whose wife successfully fought off the Indians on May 30, was shot in the side. Mr. Lynden was shot in the thigh and Henry Tucker, no doubt with his arm still in a sling, had a thumb and finger shot off. All would recover.[6]

One week before the gunfight, a newspaper reported on a brewing conflict that Lieutenant Edward Law had experienced with some of the settlers. It all came to an ugly head when a correspondent reported false information regarding Lieutenant Law's efforts to protect the settlers. Someone who knew the facts made a reply in the *Leavenworth Times and Conservative*. Perhaps it was Law himself writing anonymously:

> From the Solomon Camp, June 26th, 1869
> Seeing a communication in a New York paper
> the other day from a correspondent on Spillman

Creek, concerning our movements in this vicinity, and which was composed principally of falsehoods and untruths, I deem it my duty to correct some of these, if not all, through the columns of your valuable paper.

After giving an account of the so called defense of their families and property, but what I, as an eyewitness, would call cowardly desertion of them, he goes on to state that after the Indians massacred all the people they could lay their hands on, all in plain view of our command, they started off towards the Solomon River and we moved out after them in military precision, - as he calls it – and appeared to be in a hurry to catch the said Indians, and that we did not go, in the first place, until implored by several citizens to save their wives and families, &c, &c. Also that we proceeded to the Solomon River the next day after the Indians and on reaching the latter place we beheld a party of Indians which we conceived to be too strong for us and that therefore we fell back to Fort Harker and Fort Hays for reinforcements &c. The truth of the affair is, that we arrived at the Solomon [Saline] River Sunday May 30th. We had heard then of the Indians behind us at Fossil Creek Station, but had no idea of their being on the Saline so soon. Any of the settlers we met, if we asked them about Indians, would laugh at us and say that "Indians never troubled them." This was about 4 o'clock in the afternoon. Finding it impossible to cross our wagons over a small creek [Bullfoot], Lieut. Law sent Sergeant [2nd Lieutenant] March down the river to find a camp while he remained behind with a part of the company to effect a crossing at another point, while the men with the wagons were building a ford across the creek. Some of the men heard several shots but not very distinct, up the river about three miles [the Weichel—Meigerhoff murders and the killing of the Alderdice children], but they thought nothing of it, as they did not dream of Indians. Meanwhile Sergeant [Lt.] March had found a camp about three miles below where the wagons were, but his party had scarcely unsaddled before they noticed some commotion on the opposite side of the river among the citizens, and directly after a party of settlers came running in shouting "Indians." Sergeant [Lt.] March speedily ordered the squad to saddle up instantly, and in less than five minutes he was dashing across the bridge over the Saline, and in a short time was at the scene of bloodshed [Strange—Schmutz killings]. The "military precision" was not very great; every man was trying to see who could get there first. We started on the route pursued by the Indians, and ran them so close in a ravine that we came upon two of them, just mounting stock which they had ran off. As it was very dark we could not see how many there were of them, and aided by the darkness they escaped. We captured two of their horses here.

Sergeant [Lt.] March, finding that the Indians were too far ahead to think of following them any further with his jaded horses, accordingly returned to camp about 12 o'clock p.m.

The next day Lieutenant Law proceeded with a part of the company to the Solomon River, leaving Sergeant [Lt.] March behind with the remainder to bring up the wagons. Instead of a large party of Indians attacking Lieutenant Law and forcing him to retreat to Forts Harker and Hays, he met with nothing more formidable than a party of citizens shut up in a log shanty, who, in their cowardly terror, fired a whole volley into the Lieutenant's party, without hurting anybody though, owing probably to their shaky nerves.

Most of the citizens on the Saline manifested a great disposition to run to where the largest crowd was, forgetting all about their defenseless women and children [Whalen–Noon flight], and leaving them for us to take care of, as they probably thought we were not quite as bad as the Indians. We had several guards that night on houses where the "men folks" had all disappeared, to turn up again in the morning.[7]

110

This account is instructive in that it complements the military reports Lieutenant Law had written, plus it shows just how close the cavalry was in perhaps preventing the deadly raid. Probably, the Indians had scouted the area the day before and knew then that the military was not there. Susanna Alderdice came so close to avoiding her fate. This newspaper commentary also shows the tension that existed between the army and the outlying settlements. One newspaper article, however, did acknowledge the good work done by Lieutenant Law's Company G:

> Troops have been sent here [Mitchell County] several times for our protection, but as a general thing, too late to do much good, except the company of U.S. troops sent here from Fort Hays, last spring [1869], commanded by First Lieutenant Law [wounded at the Washita fight], G Company, 7th Cavalry, in company with Lieut. March. These officers and men bore a noble part in trying to protect the settlers of this valley, going night and day to all points where any alarm was given, and in fact were the only company of men in the regular service who seemed to take any interest in protecting the frontier settlers.[8]

Law's company remained active in the area for most of the summer, some of them camping at the Shafer property, but most moving to the north, back into the vicinity of the August—October 1868 raids between present-day Beloit and Minneapolis. Indians were reported in and around Lincoln, Mitchell, Ottawa, Republic and Cloud Counties for more than two weeks after the May 30 raid.

On May 31, Lieutenant Law wrote that he would scout along the Saline River, but if he found no signs of Indians he would move north to the settlements along the Solomon River.[9] Earlier that morning, some of his men did assist the settlers in recovering the dead along the Saline.[10] Lieutenant March was ordered, later that day, to bring the supply wagons along with his portion of Company G to Asher Creek, about twenty-five miles to the north. Law and the rest of the company preceded him there.[11]

As Law suspected, the Indians moved north of Lincoln County. In a letter dated June 2, from camp on the mouth of Asher Creek and the Solomon River, about a half-mile southwest of present Asherville, Law reported three encounters with Indians:

> About 10 o'clock on the morning of the first – inst. – one of the settlers reported to me that he saw a party of about 12 men riding down from the bluffs towards the Solomon River, about two miles from where I had bivouacked during the night. I immediately ordered the troop to saddle up and, dividing it into two equal portions of fifteen men each, placing a sergeant in command of one & taking the other myself, I started in pursuit. I had taken the north side of the river and ordered the Sergt. to move down on the south: they apparently saw my party first, as they were about to cross the river, immediately turned round and struck off to the southwest passing within about five hundred yards of Sergt. Miller's party at a gallop; he immediately gave chase and pursued them for about five miles but they drew away from him rapidly and lost themselves in the ravines. The second pursuit occurred in the afternoon just as I was going into camp and after Lieut. March had joined me with the wagons; a settler came galloping over to me and told me that he heard shots fired in rear of his house about two miles off; I was just at that moment about to start out with a detachment of fifteen men to scout the country around. I immediately started towards the point indicated by the settler. The Indians saw me very soon after I left my camp; I saw them going over the hill & gave chase at once; they had nearly two miles a start of me and after running them for about eight miles I had to give it up my horses tired by previous marching were soon out of wind. Whilst I was in pursuit of the last named party and about half an

hour after I had left camp another small party tried to stampede the horses of the remaining portion of my command; the herd was grazing within two hundred [yards?] of the camp; the Indians appeared very suddenly coming out from the river a short distance below the camp and ran through the herd shouting, waving their lances, and pricking the horses with them; they were fired upon by the herders and the rest of the command but none of them hit; they however wounded one man slightly on the head (1 Buell of "D" Troop temporarily attached to "G") and drove off two horses. Sergt. Harris and seven or eight of the men who first managed to saddle their horses started in pursuit giving them a very spirited chase forcing them to drop one of the horses & coming within two hundred yards of the last Indian, they would undoubtedly have killed him had he not expertly changed his pony for the remaining horse taken from the herd, it was a very fast one & on him he managed to escape them; the pony however they got.[12]

Law went on to report that each of these three small bands of Indians went in different directions and their trail could not be picked up except by an expert trail man, and that the Indians would not be expected to camp within forty miles of the settlements. He also felt that his timely arrival "saved the settlements here from massacre."[13] The settlers had lost several horses, but no lives at this point. The Indians, he believed, came down from the Republican River and could be found in that direction, but he was not comfortable in going there for fear of leaving the settlements unprotected.

Law was correct in his judgment as to where the Indians were headed. On June 1, in Republic County, at the town of Scandia, Indians took two horses, provisions, blankets, and clothing from Robert Watson. What the Indians did not steal, they destroyed.[14] The next day, June 2, twelve-year-old Ezra Adkins was killed near the Republican River, not far from where Sarah White had been captured the summer before. He was driving cows near his home when two Indians took his horse. When he ran, they rode up to him on their horses, one each holding him by his arms while a third Indian "came behind and shot him through the head twice, and left him on the ground dead, but not scalped."[15] A neighbor, Nels Nelson, witnessed Ezra's death. Nels and his two brothers were working on the other side of the Republican when about thirty screaming Dog Soldiers descended upon young Ezra. Only about twenty of the warriors were mounted, but the other ten Indians were holding the tails of the ponies ridden by the mounted warriors. When Ezra saw the band,

> . . . the terror stricken boy dismounted from his horse thinking his chances would be better for gaining the tall grass and bushes along the river where he might elude them by hiding, but one savage caught his horse while another, who had been hanging on the tail of the mounted Indian's pony, pursued their little victim, caught and held him fast by the hand, the boy resisting with all his strength . . . the savage on horseback seemingly ordered the boy released and then shot him twice in the head. After piercing him with bullets of their unerring rifles, they stooped over the lifeless body . . . robbing the little fellow of some of his clothing.[16]

After witnessing the murder, Nels Nelson rushed home, gathered his young family, and with his father and brothers fled across the river to the Adkins home where they informed Ezra's mother about his death. They were wise to flee their house. After killing young Adkins, the Indians then entered the Nelson home, destroying everything they didn't steal. Instead of taking the cured bacon, Nelson reported the Indians speared it with the poisoned tips of their deadly spears, hoping that the returning settlers would later eat it and die.[17] Later that night Nelson accompanied Ezra's father to recover the dead boy. The boy's faithful dog led the men to the body:

> The scene was a ghastly one, with the brains oozing from the gunshot wound that had been inflicted

about seven hours earlier. The grief of the family was terrible to behold and a scene never to be forgotten by the little group of settlers gathered there, where a few hours before the family had rejoiced in dreams of a future happy home.[18]

While Ezra Adkins was being killed in Republic County, Law was chasing raiders in Mitchell County. On June 1, Dog Soldiers came to a farm about three miles west of present Beloit. Schultz was enjoying his dinner at his neighbor's house when he saw the Indians take his horse. He and his neighbor, Andrew Pearson, were able to escape, apparently to the protection of Lieutenant Law's soldiers camped on Asher Creek. When Schultz returned to his house, he found everything in it either destroyed or stolen.[19]

On June 9, a party of four Indians followed the Solomon River past Asherville, all the way to Ottawa County, near Minneapolis, where James McHenry lost one horse and Joseph Jagger lost several. This would be the last documented Indian raid in Ottawa County.[20] On June 10, Lieutenant Law again wrote from Asher Creek. He noted several mules and a pony stolen from settlers, near where he was camped. A steer was found the next morning with an arrow sticking in its side.[21] At eleven-thirty on the night of June 11, Law wrote of more attacks:

> At about sunset this evening & as my last scouting party was just getting in, the settlements on Asher Creek were attacked by a party of about 50 Indians. I heard the firing & with a party of about 18 men, who were just saddled up, started in pursuit: they were about a mile off when we first saw them, about 10 in number and ran at full speed up Asher Creek: as we pursued this number increased: they apparently had been scattered all along the creek: we chased them for about 8 miles. Lieut. March & myself with 3 or 4 men got within about five hundred yards of the rearmost Indians, the rest of the detachment being scattered at different distances, from a quarter of a mile to a mile

& a half behind: we gave them a volley, apparently without effect.

We mounted again and kept on after them; they were mounted upon faster animals, I think, than even the best of our horses & seemed simply to desire to keep ahead of us & out of gunshot: as they were crossing a gully we got again within gunshot of them & gave another volley with the same apparent effect; darkness set in almost immediately after this and we lost sight of them entirely: it was too dark even to follow a trail, so after groping on for some little distance further and dismounting some of the men and sending them in front, in hopes of coming upon them unawares, I gave it up and returned to camp. As far as I can learn they did no damage other than wounding one man (a settler), slightly and driving away one horse. We recovered some cattle that they were driving off, a yoke of oxen and some sacks of flour, that they were taking with them. I shall start early in the morning strike their trail if possible & follow it up should there be the slightest probability of my being able to overtake them. I have left small parties of men in the houses of settlers on Asher Creek, so that should they attack again tonight, a thing not probable, they will be thoroughly able to defend themselves.[22]

The settler that Law says was slightly wounded was August Ernest. His wound turned out to be serious. He was shot behind the left knee. Ernest was returning with two other men from a trip to Junction City to obtain provisions. About two miles up from where Asher Creek joins the Solomon River, around seventy-five Indians came upon him and the other men in the wagon. All three men were able to escape. Ernest ran to the Nelson farm, visible south from where the Indians appeared. A screaming Indian chased him, wounding him before he got to the house. Before being taken to Fort Harker, where he remained for eleven months, Surgeon Renick, accompanying Law's company, removed the bullet from Ernest's knee. Ernest was unable to walk without crutches for the rest of his life. In addition to his severe injury, he also lost a horse. All the provisions in his dugout and wagon were either stolen or destroyed.[23]

The next day Lieutenant Law again tried to locate the Indians. They were still in the area because on this day Nancy Hewitt, who lost her husband in the deadly August raid the year before, once again had her home attacked, but this time only lost a horse.[24] Law reported being unable to find the Indians' trail, as "they had scattered apparently and their ponies had left no track on the thick buffalo grass." He also noted his belief that he had "understated their number in my report of yesterday, some of the settlers report them as numbering over one hundred, but fifty is as many as I had in my sight at any one time during the chase."[25]

Lieutenant Law writes something in this last letter that helps one to understand the difficulty of finding the trail of an Indian raiding party. The Indians knew where their main camp was and how to get there. But the thick buffalo grass on the Kansas prairie made it extremely difficult to find any trail leading back to the main village. In order to obscure their trail, raiding warriors were adept at scattering in all directions. This tactic of scattering, coupled with the thick prairie grass covering the ground, was a nearly perfect tactic in keeping a large Indian village hidden.

Moving a large village from one spot to another was a different matter. The larger the village, the more difficult it was to hide evidence of both an abandoned camp and its movement to another site. This fact will bear itself out later when General Carr finds Tall Bull's abandoned campsites. In the summer months, once a village was secretly set in a particular area and Indians went from there to raid, it was nearly impossible to locate the village. It was like hunting the proverbial needle in the haystack. This is precisely what occurred in Kansas in 1869. Thus, while all the raiding was occurring in central Kansas in late May and early June, the cavalry was guessing at where the Indians were coming from. The best guess was the

117

Indians were in north central or northwest Kansas, and from there coming to the south to conduct their raids. But precisely where was nothing more than guesswork. Lieutenant Law's report shows how frustrated he was trying to find where the Indians were coming from. There was simply no trail to follow.

While Lieutenant Law tried in vain to locate the Indian camp, there was another determined man with the same idea in mind. Tom Alderdice was doing everything in his power to find and hopefully rescue his wife and daughter. After burying his boys, Tom left on June 1 on his own scouting mission. If he could find an Indian trail, then he could lead the cavalry back to the village and rescue his family. While on raids, Indians generally traveled no more than 100 miles from their main village. Often the raiders would be just a day's ride from the village.[26] Tom thought he could find their main camp. He wrote of this journey:

> I started in pursuit on the 1st of June, traveled from Saline River three miles east of Spillman Creek, north by west striking the north branch of Salt Creek. Distance 12 miles. Traveled west by north up north branch of Salt Creek, striking Spillman Creek about fi mile above main fork. Distance 9 miles. Traveled up west fork of Spillman to head of creek traveling west by north, crossed to Wolf Creek striking east fork; went up east fork about 4 miles, crossed to west fork. Found trail. Followed trail to creek, name unknown. Traveled north to Solomon up north fork of Solomon. Saw Indians (3 in number) hunting, still further up creek Indians. I supposed a large camp above, secreted myself in ravine to watch movements. Could see nothing but Indians going out and returning to creek. Returned back to settlement for help.[27]

Tom had found the village! Using present-day locations, Tom had started from Lincoln, traveled northwest past Ash Grove and Hunter, from there west into Osborne County, then north near Covert, northeast past Osborne and finally up somewhere near Portis and Harlan in Smith County.

Somewhere on the north fork of the Solomon River near these present-day towns, he had discovered the village. He had traveled nearly 100 miles. The location was a perfect place in which the Indians would be able to conduct all the raids that had occurred in May and June that year. All of the raids were within striking distance of this village. The danger Tom faced and obstacles he overcame in finding this village prove his ability as a frontiersman and his devotion as Susanna's husband.

To carefully track the Indians to their village, and remain undiscovered himself, took precious time. Several days passed before Tom returned to the settlements to report his find. By then there were too few soldiers in the settlements to strike the village. Even Fort Harker did not have any troops available. It may have been at this time that settlers felt rebuffed by the military. Nearly forty years later both Eli Zeigler and J. J. Peate incorrectly recalled the military refusing to march against the village Tom had discovered, confusing this event with the murderous events of May 30. At any rate, Tom again took matters into his own hands, this time traveling in the opposite direction, all the way to Fort Leavenworth, where General John Schofield had his headquarters. Schofield commanded all the troops in the Department of the Missouri, which included all of Kansas.

When he arrived at Leavenworth on June 19, Tom discovered that General G. A. Custer was visiting there, serving as a judge in an upcoming horse fair.[28] He first met with Custer and appealed to him for help in the recovery of Susanna and Alice. He was met with the "red tape" of government policy, something that neither he nor Custer could eliminate. But it was reported in the local paper the next day as an example of a great government wrong:

> There are times when what is known as "red tape" may be excusable in military as in other matters. There are times, however, when its observance in military matters is likely to prove productive of a great wrong. A case in point was reported to us yesterday.

A gentleman living on the frontier, whose wife and youngest child, together with a young Swede girl, . . . had been captured by Indians, and whose . . . other children had been killed by these murdering savages, arrived in the city Friday afternoon, for the purposes of securing military aid in recovering those thus captured. The gentleman meeting General Custer in the city shortly after his arrival, told his story and appealed to him for aid. The General told him he had no power to act in the matter, but advised him to go at once to the Commanding General of the Department, remarking at the same time that as it was nearly five o'clock, he might not be able to see him that evening, as the offices were usually closed at that hour. The gentleman, *terribly grieved at his loss and at the threatened and probable fate of the captured*, would not rest until he had made an effort to do and have done all that was possible for their relief, and hence posted off at once to the Fort. As had been suggested by General Custer, it was after five at the time he arrived there, and he, in accordance with custom, was refused an audience until nine o'clock the following morning. . . .

The *distress of the gentleman* in question at his failure to get an audience and an order for troops to follow hard in pursuit of the flying Indians was very great, *eliciting the profound sympathy of all who saw him and heard his story*. From five o'clock in the evening till nine in the morning is a long time to wait, with such weighty and soul-harrowing thoughts resting upon one. . . . With two helpless women in the hands of these red devils, the one a wife, with a young child, who will wonder the man was nearly distracted on being refused an audience on Friday afternoon.[29]

When Tom Alderdice met with Custer, Custer had been so moved by Tom's story that he asked his wife, Libbie, who was with him, to listen to it. Tom repeated his story, and Libbie was so affected that twenty-one years later she would vividly recall when she met him:

He [General Custer] came to me after that, while we were stopping a day or two at the hotel in Leavenworth, to ask me to see a distracted man

120

with whom he had been talking. When I found that the man was almost wild with grief over the capture of his wife by Indians, and the murder of his children, I begged to be spared witnessing such a painful sight when I could do no good. The reply was that sympathy was something every one needed, and I made no further resistance. The man was as nearly a madman as can be. His eyes wild, frenzied, and sunken with grief, his voice weak with suffering, his tearstained, haggard face – all told a terrible tale of what he had been and was enduring. He wildly waved his arms as he paced the floor like some caged thing, and implored General Custer to use his influence to organize an expedition to secure the release of his wife. He turned to me with trembling tones, describing the return to his desolate cabin. . . . With the darkest forebodings – for those were troubling days to the early settler – he began to run, and, near some logs, he almost fell upon the dead and mutilated body of one child. Not far off was a little shoe, and some light hair, evidently torn from the downy head of another child, and a few steps from the door the two younger children lay in pools of blood, their little heads scalped, their soft flesh still pierced by arrows. Worse by far was the further discovery that awaited him. The silence in the cabin told its awful tale, and he knew, without entering, that the mother of the little ones had met with the horrible fate which every woman in those days considered worse than death.[30]

In addition to meeting with General Custer June 19, Tom was interviewed by a writer for the *Leavenworth Times and Conservative*. This interview probably occurred while he was waiting his audience with General Schofield the next morning. The written summary of this interview was printed in nearly all the Kansas newspapers, and also in the *New York Times* and other newspapers across the nation. Americans learned of his family tragedy. In this interview, Tom shared a graphic account of what happened to his family and his horrible discovery:

We received a call yesterday from Mr. Thomas Alderdice, who resides – or did reside, before his family was murdered and his property destroyed by Indians – on the Saline River, about one and a half miles below the mouth of Spillman Creek. . . .

On Sunday, the 30th day of last May [31], as Mr. Alderdice was returning from Salina [Junction City], and when about three miles from his home, he heard that a band of Indians had been into the settlement and murdered a large number of people and destroyed considerable property. On arriving at his home he found it deserted, and was almost paralyzed with grief at finding one of his children . . . dead on the ground with four bullets in his body, and another of his children dead, shot with five arrows. A third child had five arrows in his body, one entering his back to the depth of five inches. . . . Mrs. Alderdice and her babe, aged eight months, were carried away captive by the Indians.[31]

On the morning of June 21, Tom finally had his meeting with Major General John Schofield. General Schofield apparently left no memoir of this meeting. Tom, however, did write a letter that day for the general. In it he described his scouting activities noted earlier. But, more importantly, he gave a physical description, albeit brief, of his wife Susanna:

Description of Mrs. Susan Alderdice, captured by Indians on Saline River, Lincoln County, Kans, May 30th, 1869.

Height: Medium

Complexion: Light

Hair: Light Brown

Age: Twenty Two years

Eyes: Blue[32]

He also wrote that his wife "had a female child eight months old, with her, when captured."

Tom was, however, incorrect in noting Susanna's age. She was not twenty-two in 1869. Born in the first six months of the year 1840, she was in fact twenty-nine-years old. One can only speculate as to the cause of this error. Either Tom did not know her real age, which was one year older than he, or for unknown reasons, he chose to misstate her age.

General Schofield must have explained to Tom his thinking regarding the best strategy to find the Indians holding his wife. Telegraph communications at Fort Harker would have revealed by then that the Indians had been gone from the river valley for about a week. The belief would be that they would be moving toward the west and probably into the northern country of Wyoming and Montana. There were not enough soldiers to pursue the Indians from the vicinity of Lincoln County. Indeed, Custer's horses, after the Washita campaign, still were not recovered sufficiently for another extended expedition. But General Eugene A. Carr's 5th Cavalry could be used, and in fact was at that time in the field, right in the vicinity of where the Dog Soldiers were expected to withdraw. General P. H. Sheridan had recently learned that some of the Cheyenne who had spent the winter season in the Powder River country in the north had come down to the Kansas settlements.[33] It was these Indians who had joined Tall Bull at about the time of the fights with Carr's cavalry on May 13 and 16. Carr had earlier in the month been ordered to scout in the Republican River valley. That likely would be the Indians' destination.

The direction the Indian village was expected to travel, however, was out of General Schofield's jurisdiction and in General C. C. Augur's Department of the Platte. Still, General Schofield was aware that General Carr had already entered the field in search of Indians in the Republican River valley. He no doubt assured Tom that this expedition would find the Indians who came from the village Tom discovered. Schofield telegraphed Tom's letter to General Augur. Auger sent it by courier to Carr in the field, "with request that such efforts as may be practable [sic] be made by the troops in his department to rescue these captives."[34] In addition to forwarding Tom's letter to the Department of the Platte, Schofield also forwarded it to the commander at Camp Supply with a request to notify Cheyenne Chief Little Robe that if Chief Cardigan had not yet been released, he would "be retained as a hostage for the captives in question and 'Little Robe' notified to that effect."[35]

That was about all Schofield could do to relieve Tom's worries. Tom's letter would later be dispatched in the field to Louis Tesson, the surgeon accompanying Carr's expedition. Tom went back to the Saline valley. Probably with other settlers, but perhaps once again alone, he returned to where he had discovered the village. It was now abandoned, but amid the discarded items left by the Indians, Tom's worst fears were realized. Carr later wrote that in the empty village, probably hanging in a tree was the lifeless form of little Alice, strangled with a bowstring.[36] Alice was killed the third day of her captivity because her incessant crying annoyed the Indians.[37] Susanna witnessed this brutal murder, just as she had with her little boys.

The three pioneer accounts of Alice's death differ from this account given by General Carr. Barr, in *A Souvenir History of Lincoln County, Kansas*, says Alice was strangled on Bullfoot Creek near the settlements on her first night of captivity. Her body was hung in a tree.[38] Roenigk, in *Pioneer History of Kansas*, merely says Alice was strangled, neither giving the day nor the place.[39] Bernhardt, in *Indian Raids in Lincoln County, Kansas, 1864 & 1869*, gives two accounts, saying Maria Weichel later gave both versions. He repeats Barr's account, but adds a different one, that Alice was killed on her third day because "it was crying a good deal, which annoyed the savages so much that they then wrung its head off and threw the several parts of the body into the stream."[40] The Barr account cannot be accurate because the Indians did not camp on Bullfoot Creek the night of the raid. Lieutenant Law's report clearly shows the Indians were chased at least fifteen miles. That also eliminates the one account in Bernhardt. Bernhardt's other account that Alice was murdered on her third day of captivity would mean she was in all likelihood killed in the village that Tom discovered. All of these pioneer accounts were written *after* Carr made his claim in 1906 that Alice Alderdice was strangled with a bowstring and that Tom found her body. The three pioneer accounts were written many years after Susanna's brother, Eli, and her parents, had left the Lincoln County area. There was simply no one in Lincoln County when these were written who had contact with Tom Alderdice, except for Roenigk, who published his account in 1933. In fact, Tom would not return to Lincoln County for forty-two years, which was when Roenigk met with him.[41] Further, Carr's own report of the Republican River Expedition notes on July 20, 1869, that Alice was strangled in her third day of captivity. This account, written nine days after it was reported to Carr, must be accurate. He learned this from his translated interview with Maria Weichel after the Summit Springs fight. If Alice died on her third day of captivity, it would have occurred in the village that Tom discovered. She was probably dead for a few days when Tom first found the village. For Carr to have known years later that Tom discovered his dead daughter shows that Tom must have returned to the now abandoned village after meeting with General Schofield.

Tom Alderdice, Susanna's second husband. Susanna married Tom on June 28, 1866. Tom was a veteran of the Beecher Island Fight.
Courtesy of Orvel Criqui, Lawrence, Kansas.

Dog Soldier Captivity

*Women who returned from Indian captivity rein-
forced the emotional reaction that death was the
preferable fate.[1]*

*Alas, how many poor captive women have suffered
this to them worse fate than death! May the end of
such atrocities be near at hand![2]*

Susanna's terror that awful day of May 30, 1869 must have
been profound. Witnessing the murder of her boys would have
been immeasurably worse. Her one remaining hope was that
the Dog Soldiers would not kill Alice. Tied to a pony with her
little daughter tight against her chest, Susanna and the Dog
Soldiers left the immediate area at dusk.[3] As in Maria
Weichel's case, Susanna would be stripped of her clothing and
repeatedly raped by her captors. This was a practice known to
the Cheyenne as "staking a woman on the prairie (noha's-w-
stan)." It had its origins in Cheyenne society as a punishment
against an adulterous married Cheyenne woman. The woman
would be placed away from the village and all Indians of the
military society would take their turns raping her, allowing the
release of "all the pent-up, subconscious, frustration-bred
sexual aggression of the males."[4]

This practice of anger, rage, violence, and shame was freely
acted upon the white women who were taken captive by Dog
Soldiers. The act could be so violent that at times women would
die in the process. Susanna, of course, was not raped to the
point of insensibility because there were not enough Indians
who had captured her to cause that. She would, however, have
been repeatedly raped until her arrival at the village. Such an
experience was unimaginable to American women on the frontier.

The reference in Susanna's day to describe this ordeal was a "fate worse than death."[5]

Col. Richard Dodge graphically summarized the rape experience:

> The rule is this. When a woman is captured by a party she belongs equally to each and all, so long as that party is out. When it returns to the home encampment, she may be abandoned for a few days to the gratification of any of the tribe who may wish her, after which she becomes the exclusive property of the individual who captured her, and henceforward has protection as his wife.
>
> No words can express the horror of the situation of that most unhappy woman who falls into the hands of the savage fiends . . . she is borne off in triumph to where the Indians make their first camp. Here, if she makes no resistance, she is laid upon a buffalo robe, and each in turn violates her person, the others dancing, singing, and yelling around her. If she resists all her clothing is torn from her person, four pegs are driven into the ground, and her arms and legs, stretched to the utmost, are tied fast to them by thongs. Here, with the howling band dancing and singing around her, she is subjected to violation after violation, outrage after outrage, to every abuse and indignity, until not infrequently death releases her from suffering. The Indian woman, knowing this inevitable consequence of capture, makes no resistance, and gets off comparatively easy. The white woman naturally and instinctively resists, is 'staked out,' and subjected to the fury of passions fourfold increased by the fact of her being white and a novelty. Neither the unconsciousness nor even the death of the victim stops this horrible orgie [sic]; and it is only when the fury of their passions has been glutted to satiety that she is released if alive, or scalped and mutilated if dead. If she lives, it is to go through the same horrible ordeal in every camp until the party gets back to the home encampment.[6]

Dodge's chilling account of rape of female captives, it will be seen, was devastatingly accurate. The question might be asked, why did Indians take women and children captive? Some think revenge. Perhaps also they were to serve as slaves. Less likely might be to replenish a tribe from losses occurred in fighting.[7] But by far, the main motive for capturing frontier women was profit. Dodge: "Indians always prefer to capture rather than kill women, they being merchantable property. White women are unusually valuable, one moderately good-looking being worth as many ponies as would buy from their fathers three or four Indian girls."[8] As Rister succinctly noted, "The profit to be derived far out-weighed Indian grievances – misdeeds of the whites, slaughter of the buffalo, and settler occupation of favorite hunting grounds – as a motive for raids and outbreaks."[9]

Dodge further noted the typical experience of female captives:

> The life of such a woman is miserable beyond expression, the squaws forcing her to constant labor, and beating her on any, or without, provocation. She, however, fares and lodges exactly as the other members of the family of her owner, attends the dances, and is in no way socially ostracized. She brings her owner more or less revenue, dependent upon her beauty; and, as property, is worth quite as much as an equally good-looking girl of virtue. She is a favorite stake at the gambling-board, and may change masters half a dozen times a day, as varies the fortune of the game; passing from hand to hand; one day the property of the chief, the next day, of a common warrior. No discredit attaches to the ownership or farming out of these unhappy women.[10]

No known recorded accounts of the captivity of Susanna Alderdice and Maria Weichel exist, but six weeks of such an experience had to be horrendous. To understand their ordeal, it is necessary to review other captivity accounts during this time. If there are similarities in experiences in these other accounts, then the likelihood is that Susanna and Maria's sufferings were not different. What does emerge is the knowledge that a woman's fate in Indian captivity was indeed the most feared experience she could encounter during these tumultuous times of Indian raids along new frontier settlements. Further, if a woman were rescued, her integration back into society was not at all easy. Popular published accounts written of Indian captivity were often mere whitewashes of the truth, motivated primarily as a means to reclaim a meaningful identity for the rescued female.[11] The truth was often much worse. Indeed, the truth, known to people at the time, could not be spoken simply because it was so horrific. It was viewed as a shameful experience, and was not to be discussed.[12]

Dog Soldiers on August 8, 1864, captured Mrs. Nancy Jane Morton on the Overland Trail near Plum Creek Ranche, Nebraska. Her husband, Thomas F. Morton, had gone into partnership with Matthew G. Pratt in Sidney, Iowa, to procure and deliver goods by freight to Denver, Colorado. Mercantile goods, valued at $16,104.38 were loaded onto four freight wagons, pulled by fourteen mules and two horses. Three men were hired as freighters to drive the wagons. Other people rounding out the train included Nancy's husband, Thomas, her brother, cousin, and other relatives. The wagon train totaled thirteen people. Leaving Sidney on July 31, they only got as far as Plum Creek when early in the morning on August 8, the Indians descended upon them. In a short time all the men were dead, and Mrs. Morton, who was pregnant, along with seven-year-old Daniel Marble, were taken captive.[13]

The Indians who committed this depredation were not Sioux, as reported later by Black Kettle, but in fact Cheyenne Dog Soldiers, and some Arapahoe. They were under the leadership of Dog Soldier Chief Bull Bear. When Mrs. Morton was finally brought into the Indian village north in the Powder River country at Pond Lake, she was joined with other captives, "Miss Roper, Mrs. Eubank and five Children."[14] These captives were taken the day before Mrs. Morton was captured, along the Blue River near present-day Oak, Nebraska.[15]

Nancy Morton's Indian depredation claim depicts a horrible captivity. In a deposition taken May 11, 1865, she notes that she was traded five times to Indian traders, and four times recaptured. Mr. Coffey and Mr. Bissonette finally bought her and delivered her to Fort Laramie, Wyoming Territory, on February 20, 1865.[16] In a deposition of June 3, 1865, she stated that she "suffered from all the abuse and indignity that could be practiced toward her not only by one Indian, but many. . . ."[17] In a letter dated May 30, 1868, coincidentally, exactly one year before Susanna and Maria endured a similar fate, Mrs. Morton is noted as having survived "a long and most brutal captivity with barely her life. . . ."[18] Yet a further affidavit dated May 11, 1868, notes that the "captivity of Mrs. Morton . . . was one of hardship she having undergone great wrongs and sufferings at the hands of her barbarous captors. . . ."[19]

In addition to the information gleaned from Mrs. Morton's Indian Depredation Claim, Nancy wrote two versions of her captivity. Never intended for publication, these manuscripts did not appear in print until 1993, under the title *Captive of the Cheyenne*.[20] Nancy describes her capture shortly after leaving the Plum Creek Ranche,

> . . . when a band of Indians about three hundred in number, dashed over a hill, and came down upon us, whooping, howling, and shouting, and shooting arrows and guns.
>
> Our teams were stampeded, overturned the wagons, and the Indians commenced a general slaughter of our party, killing my husband, my brother, my cousin, and everyone of the thirteen, except myself and a boy, Daniel Marble, who was about nine years old. Those killed were all scalped in my presence. I was shot by an arrow in my left thigh, and also in my left side, causing severe wounds in each place. When the teams were stampeded, the wagon wheel ran against my left side, bruising me severely, and as I believe fractured my ribs, and from which I have ever since suffered, and often severe and excruciating pain.[21]

Nancy goes on to describe the Indians beating her with whips, "and whip stock, and other things, and finally took hold of me, and threw me upon the horse, with a limb on either side, compelling me to go with them."[22] One Indian took Daniel Marble and "whipped the little fellow severely because he too was crying."[23] Five days later, she miscarried her baby, "on account of my severe and ill treatment, and my eyes went blind."[24] Regarding cruel treatment, Nancy also reported that the Indians would take the fresh scalps of her dead relatives and throw them into her face, laughing as they did so. One scalp she recognized as that of her brother.[25]

When she was finally brought to the village, she experienced a practice that traces back to the Cheyenne Algonquin roots. She faced the dreaded gauntlet:

> They formed themselves in two lines and made me ride the gauntlet between these two lines, and meantime they threw missiles of every description and lances at me, lashed me with whips and sticks, and everything they could get hold of, while I rode both up and down the line. My body was blue on each side from their treatment, the striking of the missiles, and whips, from below the knee to the waist.[26]

Other captives of the Cheyenne describe the gauntlet experience. In 1874, four girls were taken captive in western Kansas, the rest of the family murdered. Seventeen-year-old Catherine German would later describe her frightening experience when riding into the main village three days after her capture:

> Men, women and children, also barking dogs, took after us. The Indians grabbed at me from all sides as we passed them. I wondered if they intended to tear me into pieces. They did tear my dress skirt into strips. Later, I learned that it was their custom, at that time, to grab at a captive, and if anyone could pull her from the pony she rode, she

would belong to the one thus obtaining possession of her.[27]

Catherine would elsewhere describe this experience:

> My clothes were torn from me. I was stripped naked, and painted by the old squaws, and made the wife of the chief who could catch me when fastened upon the back of a horse which was set loose on the prairie. I was made the victim of their desires – *nearly all in the tribe* – and was beaten and whipped time and time again. They made me carry wood and water like the squaws. I had to kill dogs and cook them for the Indians to eat. We had nothing but dog-meat and horse-meat.[28]

Catherine's sister Sophia, twelve at the time of capture, would later write of this event, "Like the little girls I too wore my same dress I had on when captured, until the Indians tore it off of me in the wild ride through the main camp."[29]

Would Susanna and Maria experience the gauntlet when brought to the Indian village? It will probably never be known, unless a narrative from Maria is some day found. But there is no reason to believe that they did not experience the gauntlet. After a raiding party returned to their village and their captives having experienced the gauntlet, there would be "a continuous round of revelry – feasting, dancing, and a prideful display of the spoils – the raiders would be lionized for days."[30] The Dog Soldiers had stripped Susanna's boys naked after they were murdered. Perhaps their bloody clothing was waved in Susanna's face during the Indian revelry.

Another disturbing report of child captivity by Dog Soldiers was reported in 1867. The *Nebraska Advertiser*, August 1, 1867, first reported the incident. In a raid along the Little Blue River in southern Nebraska near present-day Fairbury, Indians captured two children. The parents escaped into the house. In an attempt to get the parents out, the Indians tortured the children; but when the parents wouldn't budge, the two children were ridden away as captives.[31] A more complete story appeared a week later in the *Nebraska City News*. The family was identified as Ulberich [sic] and the children were a boy, Peter, aged twelve and a girl, Veronia [sic], who was fifteen [thirteen]. On July 24, Peter, Senior, had sent his two older children to get feed for their hogs in a field near their house:

> A few minutes afterward, about 9 o'clock in the morning, he saw an Indian riding up to the house, who endeavored to attract his attention by the usual Indian salutation of 'How-how,' and evidently wished to engage him in conversation. Upon looking toward and beyond this Indian, he saw twelve or fifteen others, four of whom were engaged in leading off a horse and mule belonging to him. From this he instantly knew they intended mischief; and hurrying into the house busied himself in preparing his arms and barricading the windows and doors with means already provided for such emergencies, calling to his wife to get the children from the field. On looking towards the field they saw the children running for the house pursued by two Indians who caught them and took them into the bushes out of their sight. After he had made the house as defensible as possible he reconnoitered from the cracks in the window shutters and saw them stealing a third horse from the stable. . . . They then commenced whipping the children to make them cry, hoping to move the sympathies sufficient to bring him out. . . . After 20 or 30 minutes, they brought the pleading children into sight and the chief called to him. 'Father come out and we will give you your Papoose.'[32]

The father pleaded with the Indians to return his children. Once the Indians saw he wasn't coming out of the house, they "laughed at him and went off tying the children on to the horses before them." Peter described his daughter as "tall, slim, yellowish hair, with light complexion blue eyes."[33] What happened next would have been lost to history had the incident not been recorded in Peter Ulbrich's Indian depredation claim.

134

It is a powerful story. Peter Ulbrich, who had homesteaded on the Little Blue, wrote in his affidavit:

In the fall of 1862, October 5, I went west from Nebraska City with my family and in company with my brother-in-law Albert Kalus, under the guidance of John Mattes, who for several years previously was operating a blacksmith-shop on the Military or Overland Road from Leavenworth to Fort Kearney, in order to take up a claim under the pre-emption or homestead laws of the United States.

I settled with my family on the best piece of government land, that I could select, to-wit: about 8 miles north of the Kansas line, close by the sixth principal meridian, on the Little Blue River, three miles south of Thompson's stage-station, 8 miles west from the Big Sandy, and the same distance southwest from Farrell's stage station, said land lying and being in what is now known as Jefferson County, Nebraska.

I broke about fifty acres and cultivated the land, put up a house, stable, corn crib, fences &c, dug a well and a cellar &c. I lived happily and prospered nicely, as I got a good price for all my farm and garden products, which I sold readily to soldiers, freighters and emigrants, taking the overland route, until <u>July 24, 1867</u>.

About 9 o'clock in the morning of this terrible day a roving band of Cheyenne Sioux, about thirty in number, came galloping down from the direction of Pawnee Ranche on the Fort Kearney road; a squad of them immediately entered my pasture and seized two horses and a mule of mine, grazing therein.

At the same time others in the party jumped over the fence into the field, where my 13 year old daughter Veeney (Veronica) and my 12 year old son Peter were pulling weeds for the hogs in the potato field, pounced upon the terrified children, began whipping them with their rawhides and driving them in the direction of the house, which we had hastily barricaded. Finding the doors and windows barred the Indians called out the words in plain English: "Father, father! Come out, we give you papooses." From upstairs I had observed Indians on every corner of the house with their guns at aim; I could see from their countenances and general conduct and appearance that they would massacre all of us, if I opened the door. Having no other means of defense but an old rusty musket, I preferred to await events. My wife implored them: "Give the papooses free, you got horses and mule, take it, that is enough!"[34]

Waiting and parleying quite a while the Indians finally went to my stable and compelled my boy in sight of the house to cut up the double harness hanging there, with a sharp knife they handed him; the bridles, lines and other straps were carried off by them.

About 10 o'clock A.M. the Indians lifted my son and daughter on the horses stolen from me, riding off with them in a due westerly course. Arrived at the eastern shore of the Little Blue River they shot and killed my boy while riding in their midst; they left him, where we found his body 4 or five months later, at the exact spot which his then liberated sister had pointed out.

This double bereavement, the uncertainty of the next hour, the fleeing of the few widely scattered settlers to the stage-stations, which were fortified to some extent, the news of the murder of my brother-in-law Albert Kalus,[35] who lived one mile east of the Bennet brothers, three miles west from us on the western shore of the Blue, the reported murder of many ranchmen and freighters on the military road, the finding of several bodies, deprived of their scalps and otherwise mutilated, in a manner too horribly disgusting to detail, their faces hacked in a frightful mass by Indian tomahawks, settled a hopeless darkness over my only recently happy and unmolested home.

As soon as I could, I traded my cattle to Mr. Fell [Farrell] on the Big Sandy for a span of horses and a set of harness, hauled my family first to Nebraska City, leaving all my crop, 45 acres of corn, one acre of potatoes, a large patch of onions, a railfence around the field, five hogs, eighty hens, forty bushels of shelled corn, two-story house, cellar, well, stable, crib and other outhouses behind.

It would have required only three months longer, before I would have been able legally and financially to make final proof on 160 acres under the preemption law and to claim 160 acres more under the homestead, by virtue of bona fide settlement and actual improvements, all of which I was compelled to abandon.

My son, Peter Ulbrich, when murdered by said Indians was twelve years old, strong for his age, and leaving the price of filial affection completely out of account, I claim and am able to proof if required, that his services on the farm during his minority and until he would have got ready to set up a household for himself, would have been worth to me not less than two thousand dollars ($2000.00).

For transporting my daughter Vinney (Victoria [sic.]) into savage captivity, for her defloration, for numberless violations of her youthful body I claim damages as her father to the amount of five thousand dollars ($5,000.00).

When I recovered her at the farm of Mr. Campbell, south of Grand Island, she was nothing but skin and bones. Campbell's three or four children and my daughter had been surrendered (or exchanged) to the military authorities at North Plate Nebraska, and forwarded by the Union Pacific Railroad to Grand Island, where Mr. Campbell received them.[36]

Mr. Ulbrich apparently was not aware that the U.S. Congress authorized no compensation via Indian depredation claims for loss of human life, or for injury or suffering. Indian depredation claims only compensated property losses. It is interesting to note his claim of $2,000.00 for lost labor of his son, but $5,000.00 for the loss of Veronica's female innocence. It seems, perhaps, his daughter's loss of virtue and innocence was a greater loss to him than the life of his oldest son.

Dog Soldiers attacked the Campbell family on the same day Veronica and Peter Ulbrich were captured. Having emigrated from Scotland a few years earlier, the family consisted of father, Peter Campbell, his wife and seven children. The youngest boys were twins. The Campbells had earlier settled on a homestead near present-day Doniphan, Nebraska, about ninety miles northwest of the Ulbrich home. Mrs. Campbell had died in the winter of 1866. On the day of the raid, Peter and one son were several miles away assisting a neighbor with an early harvest. When learning that the Indians had raided their home, Peter and his son, John, first came upon another neighbor's home, "where they found the mother of the family lying dead on the threshold of the door, clasping her infant son in her arms; and nearby a son, fourteen years of age, lay shot through the thigh."[37] On arriving at their house, they discovered one Campbell girl, nine years old, had eluded capture by hiding in a field of grain. The other four Campbell children were missing. They had been taken captive.

In August 1867, Frank North, who will perform admirably at the Summit Springs fight in the attempt to rescue Susanna and Maria, was involved in a fight with Cheyenne Dog Soldier Indians under Chief Turkey Leg. North was with a company of Pawnee Scouts that defeated Turkey Leg near Plum Creek Stage Station, where Mrs. Morton had been captured three years earlier. Seventeen warriors were killed in this fight and an Indian woman and boy captured.[38] As it turned out, the captured woman and child were the wife and son of Turkey Leg. A resultant meeting with Turkey Leg precipitated the release of the Campbell children along with Veronica Ulbrich, in exchange for Turkey Leg's family.

The account of Indian captivity left by Veronica Ulbrich is a devastating testimonial and a prime example of the onus attached to white female survivors of Plains Indian captivity. When she gave her account, she was married to Alfred Megnin. Surprisingly, her husband did not know of her experiences.

When Veronica's father made his depredation claim he wrote this letter:

Nebraska City, Neb.

June 27, 1889

To the Hon. Commissioner of Indian Affairs

Honored Sir:

My daughter Veeney (Veronika) was married in November 1887 to Mr. Alfred Megnin, who does not know that she ever was a captive among the Indians, nor exposed to their beastly assaults.

And in order to make it appear that the Indians could not use her on account of her childhood, we represent her among the neighbors and even to her husband to be only 28 years instead of her thirty-four years which she is in fact [this would make her seven years old when captured, not thirteen, as in fact she was. At seven it was easier to fool people into believing she was too young to have been sexually abused. Ed.].

It might cause trouble in the family, similar to the Roper family in Beatrice, if Mr. Megnin should find out, that my daughter was a subject of the Indian's beastiality.

If you cause a special agent to examine my claim you will please instruct him to summon me, my wife and daughter and other witnesses, to Nebraska City, or some other point, so that her husband cannot hear the testimony. Very respectfully,

Peter Ulbrich[39]

Testifying only for the government in support of her father's losses, Veronica, too, sought recovery for her personal suffering:

I am the daughter of the claimant Peter Ulbrich and am married since November 1887 [this testimonial is written in 1889] to Alfred Megnin of French descent, who assists my father in working his farm. Although it is a long time ago I remember yet vividly the hot summer day of 1867 when a band of Cheyenne Indians swept down upon our farm, captured me and my brother Peter. They

whipped us with their rawhides and we cried bit-
terly for help. More dead than alive they took us
away from home and three miles later they shot my
brother off the horse and left him, where I pointed
out the location four months later to my father and
Mr. George Moore from Lone Tree, now of Wyoming
Territory.

They compelled me to travel with them, we were
traveling from one place to another, some of the
band were on the go all the time. I did not get
enough to eat, suffered from thirst, had to wash and
do other work; sometimes they whipped me, sometimes they wanted or threatened to kill me. Soon
one Indian, soon another belonging to the band
forcibly violated my body, causing me immense
pain and anguish thereby. This was almost a daily
and nightly occurrence which would have killed me,
if I had not been liberated almost exhausted. I used
to remember the names of some members of the
band, especially of some squaws, but I cannot recol-
lect any more at this time. . . . I first saw the
Campbell children, Jessie about twenty years of
age, Catherine about 18 years, Daniel and Peter,
both small boys about 5 or 6 years old; I think they
were twins. Of course I was glad to have white
company in my misery. I was afraid I never could
get away and had to stay with these brutes and
devils all my lifetime.[40]

Veronica identified her sufferings very clearly. She never
had enough to eat. She was always thirsty. She was forced to
do the hard labor of an Indian woman. She suffered brutal
whippings throughout her captivity ordeal. She was continually threatened with punishment and death. Rape was nearly
a daily *and* nightly occurrence. It was this last act that left her
nearly dead by the time she was rescued. Obviously, this testimony of such brutal, violent daily sexual attacks lends credence to the claim that such atrocities were a common
experience of white women captives of the Dog Soldier Indians.
And the pioneer women knew this. Yet, it is often denied, both

back when it happened and today. The *Omaha Daily Herald* reported the exchange of the Campbell children and Veronica Ulbrich. Though the article did not name Veronica other than identifying her as a Danish girl aged fourteen, it stated the captivity of the children was not too bad: "They complain of no harder work than carrying water, and say they were generally well treated."[41]

Why would a newspaper distort the facts? The answer seems to be financial. Omaha was the stopping off city for the Platte River trail that went through Nebraska, and if they reported the truth it would no doubt be damaging for immigrant travel and would hinder the outfitting and supply businesses in Omaha. Obviously business merchants in Omaha did not want travelers to fear the trail. The Campbell children had been captured just south of the trail near Grand Island. Thus the Omaha newspaper would not report incidents that might hinder business.

Some people today still want to deny the brutality of Indian captivity. Father Peter John Powell, in his remarkable two-volume work, *People of the Sacred Mountain: A History of the Northern Cheyenne Chiefs and Warrior Societies 1830-1879 With an Epilogue 1969-1974*, when writing about the captivity of Sarah White and Mrs. Morgan, the two captives rescued by Custer in March 1869, states:

> Both women recounted their experiences afterward. They mentioned no hardships greater than those borne by the women of the People, especially during the days of soldier pursuit. Mrs. Morgan spoke with warmth of the goodness of her Cheyenne husband, whose proposal she accepted, believing that she would spend the rest of her days among the People. She described his thoughtfulness and generosity, saying that all he expected of her was to tend his horse when he returned from war, a mark of affection and respect. "I began to think much of him for his kindness to me, and when they [the People] brought the news that there were

two white men in camp, I did not care to see them. I was surprised to see my own brother walk into the tent. I had on Indian garb," she recalled.[42]

The source that Powell uses to make this false claim comes from another book, *Pioneer Women: Voices From the Kansas Frontier.*[43] Its author, Joanna Stratton, admits that the sources for her accounts were "written several decades after the actual events and experiences occurred."[44] Clearly, such accounts have to be assessed against accounts written at or near the time of the incidents. When this is done with Mrs. Morgan's captivity experience, Powell's account is obviously incredible to accept. Emily Harrison, in her 1907 article, "Reminiscences of Early Days in Ottawa County," wrote that

> Mrs. Morgan's story is a *pitiful one*. Both women were dreadfully abused at the hands of the Indians. . . . When they returned to their homes they were besought by newspaper men and book writers to give an account of their experiences, and furnish their portraits for publication. This Mrs. Morgan refused to do. She never told anyone what befell her while with the Indians. *She considered it a disgrace*, and that a relation of it only added to the infamy. Her brother, Mr. Brewster, felt as she did.[45]

Mrs. Custer wrote of her memory of Mrs. Morgan's captivity ordeal:

> The young faces of the two . . . were now worn with privation and exposure, and haggard with the terrible insults of their captors, too dreadful to be chronicled here. . . . The story of their life was one of barbarous treatment and brutality. . . . The conduct of the squaws, always jealous of white women, was brutality itself. . . . With the terrible physical labor required of them, in addition to revolting indignities, it was a wonder they lived. They were almost starved, some days only being allowed a morsel of mule-meat, not over an inch square at most, for an entire day. The squaws beat them with clubs when the Indians were absent. . . .[46]

142

Mrs. Custer relates a later incident when two officers who were present at Mrs. Morgan's rescue came upon her residence back in Ottawa County a few years after her release from captivity:

> When they [the two officers] asked if all went well with her, she could not help confiding in them the fact that the husband whom she had married after her return [she was married to James Morgan before her capture], instead of trying to make her forget the misery through which she had passed, often recalled all her year of captivity [five months] with bitterness, and was disposed to upbraid her, as if she had been in the least responsible for the smallest of her misfortunes.[47]

General Custer himself would write regarding the captivity of Morgan and White:

> The story of the two girls, containing accounts of wrongs and ill treatment sufficient to have ended the existence of less determined persons, is too long to be given here. Besides indignities and insults far more terrible than death itself, the physical suffering to which the two girls were subjected was too great almost to be believed. They were required to transport huge burdens on their backs, large enough to have made a load for a beast of burden. They were limited to barely enough food to sustain life; sometimes a small morsel of mule meat, not more than an inch square, was their allowance of food for twenty-four hours. The squaws beat them unmercifully with clubs whenever the men were not present. Upon one occasion one of the girls was felled to the ground by a blow from a club in the hands of one of the squaws. Their joy therefore at regaining their freedom after a captivity of nearly a year can be better imagined than described. . . .[48]

It is rather obvious, when comparing the account written by General Custer and the account written sixteen years later by Mrs. Custer, that she used the writings of her husband to refresh her memory of the captivity experiences of Mrs.

Morgan and Sarah White. But it should not be forgotten that General Custer rescued these women and interviewed them at the time of their rescue. His account, written in 1874, is a first-hand account detailing their captivity. This account alone should be sufficient to displace the account given by Powell as coming from the frontier of the imagination and not the frontier of the West. Indian captivity in the West was brutal and horrific, and it is simple nonsense to think otherwise. It is a polite understatement to claim, as historian Lonnie White did: "It is, therefore, not surprising that the women captives who survived their ordeal . . . were more than happy to be restored to white civilization."[49]

Mrs. Morgan never recovered from her captivity experiences. She was also very private about it. In a letter to a friend in 1893, she wrote: "It was the outraged heart that was so hard to bear, that was the burden I had to endure. But dear friend, rather than the world should know what I have been forced to endure, I would rather live the remaining days of life in poverty than *have these dreadful facts known*."[50] In another letter Mrs. Morgan states, "I guarded my misery from all eyes but my own. . . . Has it not been enough for one woman to bear? They say, Each cloud has a silver lining, but that has not turned to me yet."[51] It never did. She eventually broke down and was hospitalized for insanity, dying at the Kansas Insane Asylum in Topeka, July 11, 1902.[52] Mrs. Morgan had a mixed-blood child on December 7, 1869. "Let the world draw its own conclusions, mine are, that that babe's blood was as pure as any of the rest of my children [three]. I called him Ira Arthur. He died at the age of seventeen months, always a puny child."[53]

Mrs. Morgan's husband, James, apparently was not supportive in her return back to her community, and this identifies, as earlier noted by Mrs. Custer and Peter Ulbrich (when he mentioned the Roper family), another problem with captivity, namely, gaining acceptance back into white society. Mrs. Morgan wrote:

My life received a blight at that time [captivity] which will go with me to the grave. Life has been worth nothing to me since then. Do not mention my husband to me. He reproached me times without number for my misfortune, (for having been a help-less victim to the atrocities of the wild savages). I continued to live with him until 1880, then as things grew worse, I left him. He then sued, and obtained a divorce by my consent.[54]

Mrs. Morgan's co-captive, Sarah White, was married within a year of her release from captivity. She lived quietly in the neighborhood from which she was taken, raising many children and living a long life. Is it possible she was an exception from the permanent scars, both emotional and physical, of Indian captivity? The answer is no. She knew that there was no compensation for her sufferings. She tried to change it. In 1870 she wrote to her congressman, Sidney Clarke:

I write to inform you that I, Sarah White of Cloud Co, State of Kansas, was taken prisoner by the Cheyenne Indians Tribe August 13th 1868. My father was killed at the same time. I wish you to bring the facts before Congress and *appropriate me money for hardships and privations endured* until March 18th, 1869, when I was recaptured by Gen. George Custer. Please answer soon and oblige me.[55]

What, then, can be said about the captivity of Susanna Alderdice and Maria Weichel? It is probably safe to say it was the daily rapes that every woman knew would be her fate if captured that produced the single greatest fear about captivity, and this was what was not mentioned in popular captivity narratives later written by rescued captives. The accounts noted earlier verify this brutal activity. Without question, Susanna and Maria suffered greatly from this awful act. Understandably, Susanna and Maria suffered horribly during their captivity. If there was meat to eat, it was usually putrid or uncooked, and if cooked, it was only slightly cooked.[56] Cooking utensils were never or rarely cleaned.[57] The harsh burns from the hot sun were ignored and untreated. The women would be dressed in Indian fashion. Their shoes would be replaced with moccasins. And the rapes would go on, night and day. The hundreds of miles Susanna and Maria were taken in their captivity would be traversed afoot, in moccasins they would be forced to wear. Their feet would get bloody, the broken blisters untreated. Long distances would be walked without the benefit of water, all in the hot summer months of June and early July. They would be forced to carry upon their backs heavy loads of wood, camp utensils or other paraphernalia. When the Dog Soldiers left the village to hunt, scout or plunder, jealous Indian women would beat the captives, taunt them, threaten them and generally torment them throughout their captivity.

During this whole captivity Susanna would have to endure her suffering with the memories of witnessing the brutal murders of her children. Was there an act of compassion or mercy shown to Susanna during her captivity? Perhaps. Human nature is such that acts of compassion surface in even the most deplorable of conditions. Indeed, Mrs. Morgan reported that some of the Indian women treated her kindly.[58] But also, maybe no compassion was shown. One merely needs to recall the filmed celebratory acts of women and children in Pakistan after they learned of the successful attack upon American civilians in the World Trade Center in New York on that awful day of September 11, 2001. When hatred runs deep, it is often the case that what produces tremendous suffering for people of one particular culture bears approval in another. Why should it have been any different in 1869? Indian captivity was an awful fate. It was indeed a fate worse than death. And Susanna and Maria were not yet free of its grasp.

Republican River Expedition

Then I started again in June from Fort McPherson, Neb., and went south into Kansas looking for them, and finally found their trail and followed it about 200 miles, having four fights, in which several were killed . . . .[1]

When General Eugene Carr had his second fight with Tall Bull on May 16, 1869, on Spring Creek, not far inside the Nebraska border from present-day Traer, Kansas, his soldiers had been without rations for two days.[2] They were in critical need of sustenance for themselves and their horses. Scout Bill Cody, though sporting a painful head wound from the fight earlier in the day, volunteered to ride through the night in an attempt to alert personnel at Fort Kearny, Nebraska, of Carr's need. Cody's hat had been shot off during the fight. The bullet cut into his scalp for about five inches, ridging along the skull.[3] He was lucky he was not killed. It was a painful wound and had bled heavily. Carr's command was about fifty miles from Fort Kearny. The area was alive with Indians. Nevertheless, Cody volunteered to make the ride in advance of the column, "a point characteristic of him as he never shirked duty or faltered in emergencies."[4] Cody accomplished his duty, alerted the soldiers at Fort Kearny of Carr's need, and then met Carr later the next day with an advance column from Fort Kearny. His actions saved one day for Carr's men. Before the fight at Spring Creek, Carr had sent his wagons to Fort McPherson. He would soon arrive there with the rest of his command.

While Carr's troops were recuperating at Fort McPherson, Tall Bull and his Dog Soldiers had in the meantime made their devastating raids into central Kansas. At Fort McPherson, Carr was well aware of the raids. Newspaper accounts were read and studied alongside maps and Carr concluded, as did Tom Alderdice after Susanna was captured, that the Indians "must be encamped on the Solomon."[5] This would place the Indians under the military jurisdiction of the Department of the Missouri and not the Department of the Platte, which Carr was now operating from. However, it was more likely that when the Indians left the Solomon, they would travel to the west and north and return to the Powder River territory. This territory was under Carr's jurisdiction. It might be possible that Carr could intercept the Indians in their retreat.

At eleven o'clock in the morning on June 9, Carr led the Republican River Expedition out of Fort McPherson, Nebraska. This command initially included eight companies of the 5th Cavalry, and what would eventually become three additional companies of Pawnee scouts under the command of Major Frank North. One of North's subordinate officers was his younger brother, Captain Luther North. More than fifty wagons carrying forage and supplies for twenty days accompanied the expedition. Later, Company F would be sent back to Fort McPherson for duty along the Platte.[6] A third company of Pawnee scouts replaced this company. Carr now had seven companies of the 5th Cavalry, companies A, C, E, G, I, L and M, along with three companies of Pawnee Indians, two of which joined the expedition in the field. All of the cavalry companies were undermanned, making Carr's total number of men available for the expedition, including the Pawnee and teamsters, around 475.[7]

They only marched three miles the first day but made twenty-seven miles on June 10.[8] The expedition was traveling south and east toward the Republican River. On June 12, Lieutenant Charles Brady and Company L were detached to scout the country southwest down to the Republican River. Lieutenant William Volkmar led a smaller detail southeast, also towards the Republican. About ten o'clock in the morning, Volkmar's detachment encountered a hunting party of about twenty Indians. The Indians quickly fled over the hills to the southeast. Lieutenant Brady was recalled from his scout and Pawnees were sent to follow the Dog Soldiers. Brady marched fifteen miles to the Republican River before being recalled by a courier ordering him back to the main column. He did not return until midnight. The next day the main column reached the Republican River, but the Indian trail had still not been discovered.[9] Carr's objective was to return to the area near where he had his earlier fight on Beaver Creek on May 13. Perhaps near there he might pick up an Indian trail.[10]

On June 15, Carr's expedition crossed the trail near Spring Creek where he had the fight of May 16, "old lodge poles, cooking utensils &c still lying on the ground."[11] Another five miles were traversed to the southwest before going into camp in the early afternoon. About five o'clock, an unknown number of mounted Indians, apparently hiding all afternoon in the thick undergrowth surrounding the creek, made a daring attempt to stampede the horse and mule herds, which had been put to pasture. One soldier and a teamster were severely wounded, both shot with pistols.[12] The Indians, however, failed to capture any stock and quickly retreated to the south. Pawnee Indians immediately pursued them, and were soon joined by three companies of soldiers under the command of Major W. B. Royall. They chased the Dog Soldiers twelve miles until darkness ended the hunt. The soldiers returned to camp at ten o'clock. For all their efforts they only succeeded in capturing one Indian pony abandoned in the chase.[13]

On June 16, the command was issued five days' rations, and sent in pursuit of the Indians who had been chased the evening before. The rations were placed on pack mules. One company of soldiers stayed with the wagons. Indians were occasionally seen throughout the day on distant hills, but the soldiers were unable to catch them. The Pawnees reported their belief that the Indian village would be found somewhere on the Solomon.[14] They were right, as it was somewhere near this very day that Tom Alderdice had returned to the Saline valley settlements to report his finding the village on the north fork of the Solomon.

This was also about the time that the Dog Soldiers began to leave Kansas. They started their withdrawal back to the west, following the Republican River valley until it was appropriate to jaunt to the north into Sioux country. It was fortunate that Carr crossed their trail by accidentally running into an Indian hunting party on June 15. From this day forward, Tall Bull's Dog Soldiers would not be able to escape Carr's pursuit.

Carr followed the Indians in a southeasterly direction for the next three days, all the way to the north fork of the Solomon River, but was unable to locate any Indian trails.[15] Detachments of soldiers extending as much as twenty-five miles away from the main column could not find any Indian signs. Carr returned to the main encampment where the wagons had been detached. Details scouted for the next several days around the vicinity of Carr's earlier fights of May 13 at Elephant Rock and May 16 at Spring Creek. Finally, on June 21, a "trail of a small party of Indians was found, proceeding up the creek [Beaver Creek], but it was several days old."[16] A detachment of soldiers followed it until dark, then returned to camp. The pursuit proceeded west the next day. The command would alternate traveling in a westward direction along Prairie Dog Creek, Beaver Creek, or smaller tributaries. A daylong rain and hailstorm forced them to remain in camp all day June 25.[17]

On June 26, while in the vicinity of his May 13 fight along Beaver Creek, Carr decided to send a small detachment of men to try to locate the unburied bodies of the three soldiers killed and left on the field in that fight. About five miles below their present campsite, "the bones of three men were found and buried, the burial party that attempted to perform that duty in May having been chased away by a superior force of Indians."[18] One of the buried dead was Sergeant John Ford, and an unnamed creek discovered nearby was named Ford Creek in his honor.[19] In addition to burying the bones of these men killed on May 13, Carr reported having found two or three horses that had been wounded and subsequently abandoned in that fight six weeks earlier.[20] A larger unnamed creek was soon discovered and named Driftwood Creek. Here Carr's men camped for the night.

The next day the column continued in a northwesterly direction, eventually coming to the Republican River, which Carr followed in a westerly direction. On June 28, a lodge-pole trail, heading west and accompanied by numerous shod horse and mule tracks, was discovered about five miles north of the Republican. Carr himself found this trail. Leading his command down a path to cross the Republican River, Carr noticed pony tracks.

> I dismounted the command so as not to hurt the tracks and sent for "Buffalo Bill," who was hunting antelopes off to the right, and told him to look at that! He said, "By Gee Hosaphat, that is the trail!" and I felt quite cocky at being the first to find it. It had drawn close together, to make as little show as possible, when it had to cross the river, and went into the bluffs on the north side. It then went parallel with the line of the valley to the westward, crossing the ridges and ravines, keeping five or ten miles away from the river bottom, and camping on hidden springs, which the Indians knew.[21]

The Indian trail had twelve lodges, included women and children, and "anywhere from one to three hundred animals."[22] Proceeding with caution, several scouting parties were sent to follow the trail, which continued twenty-five miles. The trail "appeared to grow fresher and to be not more than a week old."[23] For Carr, this was good news. For Tall Bull, this marked the beginning of the end.

While Carr's main column was in camp on June 29, a prearranged site to receive supplies,[24] a supply wagon train arrived from Fort McPherson, accompanied by Companies D and H, commanded by Major E. W. Crittenden. Soldiers accompanying the supply train observed about forty or fifty mounted men near where the train had crossed Frenchman Creek, about twenty-five miles north of Carr's present camp. They were no doubt Dog Soldiers. They moved off the bluffs in a northwesterly direction.[25] The next day Company L and I escorted the empty wagons back to Fort McPherson, and were no longer a part of Carr's command. The two companies under Crittenden replaced them. The supply column had left Fort McPherson on June 24.

Important for Carr, along with the supplies was sent a telegraphed copy of Tom Alderdice's letter, written on June 21 at Fort Leavenworth, when he had his meeting with General John Schofield. Schofield had kept his promise and telegraphed Tom's letter to the Department of the Platte. It was now in the hands of Carr, who turned it over to his surgeon, Doctor Louis Tesson. From Tom's letter, the column learned the Indians they were trailing were in all probability carrying the captives taken in the Saline valley on May 30. With this letter was a physical description of Susanna. It would be used later at Summit Springs. First Lieutenant George Price later wrote that during the expedition,

> . . . it became known that the enemy held as cap-
> tives two white women whom they had captured on
> the Solomon [Saline] River about the 1st of June,
> and as it was evident that they were preparing to
> march northward, by way of the Laramie Plains
> and the Black Hills of Wyoming, to the Powder
> River country, it became a matter of the utmost
> importance to intercept them and rescue the unfor-
> tunate women before they could cross the South
> Platte River.[26]

William Cody's later autobiographical accounts of the Republican River Expedition said that at each abandoned Indian camp "we found the print of a woman's shoe, and we concluded that they had with them some white captive."[27] Later historians, quoting from Cody, also made this claim. Richard Walsh, in *The Making of Buffalo Bill*, writes: "A trail had been picked up which showed the prints of a woman's shoe and bits of gingham torn from a dress."[28] Don Russell, in *The Lives and Legends of Buffalo Bill*, quotes from Cody: "Wherever they had encamped we found the print of a woman's shoe."[29] Wilbur Nye, in *Plains Indian Raiders*, adds a twist: "By July 8, General Carr knew that the two captured women were still alive. His Pawnee scouts had seen their shoe prints in the sand along a stream."[30] Hercules Price, an enlisted soldier serving in the Republican River Expedition, wrote from an Old Soldier's Home in 1908 the further claim that while traveling on Frenchmen Creek "we picked up a piece of calico dress torn off, and afterward, we picked up a piece of paper with the words written in pencil – 'For God's sake come quickly and rescue us'."[31] Indeed, the challenge is to try and find a history book covering Carr's expedition that does not mention this story in one form or another.

The truth is, however, these claims are all myth, first inspired, no doubt, by Cody to give a thrill to readers of his autobiography. There are three reasons why this did not happen. First, if this were true, it would in all probability have been reported in Lieutenant William J. Volkmar's "Journal of the March," for his orders were to record such events as were significant to the expedition. Volkmar, assigned as Carr's Itinerary Officer, had daily written in his journal for the duration of the expedition. Finding verification in abandoned Indian camps that white women were being kept captive would have been just such a significant event that he would have been expected to report. That both Volkmar and Carr in their respective reports did not record it is evidence that it did not occur. Cody is the one who later wrote about it and others merely followed.

Second, Indians did not permit white women captives to wear their own shoes. In all known instances of Indian captivity the women, found dead or alive, were wearing moccasins. Indeed, Indians realized a woman's shoe print in an abandoned village would show that they were holding captives, something they did not want to advertise. White captives were made to dress as Indian women. Wearing white women's dresses and shoes was simply not permitted.

Third, Tom Alderdice's letter to General Schofield was in Dr. Louis Tesson's possession at the Summit Springs battle, as noted in Carr's report of the engagement. The expedition left Fort McPherson on June 9, twelve days *before* Tom Alderdice met with General Schofield. How, then, did the letter end up in Tesson's possession? The answer is easily seen when noting that the supply wagon that arrived at Carr's prearranged re-supply camp had left Fort McPherson on June 24, three days *after* Tom's letter was forwarded by Schofield to General George D. Ruggles at the Omaha headquarters of the Department of the Platte. From there it was received via tele-graph at Fort McPherson in time to accompany the supply wagon that met with Carr's command on June 29.[32] How else could Surgeon Tesson have a telegraph copy of Tom's letter if it was not delivered when the Fort McPherson supply wagons arrived in Carr's camp on June 29?

It was the receipt of this letter on June 29 that Captain George Price refers to in his book, *Across The Continent With The 5th Cavalry*, when he writes that during the expedition the command became aware that two women captives were proba-bly with the Indians they were pursuing. Further, Tom's letter gives a detailed description of where he had found the Indian village after Susanna was captured. This description verified for Carr and his officers that the Indians they had encountered on the Solomon, shortly after starting the Republican River Expedition, and whose trail they were then following, were in all probability the same Indians who had committed the mur-derous depredations along the Saline River in late May. Thus, the Indians Carr was pursuing very likely had with them the captives that Tom's letter reported.

As much as it dramatizes Carr's attempt to find the Dog Soldier village and rescue the captives to visualize seeing shoe prints, pieces of calico dresses, or even desperate notes for rescue in abandoned Indian villages, it simply did not happen. These later accounts merely built a fashionable myth upon the simple incident of Tom Alderdice's letter being received by

Carr when the supply wagons arrived in his camp. Having learned of Tom's discovery of the Indian village on the North Fork of the Solomon River, Carr could now be virtually certain that the Indians he was pursuing were the same band that Tom had identified in his letter.

On June 30, the day after the supply wagons had arrived, Major E. W. Crittenden took the two companies that had accompanied him with the supply wagons and scouted back north in the area where the Dog Soldiers were observed the day before. Crittenden's orders were to "follow the trail, ascertain where it goes, whether it increases in size, goes towards a village, &c &c."[33] The rest of the command would remain in camp that day and the next. Crittenden returned the next day and reported not finding any Indian trail. On July 2, the whole command moved fourteen miles north, camping a mile and a half below where the South Fork of the Republican joins with the Republican in Dundee County, near present-day Benkleman, Nebraska. Coincidentally, Custer had camped in the same area almost exactly two years earlier when he was leading the Hancock Expedition. On July 3, the command proceeded west on the north side of the Republican. Nearly fifteen miles were marched before going into camp between present-day Parks and Haigler, Nebraska.

Scouting parties were sent to the sand hills north of the river and there they found the Indian trail that had earlier been discovered on June 28. The trail was getting fresher. An abandoned Indian camp was found, and judged to be not more than thirty-six hours old.[34] Indians, burdened with large numbers of horses and mules carrying heavy loads of buffalo meat and plunder from their raids, traveled about fifteen miles a day. Carr was averaging about thirty miles, gaining one day on the Indians for every day they traveled.[35] The Pawnees, examining the abandoned village, concluded it contained "not more than 400 warriors. They had a lot of shod mules, in every camp they had been pulling off shoes."[36] This would mean the village contained between 160 and 200 tepees.

On July 4, Major W. B. Royall took Companies A, E, and M and one company of Pawnees, and followed the Indian trail to the west. Meanwhile, Carr, with the rest of the command, crossed the Republican to the south side and proceeded south on the Arikaree Fork of the Republican. He was now close to the site of the Beecher Island fight that occurred ten months earlier. They crossed an Indian trail, apparently a war party returning to the main trail Royall was following on the north side of the Republican River. Instead of following this trail to the north, Carr followed on the south side of the Arikaree for about ten miles before camping.[37]

On July 5, a courier reported to Carr that Royall's four-company unit had passed several abandoned Indian camps, and that the trail was getting fresher. On July 6, Carr marched in a northwesterly direction for twenty miles. On July 7, Royall returned to Carr's camp, reporting a fight on July 5. About thirty miles north of the Republican River, Royall had come across a war party of a dozen Indians carrying a wounded Indian boy. A sharp fight ensued. The Pawnees killed three Dog Soldiers, including the boy, and wounded three others. Eight head of stock were captured. The remaining six Dog Soldiers fled to the southeast. The Pawnees told Royall that the village would be warned and it would now be impossible to catch them.[38] Royall was out of rations and therefore returned to the main command. On July 8, the reunited command traveled back to within a mile of their July 4-5 campsite.[39]

On July 8, Corporal John Kile and two men from Company M were sent back on Royall's trail to recover a horse that was left exhausted after Royall's fight on July 5. No sooner had Kile found this horse than a band of eight Dog Soldiers surprised and attacked him and his small command. A large boulder was used as one breastwork and the recovered horse was quickly killed for a second breastwork. A sharp fight ensued. After two Indians were badly wounded, the Dog Soldiers had enough and withdrew. Kile and the two men safely made it back to Carr's camp and reported their fight. About midnight a party of about thirty Indians charged the camp, firing a couple of volleys at the soldiers. The Indians were getting bolder.[40] Carr was getting closer to finding their main camp. For Kile's brave conduct on July 8, Carr would recommend him for the coveted Congressional Medal of Honor.[41]

Another Medal of Honor was awarded for the engagement in Carr's camp later that night. Pawnee Indian Sergeant Co-rux-te-chod-ish (Mad Bear) boldly ran out of the camp in pursuit of the Dog Soldiers that had charged the camp but was accidentally shot and badly wounded by a soldier who was firing at the fleeing Dog Soldiers.[42] Co-rux-te-chod-ish (Mad Bear) eventually recovered from his wound, but missed the Summit Springs fight. Controversy later surrounded this Indian Medal of Honor. Carr biographer James King, following statements made by Luther North, claimed that this Medal of Honor was actually meant for Traveling Bear, who distinguished himself in the Summit Springs fight and later died in the incident at Massacre Canyon.[43]

Massacre Canyon, in Hitchcock County near Trenton, Nebraska, was an ugly engagement on August 5, 1873, between the Sioux, under Pawnee Killer, and a large Pawnee buffalo hunting party.[44] In that fight, 1,000 Sioux attacked 350 Pawnee men, women, and children. The Pawnee dead included twenty men, including Traveling Bear, thirty-nine women and ten children.[45]

Luther North claimed that Traveling Bear (Co-rux-ah-kah-wah-dee) killed four warriors at Summit Springs:

> My brother reported this to General Carr, and General Carr in his report of the battle mentioned him for his bravery, but in some way the name got confused with the name of the man Co-rux-te-cha-dish, Mad Bear, who was wounded in the night attack on the Republican about a week before. Later Congress had a bronze medal struck for him. The name on the medal was Mad Bear, but the medal was given to Traveling Bear by my brother [Frank North]. Mad Bear was in an ambulance the

day of the battle, for he was not yet well enough to ride on horseback.[46]

North is in error in saying that Traveling Bear received the Medal of Honor at the Pawnee reservation. A letter dated September 29, 1869, at Pawnee Agency, Nebraska, bears the 'X' mark for Co-rux-te-chod-ish, Mad Bear, acknowledging receipt of the Medal of Honor.[47] Also, Carr made no mention of Traveling Bear in his report of the Summit Springs fight. When one looks at Carr's written recommendation for the Medal of Honor, it is clear that Carr meant Mad Bear and not Traveling Bear. In his July 20 report, Carr noted that Mad Bear had chased the Indians who had tried to stampede the mules and horses on the night of July 8. Mad Bear mounted his pony and gave chase. As he was about to catch and kill one warrior, his horse fell and threw him. At the same time he was accidentally shot by one of the soldiers firing on the fleeing Dog Soldiers. Carr noted his bravery here "and also for killing two of those killed by Colonel Royall's command [on July 4]."[48] Carr, in his reminiscences, would again write of this incident: "His [Luther North's] corporal of the guard followed them in a most daring manner and got wounded, *for which I got him the medal of honor.*"[49] From all this evidence, it is rather obvious that North was mistaken regarding whom Carr recommended and intended for the Congressional Medal of Honor. It was meant for and awarded to Mad Bear, not Traveling Bear.

After John Kile's heroic stand on July 8, he was promoted to First Sergeant. Earlier, it had been learned that Kile was a deserter from Custer's 7th Cavalry. Although he had indeed deserted the 7th Cavalry, he almost immediately joined the 5th Cavalry. He was relieved from his desertion charge by Special Order Number 220, Headquarters, Department of the Missouri and promoted to Corporal May 1, 1869.[50] After the Republican River Expedition, Kile was placed on detached service to the Department of the Missouri by Special Order of August 24, 1869, the same day he was awarded the Medal of Honor.[51] When his enlistment expired, Kile re-enlisted and was reassigned back to the 7th Cavalry. When he arrived at the 7th Cavalry camp on Big Creek, near Fort Hays, he was recognized as a deserter. His papers, however, revealed his receiving the Medal of Honor and his meritorious service under Carr in the 5th Cavalry.[52]

When Kile reported to the 7th Cavalry, there had been ongoing trouble between soldiers and civilians in the nearby town of Hays, Kansas, where former 7th Cavalry scout Wild Bill Hickok had earlier served as sheriff. Kile and another soldier went into Hays and got into a scuffle with Wild Bill. Both soldiers approached Wild Bill from his blind side, and together jumped him. In a fierce struggle Wild Bill was getting the advantage over the other soldier, grabbing one of his pistols to shoot him when Kile pulled his own pistol from its holster, placed the barrel into Hickok's ear, and pulled the trigger. Seventh Cavalryman John Ryan reported what happened next:

> It missed fire, or it probably would have ended his [Hickok's] career right there. Longeran [the other soldier] was holding Wild Bill's right wrist, but Wild Bill turned his hand far enough to one side, and the first shot he fired shot Kelley [Kelley was the alias last name of Kile when he first enlisted in the 7th Cavalry before deserting] through the right wrist. He fired a second time, and the bullet entered Kelley's side and went plumb through his body and could be felt on the other side. Of course that put an end to Kelley [Kile] then and there in a few moments.[53]

Returning to Carr's pursuit, July 9, 1869, was a hot day. The column marched northwest for thirty-two miles, camping on some water holes that were found just inside the Colorado border from Kansas. Lieutenant Volkmar reported that the hot winds rendered the day's march "very trying. Large quantities of slaughtered buffalo were found during the day. *And the Indian trail became very heavy.*"[54] By eleven-thirty the next morning, the cavalry had traveled nearly nineteen miles and reached Frenchman Creek near present-day Holyoke,

Colorado. Soon, a large abandoned Indian village was discovered, several Indian parties having brought in "quantities of shod horses and mules."[55] By four o'clock that afternoon, the command traveled another thirteen miles northwest near present-day Haxtun, Colorado, where another Indian camp was found along Frenchman Creek. It was a fresh camp, for the skins of the dead animals found there were still moist.[56] The command was quickly overtaking the Indians. Because no Indians were sighted for two days, it was likely that the command was undetected.

Were the Dog Soldiers getting careless? Captain Luther North hinted such when he wrote that when an Indian "knows that an enemy is after him it is impossible to take him unawares but let him think himself safe and he is the most careless being on earth. . . ."[57] Where did the Dog Soldiers get the belief that they were no longer being followed? Carr wrote later that after Royall's command had fought the small war party carrying a wounded Indian on a litter on July 5, Royall returned to the main command, arriving back July 7. "About 50 of the warriors had followed Royall back, and seeing that I was marching east, thought that I had given them up and was going home, and made a dash at me and gone back to their main body."[58] He was referring to the attempt to stampede the stock on the night of July 8. The camp was about a mile east of where the command camped on July 4,[59] giving the appearance that the soldiers were withdrawing. It fooled the Dog Soldiers and they did not do anything to assure themselves that the cavalry was withdrawing. This carelessness by the Dog Soldiers would prove to be a fatal mistake, for the cavalry later followed up on the trail Royall earlier discovered, and by July 10 they were within striking distance of the village.

By the time the soldiers had gone into camp late on the afternoon of July 10, they had marched thirty-two miles, gaining another day on the Indians. The command had now marched a total of 453 miles since starting from Fort

McPherson on June 9.[60] The march of thirty-five miles on July 11 would bring them to the unsuspecting village.

Sunday morning, July 11, began under clear skies. Five days' rations were prepared and packed on mules. The wagon train followed at a slower pace, protected by Company M.[61] By five-thirty that morning, the command followed the fresh and well-defined Dog Soldier trail. By eight o'clock, Carr's men had traveled more than ten miles. A little more than four miles later, at nine o'clock, the soldiers came to a high ridge, overlooking the South Platte River, visible a few miles to the north. This would be south of present-day Iliff, not far from Riverside Station. Loose horses were observed in the river bottom to the north. The Pawnees informed Carr the village was quite near. Volkmar wrote: "Great caution was observed by the column, everybody dismounting and leading the horses quickly over the ridges, and down through steep ravines to the 'bottom'."[62]

For the next ten miles the command stayed in the low lands of the sand ridges and hills, following a west course parallel to the south side of the South Platte River. They almost got to present-day Sterling, when, at eleven-thirty, the trail divided. Pawnee scouts reported what they believed to be a large herd of horses to the north on the river bottom of the South Platte, in the general direction of one of the trails. It was quite hot with a stiff wind. The command had had no water since leaving early in the morning. Some Pawnees also reported seeing two men on horseback. Carr quickly and quietly moved the command into a ravine to avoid being detected.[63]

Carr then divided his command. Royall took half, which included Companies E and G, and two companies of Pawnee scouts, and galloped north to the South Platte River where the suspected herd of horses had been spotted. Royall took Cody and scouted the area to learn if the Indians had crossed the river. Carr, with the remaining four companies of the 5th Cavalry (A, C, D and H), and one company of Pawnee scouts,[64] comprising 244 soldiers and fifty Pawnees, followed the main trail, which led southwest across the tableland.[65] Soon Pawnees told Carr they believed the village was nearby. Carr's command then galloped west for about eight miles.

General Eugene Asa Carr
Courtesy of Quito Osuna Carr, M.D., Albuquerque, New Mexico.

The Battle of Susanna Springs
(Summit Springs)

*...on the 11th under command of Bvt. Maj. Gen. E.
A. Carr, took an active part in the engagement at
Susanna Springs, C.T.[1]*

It was now one-thirty in the afternoon of July 11, 1869. The
Dog Soldier village was a mere three miles away to the southwest, but not yet discovered. A Pawnee courier had been sent
to recall Major W. B. Royall's portion of the command. Royall
had been traveling northwest while General E. A. Carr was
going west. Royall did not have far to travel to rejoin the
command and soon he was back, reporting that the "horses"
thought to be in the river bottom were in fact bushes. He found
no evidence that the Dog Soldiers had crossed the river. Within
ten minutes after Royall rejoined Carr's battalion, the village
was found, the horse herd visible outside it. The ground here
was hilly, and this allowed Carr's reunited command to get
within about two miles of the village, still undetected.[2]

Lieutenant W. J. Volkmar's report states that Carr divided
the command into four separate columns. Lieutenant George
Price would write that there were three columns, the Pawnee
Indians with one column.[3] Carr reported placing the three
leading companies into "parallel columns of two's, directing
Major Crittenden, 5th Cavalry, to take command [of the center
column] and sounded the charge."[4] Captain Samuel Sumner
wrote that the Pawnees were on the left, his Company D next
to them, and Companies A, C, E, G, and H on the right.[5] Before
the order was given to charge the village, the Pawnees prepared themselves for battle. They stripped themselves of all
their clothing except for their blue cavalry pants, in order that
the soldiers might distinguish them from the Dog Soldiers

during the battle. The Pawnees also removed the saddles from their horses, preferring to ride bareback into the fight. Captain Leicester Walker took the left position with Company H. Lieutenant George Price took the right position with Company A. Captains S. Sumner (Company D) and Thomas Maley (Company C) took the center with their respective companies, Major Crittenden commanding. The Pawnees joined the center column. One company of the 5th Cavalry (E or G) was kept in reserve. General Carr would soon lead this reserve company into the middle of the village.[6]

About two o'clock, "the trumpets rang out the 'charge' and with hurrahs the columns and reserve dashed over the hill, down the slope toward the village."[7] The strong wind coming from the west prevented the Dog Soldiers from hearing the charging men coming from the east. Lieutenant Price reported the wind so strong that only those men next to the chief trumpeter could hear the sounds for the charge, but everyone knew instinctively what to do and commenced the attack.[8] Carr remembered:

> When we all got started I told the bugler behind me to sound "the charge." He put up his trumpet to his mouth but no sound came out. I asked him why he did not sound the charge, and he said, "I, I, disremember it, sir," but it came to him directly and he sounded it while all were going at full speed; and we were among the enemy before they had any idea we were within a thousand miles.[9]

As the advancing columns raced toward the village as fast as the tired horses could carry the men, a young Indian warrior spotted the charge. He was herding several hundred ponies the same distance south of the village as Carr's command was to the northeast, a little more than half a mile away. When the herder saw the soldiers, he bravely drove the horse herd into the village rather than escape to the south. That was the only way he could alert his people of the impending attack. It now became a race to the village. If the herder won, the village would be warned, albeit barely. Still, every moment was important. Lieutenant Price remembered, "if the herder should gain the village but one minute before the advancing cavalry could strike it the advantage arising from a complete surprise would also be lost."[10]

The young Dog Soldier did not win the race, but he did not lose it either. He arrived just ahead of the advancing columns, yet not with enough time to be able to prevent the surprise that Carr sought. Luther North wrote:

> About a half a mile from the village, and off to one side from our line, a Cheyenne boy was herding horses. He was about fifteen years old and we were very close to him before he saw us. He jumped on his horse, gathered up his herd, and drove them into the village ahead of our men, who were shooting at him. He was mounted on a very good horse and could easily have gotten away if he had left the herd, but he took them all in ahead of him, then at the edge of the village he turned and joined a band of warriors that were trying to hold us back, while the women and children were getting away, and there he died like a warrior. No braver man ever lived than that fifteen year old boy.[11]

Lieutenant Price wrote that the herder and his horse were killed in the middle of the village. He also reported that the soldiers

> . . . were not seen by any of the enemy, except the herder, until they were within fifty yards of the village and charging upon it at a terrific pace. The warriors had no time to seize their arms or secure their ponies. They were completely dazed and bewildered, and fled panic-stricken in every direction.[12]

Captain L. Walker in his report of the fight said the village "was charged with the most frantic enthusiasm. The Indians, Sioux, Cheyennes and Arrapahoes, [sic] numbering about 500 warriors, were taken with panic, and almost paralyzed with fear, they ran, offering but little resistance, leaving over 50 killed. . . ."[13]

If it is true that the Dog Soldiers offered but little resistance to the attack, then indeed the young herder acted in a most impressionable and brave manner. The actual fight inside the village lasted only about twenty minutes.[14] When the fight was over, fifty-two dead warriors were officially counted. Only one soldier had a wound, "slightly scratched by an arrow."[15] It is amazing that such a conflict could produce such staggering differences in casualties.

There are perhaps two possibilities that may explain this discrepancy in casualties. One is the Indians were filled with fright, fled for their lives, and were killed without much resistance. The other explanation might be that the complete surprise of the village didn't permit the Dog Soldiers time to ceremonially prepare for battle. This does not mean that the Indians were unable to secure weapons to defend themselves. Rather, it meant they weren't able to perform their rituals for battle and thus they did not have with them their medicine that sanctified, according to their beliefs, their *ability* to perform in battle. If this were the case, it better explains why the Dog Soldiers made such little resistance.

Carr reported that one horse was killed during the fight, but another twelve were ridden to death in the ensuing chase of several miles. One Indian caught in the village, seeing he could not escape, tried to pass as a woman covered with a blanket, and when discovered, replied, "Me good Indian, talk heap." Such a plea had no efficacy and he was quickly killed.[16] Carr reported soldiers chasing Indians for about four miles. Volkmar wrote that the pursuit lasted six or eight miles.[17]

There were steep ravines southeast of the village, where Tall Bull and about twenty Indians fled. It was here that a sharp resistance was encountered. Carr:

> Tall Bull, the chief finding how matters were going, determined to die. He had a little daughter on his horse and one of his wives on another. He gave the daughter to his wife, and told her to escape and take the white woman who was prisoner, and she

might use her to make terms for herself when peace was made. The wife begged him to escape with her, but he shut his ears, *killed his horse*, and she soon saw him killed, fighting. She then surrendered and was saved with her daughter of eight, and brother of twelve years.[18]

In an 1887 letter Carr basically repeated his earlier account in his official report:

I may add that Tall Bull the chief . . . was killed. He had started off with his favorite wife and little girl and they were hoping to escape when he looked back and saw the destruction of his village and band of robbers in which he had taken great pride. He told his squaw that he could not bear to live after that and was going to turn back and fight and be killed. . . . The squaw said that he turned back and met the soldiers and was killed and that she sat down facing them with her little girl in her lap and they came up and took her as prisoner into camp – she with all the seventeen prisoners were afterwards sent up the Missouri to their friends.[19]

Volkmar reported that Tall Bull died "after a desperate personal defense."[20]

It is with the death of Tall Bull that controversy surrounds the fight at Susanna Springs. There are five different individuals claimed to have killed Tall Bull. They are Major Frank North, Buffalo Bill Cody, Lieutenant George Mason, Sergeant Daniel McGrath, and an unidentified Pawnee Indian. Don Russell, in *The Lives and Legends of Buffalo Bill*, does an incisive job of revealing the inadequacies of the claim that Major Frank North killed Tall Bull.[21] The North claim comes from Frank's younger brother, Luther, who gave ten different published accounts, no two of them agreeing.[22] Russell demonstrates the inadequacies of each account, making it clear that Luther North had unresolved animosities against both Cody and officers of the 5th Cavalry, including Carr. These animosities motivated him to make his claims on behalf of Frank, who had died as a result of injuries while performing in Cody's Wild West Show.[23] Since North gave so many accounts, it really doesn't matter which one is used:

> As we were going along this coulee, a Indian rose up to fire and then dodged back. We stopped and waited for him to rise up again, and Frank suggested that if we would go on, the Indian would rise up again as soon as he would hear the noise of our horse's hoofs. So we started on and Frank (personally) remained with his gun drawn and the instant the Indian rose to fire at me, Frank shot him dead. This was Tall Bull.[24]

J. E. Welch, a teamster accompanying Carr's expedition, wrote in 1904 that Lieutenant George Mason of Company A killed Tall Bull, "who rode up to him and shot him through the heart with a derringer."[25] Welch's account of the Susanna Springs fight is riddled with errors and exaggerations, but it is also accurate in ways that would be unknown to someone who was not with the expedition. For example, he reports that Carr turned the captured Indians over to the charge of the Pawnees. Carr, writing in his reminiscences, said, "I put the women and children prisoners under charge of the Pawnees, as I was not going to have any scandal with my soldiers."[26] Welch also notes that nineteen prisoners were taken in the fight, four of whom were women, the rest children. Carr writes that there were seventeen prisoners taken, but does not discriminate the number of children and women.[27] This account of Lieutenant Mason having killed Tall Bull cannot be dismissed as outright false, as can the North accounts. Carr himself says in his reminiscences that Tall Bull's wife saw him fall when he was shot.[28] It should be remembered, though, that Welch was a teamster with Carr's expedition and thus could not have been at the fight, for the simple reason that the wagons did not arrive at the scene of the battle until nine o'clock that evening.[29] Welch's responsibilities would in all probability have him with the wagons. But he was there the evening of the fight and would have heard the immediate camp talk about the fight. Thus, his report of Lieutenant Mason killing Tall Bull may be correct.

Carr, unfortunately, names three different people who killed Tall Bull. Major Frank North is not one of them. Carr names Cody, but he also identifies Sergeant Daniel McGrath as killing Tall Bull. And, in a letter to Cody in 1906, Carr declares that the Pawnees killed Tall Bull. Carr there writes:

> My recollection is that Tall Bull's wife said they were escaping on foot when he looked back and saw the destruction of the village and the Dog Soldier band which had taunted the other Indians saying "you call us dogs because we fight the whites you are squaws and we are Dog Soldiers." Tall Bull told his wife that "his heart was bad" and he could not live after this; that she must escape and treat the white woman well and the whites might treat her well. *He turned back and the Pawnees killed him.*[30]

When Cody became famous and did his Wild West shows, he featured the Susanna Springs fight in several seasons of shows. By this time Carr was endeared to Cody as a friend. He provided for Cody another account of the Susanna Springs fight, which Cody published in his illustrated booklet that accompanied the appearances of the Wild West show. There Carr gives credit to Cody for killing Tall Bull:

> Buffalo Bill got pretty well around the village when he went in on Capt. Price's right. He had with him two soldiers and a Pawnee. He saw the women and children getting away and hiding in ravines and sand washes. As he advanced he saw a chief on a horse charging about, and haranguing his men. He and his party laid for him and, as he came near, Buffalo Bill shot him off his horse and got the horse. This was the celebrated race horse "Tall Bull," which he, Cody, rode for a long time, and won many exciting races. So that left no doubt that Buffalo Bill killed Tall Bull.[31]

In 1901, Carr wrote a letter of recommendation for Sergeant Daniel McGrath, who by this time had retired as a career soldier with the 5th Cavalry. This letter credits McGrath with killing Tall Bull:

> I take great pleasure in recommending Mr. Daniel McGrath, ex-Sgt. 5th Cavalry, for any position for which he professes himself capable.
>
> He is most intelligent, reliable and faithful. He served under my command for ten years, and particularly distinguished himself at the Battle of Summit Springs, Colorado where he killed the Chief Tall Bull.[32]

Cody, in his 1879 autobiography, gives himself the credit for killing Tall Bull. Noticing an Indian giving orders and mounted on an impressive horse, Cody believed he could kill the Indian and thereby capture the horse:

> When he [Tall Bull] was not more than thirty yards distant I fired, and the next moment he tumbled from the saddle, and the horse kept on without his rider. Instead of running towards the Indians, however, he galloped toward our men, by one of whom he was caught. Lieutenant Mason, who had been very conspicuous in the fight and who had killed two or three Indians himself, single-handed, came galloping up to the ravine and jumping from his horse, secured the fancy war bonnet from the head of the dead chief, together with all his other accouterments. We both then rejoined the soldiers and I at once went in search of the horse; I found him in the possession of Sergeant McGrath, who had caught him. The sergeant knew that I had been trying to get the animal and having seen me kill his rider, he handed him over to me at once.[33]

What is interesting about this early account of Cody killing Tall Bull is that Cody mentions Lieutenant Mason and Sergeant McGrath, both of whom are also given credit by others for killing Tall Bull. Cody, having placed both of these men in his story actually lends credence to claims that they respectively killed Tall Bull. Carr, giving credit to three different people, seems to eliminate himself as a credible witness. What appears clear, though, is that Luther North's story that his brother killed Tall Bull is false. After that, perhaps Cody has an edge as the one who killed Tall Bull, but it must be seen as slight. McGrath comes in a close second, with Mason and a Pawnee as a distant third. The proper conclusion, unless other yet undiscovered evidence surfaces, is that we cannot say today who really killed Tall Bull. But, indeed, there does exist such evidence.

An unpublished enlisted man's version of the Susanna Springs fight by a soldier who served in the 5th Cavalry shortly after the battle, also credits Sergeant McGrath as the killer of Tall Bull.[34] John Stevenson, serving several enlistments under the name of Charles Abbott, joined the 5th Cavalry in 1872. Writing his memoirs after retiring as a first sergeant, Stevenson wrote his understanding of who killed Tall Bull. It is Sergeant McGrath. Though Stevenson was not at the fight, it is likely that his account reports what the enlisted men understood about who killed Tall Bull:

> Buffalo Bill claims to be the man who killed Tall Bull. So, also, did Lieutenant Mason, Regimental Quartermaster, but neither one is entitled to the claim. Tall Bull was killed by Sergeant Dannie McGrath, Company H, 5th Cavalry. Cody was all of three hundred yards from where Tall Bull fell. It is true that this is not an extraordinary range for such a expert shot as he is, but when men were galloping through a line of fire as these men were, it is almost impossible. Lieutenant Mason was only about half the distance from Bull that Cody was, but was armed with a revolver, so it seems to me that it was rather preposterous for him to make the claim, not withstanding the fact he was an expert pistol shot. My experience in pistol shooting is that when mounted and going on the dead jump it is necessary to burn your opponent with your powder to get him. Still a lucky shot might get a fellow even at long

range. Now, McGrath's horse was shot and he was on foot at a distance of less than fifty yards. He deliberately kneeled on one knee, took careful aim and fired and shot Tall Bull through the heart.[35]

What is interesting about this account is that it acknowledges the three important possibilities of who killed Tall Bull, and then provides the evidence for the claim that McGrath, and not Cody or Mason, killed Tall Bull. This account, placed alongside Carr's letter giving credit to McGrath, gives a slight edge toward him over Cody as the killer of Tall Bull. Stevenson's account also identifies McGrath as the soldier who had his horse killed in the fight, and places that incident near the ravines where Tall Bull was killed.

What did surviving Dog Soldiers tell in their accounts of the fight at Susanna Springs? George Bent wrote that when the Dog Soldiers arrived at Susanna Springs, a war party of Sioux Dog Soldiers had informed Tall Bull that soldiers were following the trail left by the traveling village and they should not tarry there. But recent rains had produced high waters in the South Platte, making it too dangerous to cross with the women and children. Tall Bull, therefore, made the fatal decision to wait at Susanna Springs for two days while the water subsided. Some Sioux Dog Soldiers did not want to stay and left the village the evening before Carr's attack.[36] Bent helps to explain the discrepancy of the actual number of tepees found at Susanna Springs with what Carr had expected to find. The eighty-four lodges captured at Susanna Springs would indicate a warrior presence of about 200. The Pawnees had earlier calculated about 400 warriors, given the tepee rings counted at the abandoned campsites prior to surprising the village at Susanna Springs.[37] There should have been around 150 to 175 tepee lodges at Susanna Springs. About half the village had indeed departed before Carr's surprise attack.

While one part of Bent's account sounds logical, his claim that the Indians knew the soldiers were still following their trail is questionable. If true, it seems only to indicate a tremendous carelessness by the Indians in not anticipating the soldier's continued pursuit and thus getting caught in such a complete surprise at Susanna Springs. Either the Indians were unconscionably careless, which is even more incredulous given that they chose to remain at Susanna Springs longer than it was thought safe, or they did not suspect their trail was being followed, a careless act but not unconscionably careless. Given Lieutenant Volkmar's report that the trail was not being hidden as the command advanced to Susanna Springs, it seems obvious that the Indians did not suspect soldiers were trailing them. Thus, contrary to Bent, it is unlikely the Dog Soldiers were aware that Carr's command was following their trail. Even so, the Dog Soldiers still remain guilty of carelessness in not having scouts out to protect their trail from surprise. Indeed, Bent wrote that the Cheyenne later blamed Tall Bull for the surprise at Susanna Springs: ". . . it was poor judgment for Tall Bull to insist on going into camp instead of crossing the South Platte that evening, and this error was the cause of the village being surprised the next day."[38]

According to Bent, Cheyenne accounts gave more credit to the Pawnee Indians at Susanna Springs than the soldiers, the Pawnee doing most of the killing and capturing most of the pony herd.[39] Bent said: "The reason this command did so much damage, the Indians say, was because of the presence of the Pawnee scouts. They always showed up first and the Cheyennes mistook them for friendly warriors."[40]

A further question concerns the number of Indian dead at Susanna Springs. The official report from Carr lists the dead at fifty-two.[41] Volkmar lists the Indian dead at fifty-three,[42] while Price says it was sixty-one.[43] Sumner reported seventy-three killed.[44] In a long letter to Washington Smith, written in 1887, Carr amends his figures of Indian dead at seventy-six.[45] Washington Smith had been victimized in the Lincoln County raids, both in 1868 and again in 1869. His son, Chalmers Smith, had fought with Forsyth at Beecher Island. Two anonymous accounts in the *Army and Navy Journal* list fifty-two and seventy-three Indian dead.[46] But none of these figures discriminate between warrior and non-warrior dead. Bent wrote that a "large number of women and children were killed."[47] In his reminiscences Carr adds further details regarding the Dog Soldier dead on the battlefield, and non-warrior dead. The day after the fight, wrote Carr:

> The surgeon [Louis Tesson] and I walked over the field to look at the dead. He wanted a skull to send to the Smithsonian, but all had been broken by the Pawnees. *Only a few women and no small children had been killed.* We saw the body of what looked like a tall warrior lying on its back with a smaller one on each side. The doctor found it was a woman with a very light complexion. On one side lay a girl about 13, who was very dark, on the other a boy of 10, who was probably her son, as he was light like her. The Pawnees told me she was trying to escape, and when she found that she could not, stopped and knifed the children, and they [the Pawnees] killed her.[48]

If Carr is correct, non-warrior deaths did occur, but were minimal. And, as both Carr and Bent note, the Pawnees were responsible for nearly all of them. The Cheyenne, Two Crows, is one Dog Soldier who escaped and did much to help protect the fleeing women and children, but he regretted "leaving so many Cheyenne and Sioux women and children to be killed by the Pawnees."[49] Grinnell gives accounts of seven Indian women and four children killed. The Pawnees killed all of them during the frantic retreat from the village.[50] Given the long festering animosity that existed between the Pawnees and the Sioux and Cheyenne, it should not be surprising that the Pawnees did most of the non-warrior killing at Susanna Springs. Another Dog Soldier account says the Pawnees early in the fight killed two Indian women and a young girl:

> I do not belittle the Pawnees for their killing of women or children because as far back as any of us could remember the Cheyenne and Sioux slaughtered

every male, female and child they could run across of the Pawnee tribe. Each tribe hated the other with a deadly passion and savage hearts know only total war![51]

These non-warrior deaths noted above might help to explain the discrepancies between the later Carr and Price accounts of Indian dead at Susanna Springs with the earlier Carr and other smaller number accounts. Perhaps the higher numbers include non-warrior dead, however, the number was not great and the Pawnees did most of the killing.

Carr commented on soldier behavior at Susanna Springs:

We have, however, no pleasure in killing the poor miserable savages, but desire, in common with the whole Army, by the performance of our duty, to deliver the settlers from the dangers to which they are exposed on account of the past mistaken policy, or rather want of policy, in Indian affairs, which render it necessary to chastise them until they submit.[52]

When the village was attacked, all knew that it probably contained the captives taken in the Kansas raid six weeks earlier. The problem was, where were they? Could they be rescued? All knew it was common practice for the Dog Soldiers to kill captives when a village was under attack. Tom Alderdice knew this fact, one Kansas newspaper noting Tom's awareness that "a hostile attack upon the band would be the signal for the death of the women."[53] What were Carr's options? One, apparently, was to hope that the women would be found and rescued before they could be killed. Unfortunately, such was not to be the case. The captive women were no doubt frightened at the moment of attack. Would this be their liberation? This they could not know, for perhaps it was another hostile band of Indians attacking the Dog Soldier village. Further, the signal for their liberation might in fact be the signal for their death. The buzz within the village, at the moment, must have been frightful for both Susanna Alderdice and Maria Weichel. On the one hand was their prayerful hope for deliverance, but at the same time they had to know the extreme danger they faced if the attack signaled soldiers seeking their liberation.

It will never be known what Susanna's thoughts were at this crucial moment in her captivity. It can only be speculated what her thoughts might have been at her moment of death. What is known is that she was mortally wounded when the village came under attack. Carr's report lacks emotion in simply reporting, "There were two white women in the village, one of whom they murdered, and the other they attempted to murder; but we were too quick for them, and she escaped with a painful wound."[54] Susanna was mortally wounded. Maria was painfully wounded and would recover. Lieutenant Volkmar merely reported a "captive white woman supposed to be Mrs. Susanna Alderdice, was killed by the Indians during the fight."[55] An unidentified officer wrote an account of the fight that was printed in the *New York Times*. It merely stated the village contained "two white women, captured at Selina [sic] last May. One of these was killed, and the other, although wounded, will in all likelihood recover."[56]

Other accounts of Susanna's death and Maria's painful rescue surfaced later, and it is from these that further details are learned regarding their experiences. Probably the most detailed account comes from Luther North. In an interview with Walter Camp in 1917 North claimed:

> When we charged into the village, Cushing [North's brother-in-law and one of the officers commanding a Pawnee Company] stopped in a teepee to get a drink of water out of a keg and the wounded white woman ran up and grabbed hold of him almost frightening him to death. She afterwards said Tall Bull in person had shot her.
>
> The other white woman had been killed by some Indian when the Indians ran out of the village. She had been struck in the head with a hatchet or like instrument.[57]

In Luther North's memoirs he adds more details to this encounter. Cushing, after taking a drink, handed the water jug to Frank North:

> About this time a woman came crawling out of the lodge, and running to Capt. Cushing fell on her knees and threw her hands about his legs. We now saw she was a white woman. She was bleeding from a bullet wound through her breast. She was a Swede [German] and could not talk English, and had been taken prisoner several months before [six weeks to the day], when this band of Cheyennes had raided a Swedish settlement in Kansas. Tall Bull had taken her for his wife, and when we charged his camp he tried to kill her, but only made a flesh wound through her breast.

Soon after this Luther saw an untended saddled horse up the small stream flowing from the springs. As he went to retrieve it,

> I had gone only a little way when I came to a dead woman, and upon examination found she was white. She had been killed with a tomahawk. We afterwards learned that she had been taken prisoner at the same time the other woman was taken, and when we charged the camp they killed her.[58]

Yet more information comes in another account by North. Here, Maria was inside the tent when discovered by Cushing: "She was sitting on a mat in the tent [tepee], suffering intensely from the wound, but when Captain Cushing stepped up to her she seemed to forget her pain, and grabbing him around the legs she hugged him again and again and wept for joy."[59]

In still another North account, he repeated this story but added the detail that Susanna "was big with child."[60] Teamster Welch also noted Susanna's obvious pregnancy: "She had the appearance of being far gone in pregnancy."[61] Carr said in his report on the fight that "both women were pregnant and both were no doubt raped by a dozen of the savages."[62] In his memoirs Carr was more specific about Susanna: "She

[Susanna] was shot over the eye and had her skull broken in. .
. . She was of middle age [she was twenty-nine] and looked
badly, and evidently had been hardly [i.e., badly] used and
treated as a slave."[63] Luther North said in a 1932 letter, "Mrs.
Alderdice was killed as I supposed by a blow from a tomahawk
there was a small hole in her temple."[64] It is likely then that
Susanna had two separate head wounds, either of which would
have proven fatal.

Perhaps the most graphic description of what happened to
Susanna and Maria comes not from the side of the military but
rather from an obscure account from one of Tall Bull's wives,
Sun Dance Woman, who was taken captive at Susanna Springs:

> She said that both white women were in Tall Bull's
> Lodge when the Pawnees made their run through
> the village and the chief grabbed his rifle, and with
> no time to lose, brained the one called & later iden-
> tified as Susanna Alderdice and jabbed the other in
> the breast with the barrel of his gun, a vicious
> action that left her breast torn and bleeding. This
> was the other white woman prisoner a Mrs. George
> (Maria) Weichell. Both had been used as wives of
> Tall Bull and one was with child. Sun Woman
> didn't like either and shot Mrs. Weichell in the
> same breast again with a pistol before she ran from
> the lodge and jumped up behind her husband and
> small daughter waiting on horse back. She said
> that she knew that Susanna was dead or would die,
> from the sound of the rifle blow when it hit her
> head. It cracked like a split from a ripe pumpkin.[65]

When the command camped on the night of July 12 at
Wisconsin Ranch on the south side of the South Platte River,
four miles west of present-day Sterling, Colorado,[66] Maria saw
Sun Dance Woman, herself now the captive. She reported Sun
Dance Woman's cruel treatment to her during her captivity.
This included frequently pounding on her and whipping her,
treating her "most cruelly and shamefully," usually when Tall
Bull was away hunting.[67] Sun Dance Woman's cruelty was
apparently inspired by jealousy. When Maria reported this to

her rescuers, the Pawnees wanted to kill Sun Dance Woman then and there. However, Major North intervened and thus saved Sun Dance Woman's life, warning her, though, that if she tried to escape he would allow the Pawnees to kill her. It is interesting to note that Carr later wrote that Maria told him that Tall Bull treated her "pretty well" but not the women.[68]

Carr said that Maria was shot "with a pistol bullet in the back – it broke a rib, but passed around and lodged under the left breast, and was removed by my surgeon."[69] An army tent was put up in the village and there the surgeon, Louis Tesson, removed the bullet. Private Hercules Price of Company G later wrote of seeing Maria in the surgeon's care. The trumpeter for Company G, Henry Voss, was the interpreter for her, as she could not speak English.[70] Hercules Price recalled leading his horse past the tent where the surgeon was treating her. When seeing him pass in front of the tent, Maria "modestly covered her breast as I passed by."[71] He described Maria as well built and attractive. Perhaps it was no accident he walked past the surgeon's tent when he did. Henry Voss died alongside Custer at the Little Bighorn June 25, 1876. He served as Custer's chief trumpeter, having re-enlisted in the 7th Cavalry after his 5th Cavalry enlistment expired.[72]

Shortly after the fight was over, about four o'clock, a thunderstorm passed over Susanna Springs, accompanied by dangerous hail and lightning. Lightning struck one horse, "while a trooper was astride of him."[73] The horse was killed, but the soldier was unharmed, though he probably had the living hell scared out of him. All took shelter in the captured tepees. This storm eventually traveled east to Fort Sedgwick, breaking most of the windows in the post buildings, ripping the roof off of one of the company buildings, the baker's house, and a portion of the roof from the officers' quarters and the post trader's store. One mule was killed from the flying debris.[74]

That night, Doctor Tesson, working in his tent, prepared Susanna for burial. Sometime during the night, while Tesson was working with Susanna's body, movement was observed from the top of the ravines where Tall Bull and several of his Dog Soldiers died during the short fight earlier in the day. At first it was thought to be a coyote, "but it proved to be a small Indian child, three or four years old, who had known enough to hide in the breaks above the canyon during the battle."[75] This little boy, no doubt horribly frightened, wet, cold, and hungry, was brought into the village and reunited with the other prisoners. It was still raining when the wagons arrived at the village, at nine o'clock, traveling almost thirty-six miles from the camp of July 10.[76]

After the battle was over and the village secured, Carr ordered a board of officers to take an inventory of everything that had been captured. The report is staggering as to the contents:

56 rifles	67 brass & iron camp
22 revolvers	kettles
40 sets bows and arrows	200 raw hide lariats
20 tomahawks	16 bottles strychnine
47 axes	84 lodges, complete
150 knives	125 travois
50 pounds powder	9300 pounds meat, dried
20 pounds bullets	160 tin cups
14 bullet moulds	180 tin plates
8 bars lead	200 dressing knives
25 boxes percussion caps	8 shovels
17 sabres	75 lodge skins (new)
17 war shields	40 saddle bags
9 lances	75 bridles
13 war bonnets	28 woman dresses
690 buffalo robes	50 hammers
552 panniers [baskets	9 coats
carried on horses]	100 pounds tobacco
152 moccasins	200 coffee pots (tin)
319 raw hides	1500 dollars (in gold &
361 saddles	national bank notes)
31 mess pans	horses & mules killed 25
52 water kegs	

The board continued with this report:

> Besides the above mentioned articles the Board is of the opinion that there was at least ten (10) tons of various Indian property, such as clothing, flour, coffee, corn meal, saddle equipments, fancy articles, etc., destroyed by the command before leaving the camp, by burning [July 12].

> There was also found in the different lodges, articles which had undoubtedly been stolen from white settlements: albums, containing photographs, daguerreotypes, watches, clocks, crockery ware, silver forks and spoons etc. In making examination preparatory to burning the camp, quite a number of white scalps were found attached to wearing apparel, lances and children's toys, some of which appeared to be very fresh.[77]

Carr also reported the gruesome discovery of a necklace containing fingers of white people. 274 horses and 144 mules were captured. In addition, Carr noted letters recovered that "certify to the high character of certain Indians, whom must have greatly degenerated since they were written."[78] Two letters identified Cheyenne chiefs Slim Face and Pretty Bear, another letter was for Sioux chief Whistler, and four letters were for Tall Bull. Tall Bull apparently had learned that such letters helped him when he had contact with military or civilian authorities. One letter, dated October 28, 1867, and signed by N. G. Taylor, Commissioner of Indian Affairs, says Tall Bull "is a friendly Indian, to whom a Peace Medal has been presented by the Indian Peace Commission, and all persons – citizens or soldiers are requested to assist, protect and respect him accordingly."[79] Edward Wynkoop signed another letter dated May 17, 1868. His letter is a little more menacing in that it hints Tall Bull's propensity for violence:

> . . . he is peaceably disposed, and will do nothing that is wrong, *unless forced to do so by imprudent acts of white men*; it were well that he be treated friendly by all he may meet, as it is the object of the

government to have all these Indians shown proper consideration for the purpose of avoiding trouble.[80]

Six wagons were used to load captured material to be taken to Fort Sedgwick. The rest of the captured bounty was ordered burned. When the command left Susanna Springs the morning of July 12, there were "160 fires burning at once to destroy the property."[81] One unique find at Susanna Springs was a ledgerbook containing more than seventy detailed Indian pictographs. It has been in the possession of the Colorado Historical Society since 1903 but was not published until 1997. It is an amazing Indian pictograph history of the Dog Soldier Society from 1865 up until its demise at Susanna Springs.[82]

It will be recalled that when Maria was captured on May 30, her husband's finger was cut off for the purpose of obtaining a ring he wore. That ring was found in the village and returned to Maria.[83] In addition to recovering her husband's ring, Maria also told Carr, through Voss the interpreter, that she had lost a lot of money when her husband was killed. When the column camped at Antelope Station Stage Ranch on July 14, one day before going to Fort Sedgwick, much money that had been found in the village was turned over to Maria. Though unable to read or write English, Maria signed a statement acknowledging receipt of this money,

> This donation is made to me in consequence of the murder of my husband and the capture of myself and other property on the Saline River Kansas, in May 1869 and also to relieve my present condition I having been shot through the body by said Indians while their camp was attacked and captured by the 5th Cavalry USA, on the 11th day of July 1869.[84]

The amount of money was significant, $838.35. One soldier gave $100.00, another gave $20.00, another gave $15.00 and still another gave $1.85. The Pawnees gave $329.00 to Maria. Company H gave $2.25, Company M, $122.25. Private Richard Tully of Company G gave a large amount for one individual,

$295.00.[85] Hercules Price said years later that there was one soldier rumored to have found $38,000.00 in the Indian village. He was then alleged to have deserted.[86] If nothing else, outside of Price's rumor, this unprecedented goodwill gesture to Maria shows sympathy and kind-heartedness for all she had endured in her captivity. It also shows that the Dog Soldiers knew the value of money when they conducted their devastating raids on the pioneer settlements.

Susanna Springs goes down in history as a great victory for the U. S. military. What marks Susanna Springs as an important victory is, among other things, that the guilty Indians were captured and punished with no loss of life to the military. These were, indeed, the Indians who wreaked so much havoc upon the pioneer settlements. Lieutenant Volkmar reported that "from articles and records found in the village" it proved that the Indians at Susanna Springs were the same Indians Carr had earlier fights with in May at Elephant Rock and Spring Creek.[87] The depredators had been caught and punished. There was no question that the Indians who held the captive women from Kansas were the same Indians who had caused all the problems necessitating the Republican River Expedition.

Another important result of Susanna Springs is that it broke the Dog Soldier military society and made the outlying settlements much safer in Kansas, Colorado, and Nebraska. Indian depredations did continue in Kansas the next year, but, with the exception of the Cheyenne outbreak of 1878, they were the exception and not the rule during summer months. This had not been the case in Kansas in the two summers before Susanna Springs. Carr's victory ended the certainty of deadly Indian raids in and around Kansas each spring, summer, and fall.

Both legislatures in Colorado and Nebraska recognized the significance of Susanna Springs and sent official notices of thanks to Carr and the 5th Cavalry for their outstanding victory. Kansas, however, did not and Carr later resented it. Carr: "The Legislatures of Nebraska and Colorado each voted me resolutions of thanks, which I have framed and hung up in my quarters, but I have received no recognition from Kansas."[88] Even Custer wrote Carr a congratulatory letter. Carr wrote back saying it "was very gratifying to receive the commendations of an officer so distinguished as yourself in our profession."[89]

Before the soldiers set fire to the captured property and moved on to Fort Sedgwick, there was one more task remaining before leaving Susanna Springs. Susanna was to be buried. She was carefully wrapped in a buffalo robe and lodge skins and a deep grave dug. Under clear skies, at eight o'clock in the morning of July 12, Susanna was buried in the middle of the village, on a small knoll near the surgeon's tent, and near where she was found dead the afternoon before. With all the men gathered near her, this young pioneer mother was carefully placed in her grave and given a military salute. Doctor Tesson read an Episcopal service for the dead. As one person reported, ". . . the cavalry sounded the funeral dirge, and as the soft, mournful notes died away many a cheek was wet that had long been stranger to tears." Carr had placed above her grave a headboard "with an inscription stating that we knew of her."[90] The lonely prairie received one more pioneer mother.

Years later, both Luther North and Hercules Price told Susanna's brother, Eli Zeigler, about her burial. North wrote:

> While we were in camp on the Saline [1870] two young men came into our camp, and in talking to them I found that one of them was a brother of Mrs. Alderdice that had been killed by the Cheyennes when we attacked their village. I told him that I was the first man to get to his sister, but that she was dead when I got to her. He seemed quite relieved when I told him that they had not tortured or mutilated her. I told him of having seen her buried, and that one of the officers of the Fifth Cavalry had read the burial service at the grave, and this pleased him.[91]

184

Hercules Price wrote to Eli about 1910, concerning Susanna's funeral. Eli wanted to know the grave location, so that he might one day visit the area. "The poor fellow was very thankful for the kind manner in which we disposed of his sister's remains and I believe he has taken a journey to that place in N. E. Colorado this summer."[92] Eli died at the age of sixty-three, April 5, 1916, while residing on a farm just outside Salem, Oregon.[93]

As the command left the battlefield at Susanna Springs, with all the fires burning, about twenty-five now homeless canines watched everything from a distance. Carr remembered ". . . they gathered on a hill and set up a Wagnerian accompaniment in a gamut of discontent howls, as we marched away from the field of Summit Springs."[94] As the dogs' final howls faded into the air and the quiet silence of the prairie returned to Susanna Springs, Susanna's ordeal was finally over.

Willis Daily as a young man, at about the time of his marriage to Mary Twibell. Willis survived the deadly May 30, 1869 Dog Soldier raid in Lincoln County, Kansas. Severely wounded at the time, he was not expected to live. Author's collection.

*Veronica Ulbrich was captured near present-day Fairbury,
Nebraska, on July 24, 1867. This picture was taken about the time
of her brief marriage to Alfred Megnin. Her sad story is on pages
133 - 141.* Courtesy of George Ulbrick, Lawrence, Kansas.

William J. Volkmar's 1868 West Point class picture. 2nd Lieutenant Volkmar served as Carr's Itinerary Officer during the Republican River Expedition and kept a daily journal of the command's activities, including the fight at Summit Springs. Author's collection.

John Alverson, left and Eli Zeigler, right with two of Eli's daughters and Mrs. Eli Zeigler. John was Susanna's brother-in-law and Eli, her brother. Eli survived the Beecher Island fight. Courtesy of Nebraska State Historical Society.

Eli Zeigler, Adolph Roenigk and John Alverson. Roenigk later wrote Pioneer History of Kansas *(see his story on pages 81 - 84). Zeigler and Alverson escaped from Dog Soldiers May 30, 1869 (see pages 89 - 93).* Courtesy of Nebraska State Historical Society.

Eli Zeigler.
Courtesy of the Kansas State Historical Society, Topeka, Kansas.

Willis Daily's family, c. 1910. His three children standing in back from left to right: Rhoda Ann "Anna" Daily Watters, James Alfred "Jim Boy" Daily, and Elsie Daily Horton. Willis and his wife, Mary Twibell Daily, are seated in front. Author's collection.

Willis Daily and granddaughter, Leta Daily, c. 1918. This picture was taken at Fort Riley, Kansas, while James Daily, Leta's father, was in the army. Author's collection.

*Willis Daily family home, top. Bottom photo is an
enlarged detail of family seated on the front porch.
Willis, left, three grandchildren and wife, Mary.*
Author's collection.

Willis Daily's family, c. 1918. From left: Anna Watters with son, Wayne, Willis, "Jim Boy" with daughter Leta, wife Mary, and Elsie Horton with daughter Bernice.
Courtesy of Joeleen Passow, Humboldt, Iowa, granddaughter of Anna.

Standing: General Eugene Asa Carr, his son, Clark McGuire Carr and Mrs. Clark M. (Virginia Morrison) Carr. Seated in front is General Carr's wife, Mary McGuire Carr, June 1891.

Courtesy of Quito Osuna Carr, M.D., Albuquerque, New Mexico.

Bogardus—Bell cemetery with markers denoting graves for Elizabeth Bell, Braxton Bell and David Bogardus, August 12, 1868. See pages 18 - 24. Author's collection.

Close-up of inscription on Bogardus— Bell memorial marker at the site of their murders, August 12, 1868. Author's collection.

Grave of David Bogardus, killed near gravesite August 12, 1868. Author's collection.

James Alfred Daily headstone at Fort Leavenworth National Cemetery,
Kansas. The original 1873 marker (left) misspelled James Daily's name.
The author discovered the error and was responsible for getting this new
marker, right, replacing the old in November 2002. Author's collection.

Mr. & Mrs. Willis Daily tombstone at Spillman
Cemetery, Ash Grove, Kansas. Author's collection.

Pioneer monument at Lincoln, Kansas, 1909.
Author's collection.

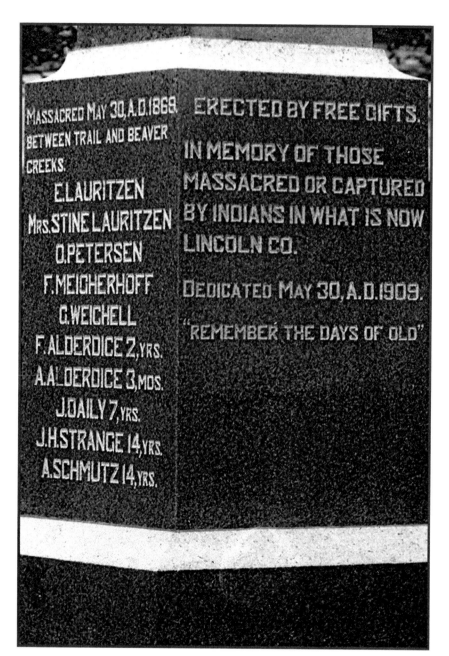

MASSACRED MAY 30, A.D.1869
BETWEEN TRAIL AND BEAVER
CREEKS.
E.LAURITZEN
Mrs.STINE LAURITZEN
O.PETERSEN
F.MEIGHERHOFF
G.WEICHELL
F.ALDERDICE 2,YRS.
A.ALDERDICE 3,MOS.
J.DAILY 7,YRS.
J.H.STRANGE 14,YRS.
A.SCHMUTZ 14,YRS.

ERECTED BY FREE GIFTS.

IN MEMORY OF THOSE
MASSACRED OR CAPTURED
BY INDIANS IN WHAT IS NOW
LINCOLN CO.

DEDICATED MAY 30, A.D.1909.

"REMEMBER THE DAYS OF OLD"

Close-up of pioneer monument at Lincoln, Kansas, 1909.
Author's collection.

Close-up of pioneer monument at Lincoln, Kansas, 1909. See full view of this side of monument on page xxii. Author's collection.

Four generations of Willis Daily's family. Top center is Anna Daily Watters. Seated from left, holding her son James' daughter Leta is Mrs. Willis (Mary) Daily; her mother, Mrs. Twibell, is on the right. Courtesy of Floy Bowers and Wayne Little, Abilene, Kansas.

The Rest of the Story

Therefore the pioneer monument on the Lincoln County Court House is a fitting recognition from the present generation to future generations, of the hardships the pioneers had to do in order that we of the present time may live here in safety.[1]

Susanna's sufferings were over. The Indians took her life and her dreams. Gone were all her hopes, wishes and aspirations for each of her children. Gone was everything. It was all gone, every dream and every hope, violently taken from her by the simple barbarity of human nature motivated by hate. Such senseless acts have been perpetrated in every generation of civilization, including today. Susanna's sad fate was that such suffering marked the end of her life. Never was a harder price demanded in the settlement of the West. It was a horrific ordeal she was required to endure.

When Susanna and little Alice were captured late in the day of May 30, there on the Kansas ground lay her young boys, stripped of their clothing and life's blood slowly seeping into the roots of the prairie grasses. Though the boys were not mutilated as were other pioneers killed that day, they had been covered in thick brush, as if to intentionally hide their bodies.[2] It took one more day to discover them. Young John Daily, not yet six years old, Willis Daily, four-and-a-half years old, and toddler Frank, only two years old, all had multiple wounds. In addition to five arrow wounds in Willis's back, one of which had nearly gone through his body and stuck fast in the back of his sternum, he was also shot twice and speared in either the hand or the back.[3]

187

But wait! Incredibly, Willis was not dead. Against all odds, he had not surrendered his spirit to death. Unconscious and gravely wounded, he was yet alive!

During the night of May 30, alarmed settlers gathered at the Schermerhorn Ranch, a few miles southeast of where Willis lay. A search party left the Schermerhorn Ranch the next morning, headed toward the Saline River, and intending to follow it over to and up Spillman Creek. J. J. Peate wrote, ". . . in the first bend of the Saline river about a mile west of the mouth of Lost Creek . . . they found two murdered children of Mrs. Alderdice and one that was badly wounded."[4] Four-year-old Willis was carefully moved, first to the Schermerhorn Ranch, and then shortly after that back across the Saline to the Hendrickson home. Willis was not expected to live.[5]

Peate adds that the surgeon accompanying Lieutenant Law's 7th Cavalry (camped at the junction of Bullfoot Creek and the Saline River the night of the murderous raid) was contacted. He refused to treat either the gravely wounded Willis or the mortally wounded Arthur Schmutz. When Peate wrote his reminiscences, he could not remember the doctor's name, but he did have this to say about the man: "I have met many army officers and found them to be honorable men, and grand comrades. This one was in the shape of a man, but it ended there."[6]

Some historians have denied this ugly incident. Ray Sparks is one:

> It was also said that the surgeon, a beast in uniform refused to aid the wounded Willis Daily, etc., etc., and that these soldiers pulled out immediately without any assistance of any kind to the settlers.
>
> The astounding and shocking facts are that there is no justification for the accusations. Lack of communication must have been the reason for this very unfortunate attitude and belief. Stories were told, added to, magnified by each teller, even by some who professed to be speaking from personal knowledge who could not possibly have seen or talked to these particular troops. The stories were told and

retold until everyone, except the troops involved, who probably never heard them, believed them and thus they became accepted as historical fact.[7]

However, Sparks lacks any justification to make this disclaimer, for the incident *did happen*. Not only did it actually occur, it was widely discussed during that time, both by pioneers and soldiers. It even made its way into the Kansas newspapers. Recall from the events noted in an earlier chapter that after the May 30, 1869 raid, Lieutenant Edward Law divided Company G, 7th Cavalry into two groups. Using the rested horses, he took one group of men and scouted about the Saline River. When he failed to find an Indian trail, he moved his small command up north to the settlements on the Solomon River. He instructed Lieutenant Thomas Jefferson March later that day to bring the supply wagons to the juncture of Asher Creek and the Solomon River, which was where Law would already be with his portion of the command.[8] The surgeon no doubt stayed with Lieutenant March's partial command, for it would have been the men with March who were still in the vicinity after Willis was discovered. This is when the surgeon refused to treat Willis. Further, the fact that Lieutenant Law wrote his last report for May 31 from the Schermerhorn Ranch shows why Willis had been moved there. It was because that was where the surgeon was staying.

Why the surgeon refused to treat Willis is a mystery. Perhaps he did so because he would have had to stay behind while March moved the wagons north to Asher Creek, leaving him without military protection. Maybe he feared encountering Indians if he stayed to treat Willis. He would have had to make his journey to rejoin the wagon detail alone, or perhaps with just one or two men, as there would not have been enough soldiers available to safely escort him if he stayed behind to treat Willis and Arthur Schmutz.

Lieutenant Law had been ordered to send a courier to Fort Harker daily to report on incidents.[9] On June 2, he asked to be relieved of this obligation, as sending a courier required an escort of five men. Each time he sent a courier, it left him short-handed, so he asked to be allowed to report every five days, or as an emergency arose.[10] Indians had attacked Company G farrier, Benjamin Wells, on June 1, when he was sent with dispatches to Fort Harker. Wells successfully fought off the Indians this time.[11] He was not so lucky seven years later when at the Little Bighorn in Montana he participated in the beginning skirmish there. His horse bolted at the start of the fight, and carried Wells straight into the Indian village. His body was discovered after Custer's last fight.[12] Knowing the dangers of riding from one command position to another, perhaps the surgeon was too afraid to take such a ride after treating Willis.

It is a fact that this surgeon refused to treat Willis, and it was not long before this was reported in the newspapers. The newspapers were justifiably indignant about the surgeon's actions. *The Topeka Commonwealth* initially reported the story and other newspapers reprinted it:

> We would like to know the name of the surgeon who accompanied the company of Seventh Cavalry on the march from Fort Harker to Asher Creek. We would like to see what kind of a name is disgraced by such an ownership. We are informed that this company was within a mile or two of the scene of the massacre on the Saline a week ago Sunday evening. A Mr. Alderdyce [sic], who happened to be away from home had two boys killed, his wife and babe carried off, and his only remaining child, a little boy four or five years of age, seriously wounded, and two arrows left sticking in his back. Word was sent to the surgeon and he was urged to go to the assistance of the wounded, a boy named Smart [Schmutz], and the one already referred to. He steadfastly refused, and no entreaties could prevail on him to go. The Lieutenant in command wanted him to go, but had no authority to order him. After failing to procure a physician at Salina and at Fort Harker, one was finally obtained at

Ellsworth. These boys laid without medical atten-
dance from Sunday evening until last Saturday
night. Meantime the arrows were pulled out of the
little Alderdyce by unprofessional hands, and he
withstood the agony of the operation with the
heroism of a youthful martyr. The boy Smart
[Schmutz], having been in feeble health at the time
he was wounded, is not likely to recover [he died
ten-and-a-half weeks after being wounded].

Decent humans will want appropriate epithets
with which to characterize this surgeon, if his
conduct be correctly reported. He is a wretch, who
would deserve little sympathy were he disembow-
eled by the savages and hung up by the sinews of
his limbs.[13]

A friend of the doctor wrote on June 10 in defense of him.
Mister Jackson named the doctor: Renick. Jackson said that
Renick had duties so pressing that he could not render medical
aid to Willis. But he did render aid to Arthur Schmutz.
According to Jackson, Doctor Renick

. . .did call upon this boy and administered to him,
and saved his life, and that Dr. Renick went to his
camp and returned the second time, and brought
stimulants and plasters, the latter of which he
placed on the wounds where the arrows were withdrawn, and stopped the flow of blood, and saved the
life of this boy. I am told that Dr. Renick did not go
to see the Alderdyce boy, although twice called
upon his camp not half a mile distant, and the
arrow was drawn from the boy's body twenty-four
hours afterwards by Mr. W. Smith, a farmer who
lives near.[14]

Surgeon B. E. Fryer, the Fort Harker post surgeon nearly
thirty-five miles to the south, upon learning of Renick's refusal
to treat Willis, tried to go to the little boy's assistance. Fryer
asked the post commander, Colonel Nelson Miles, for an escort
of five men but was denied because only ten men at Fort
Harker were present for duty. "Dr. Friar [sic], thinking he
would go without the escort, then went to the Quartermaster

191

for an ambulance and was told that he had none that he could give him."[15]

This attempt to exonerate Doctor Renick for his calloused dereliction of duty to young Willis was quickly rejected in another newspaper editorial:

> It seems that some comments we made a few days since, in relation to the conduct of a surgeon of the 7th Cavalry, in refusing to go to the relief of the wounded on the Saline, has kicked up considerable dust at Fort Harker. Our information came from what we considered a reliable source, and, as we read it, the explanation of Hon. Z. Jackson, in another place, is not altogether satisfactory. Mr. Jackson and the friends of Dr. Renick will remember that our indignant paragraph was principally directed against the Doctor because of his refusal to visit the little Alderdyce [sic] boy, and as Mr. Jackson states (upon information) that he did so refuse, after being twice called upon, we see no occasion to modify our language.[16]

It is unlikely that Renick ever made another visit to the Saline Valley, after joining Lieutenant March in the trek up to Asher Creek. He certainly would not have been welcome. The settlers never forgot his unjustifiable behavior. It was not a false story that became imbedded in the imagination of pioneers in later years, as Sparks claims. When Renick left the area to accompany the soldiers to Asher Creek, Willis was taken from the Schermerhorn Ranch to the Hendrickson house. There he laid in agony for another day, as the beleaguered community vainly hoped that a doctor could be summoned from Salina or Fort Harker. Finally, after Willis's severe and painful wounds went untreated for two days, and listening to his agonizing cries for help, the settlers had no choice but to try to remove it themselves. C. C. Hendrickson, himself a young boy at that time, recalled that Willis

> . . . begged so hard to have it taken out that a man by the name of Phil Lantz said that if someone

would hold him down, he could pull it out and a man by the name of Washington Smith said he would hold him. Lantz pulled the arrow out with a pair of bullet molds of my father's and as luck would have it, the spike came out but no one thought he would live. . . .[17]

That Willis survived this terrible ordeal is simply incredible. Tom Alderdice was not his blood father, and would have trouble raising him while working his farm full-time. Willis needed the care of a woman while still a young child, and so Susanna's parents, Michael and Mary Zeigler, raised him to adulthood. They moved from their homestead near present-day Beverly to a small hamlet in Cedron Township, about twenty miles northwest of Lincoln. Susanna's sister, Sabra Anglin, and her husband, Houstan, lived on the adjoining property. Their homes were nestled near the north side of the split of Spillman Creek, just a little west of present-day Ash Grove, Kansas. Cedron no longer exists today. Here Susanna's parents raised tough little Willis, along with their remaining children, Ellen and Frank Zeigler.

In May 1875, Michael Zeigler began the legal process to secure a government pension for Willis. He qualified because he was the surviving minor child of his father, James Alfred Daily, who died of typhoid fever at Fort Leavenworth at the end of his enlistment in the 17th Volunteer Kansas Infantry. James Daily died just seven weeks after Willis was born in 1864. Willis never knew his father, but he never forgot him either. He later named his only son after his father.[18] The pension claim was finally completed March 16, 1878, but it was not approved until April 8, 1880. Willis received eight dollars each month, due from the time of his father's death in 1864 until he turned sixteen the following October. Because his pension was not approved until six months before it expired, Willis received a lump sum of $1,480.00.[19]

Willis remained in Cedron Township, Lincoln County, during his childhood. He married Mary Twibell on March 25,

1886. Her family lived on the land adjoining the Zeiglers. Together Willis and Mary had three children. James Alfred was born April 3, 1887. Rhoda Ann ("Anna") was born February 12, 1889. Elsie Ellen was born June 16, 1891. In 1893, Willis moved his family from Lincoln County to Marshall County, four miles east of Blue Rapids, Kansas.[20] Here Willis farmed and raised his young family. Willis's son, James "Jim Boy" married Fern Tidball June 30, 1909. He served in the Army during World War I. James and Fern had two children, Leta Carroll, born February 26, 1911, and Wilma Jean, born March 10, 1919. James died in Denver, Colorado, February 23, 1954. Willis's daughter, Anna, married William A. Watters December 31, 1907. They had a son, Wayne Daily Watters, born November 27, 1909. Anna died at Fort Dodge, Iowa, on September 25, 1970. Willis's daughter, Elsie, married Jake Horton September 22, 1910. Together they had two children, Berniece, born June 19, 1912, and Maurice Eugene ("Gene"), born January 21, 1921. Elsie died at Fort Dodge, Iowa, on July 1, 1975. These five grandchildren had a total of eighteen great-grandchildren. Even more descendants are living today.

When Susanna was killed at Summit Springs, her husband, Tom, was still in the Saline valley. He feared correctly that a military attack upon the Indian village holding Susanna would in all likelihood result in her death.[21] On the other hand, ignoring her fate would have been worse. He could only hope for an outcome such as Custer achieved earlier that spring in the Texas Panhandle with his neighbors, Sarah White and Mrs. Morgan. The wait for news must have been excruciating. Before he embarked on his scouting journey that eventually led him to the Dog Soldier village early in June, Tom had attended to the burial of his little son, Frank, and stepson, John. They were both buried on their grandfather's land near present-day Beverly, Kansas. Michael Zeigler, of course, later moved his family twenty miles northwest to Cedron Township, where Willis was raised. Today these graves are lost. They were reported to be buried "on the northwest quarter of section 22, Colorado township. . . ."[22]

With Willis slowly recovering from his brutal wounds in the care of Susanna's parents, Tom occupied his time assisting the military still stationed in the Saline valley. On June 9, Company K, 7th Cavalry, arrived from Fort Harker. They remained stationed among the settlements until the end of October, when the threat of Indian attacks lessened.[23] News of Carr's victory at Summit Springs was slow to arrive among the pioneer settlements devastated by the spring raids. It was not until July 23 that Tom first heard that Susanna had been killed. Private William McConnell, Company K, 7th Cavalry, recorded in his diary the events of the day from the military camp on the Saline River:

> The morning cool. Reveille at four o'clock. Started at five. Got into camp of L Troop at about 10 a.m. Got some bad news: the 5th U.S. Cavalry had a big fight on the Platte River and captured both of the women back from them [Indians] by killing one and wounding one; also capturing some prisoners. Mrs. Alderdise [sic] was killed and her little babe also. *Her husband is with us.*[24]

Tom's worst fears had been realized. He already knew that his daughter had been killed, and now he learned his wife was also murdered. On July 27, he received a letter from the military, sent from Fort Harker, informing him of Susanna's death. The letter also included a small report written nine days earlier by General Carr:

> Sir:
>
> I have the honor to inform you that your written description dated June 21/69 of Mrs. Susan Alderdice, captured by Indians May 30/69 was forwarded by Major General Schofield to the Commanding General Department of the Platte, with a request that he would take such measures as were practicable for the rescue of Mrs. Alderdice, her child and the other captive woman. . . . The Comd. General Dept. of the Platte, referred the

paper to Bvt. Major General E. A. Carr, whose command recently had a fight with Indians at "Valley Station" in that department. General Carr's endorsement is as follows:

Headquarters Republican Expedition
Camp near Fort Sedgwick, C.T.
July 18, 1869
Respectfully returned, through Headquarters District of the Republican. A woman corresponding to the description of Mrs. Alderdice was found dead in the Indian village at the time of the capture on July 11, 1869. The woman, Mrs. Weichell, who was captured at the same time as Mrs. Alderdice, although wounded, was saved alive, and from her I learn that the murdered woman was named Susannah and had with her a child about 8 months old, which child was strangled on the 3rd day out.[25]

Thus, Tom received official notification of his wife's death. Willis belonged with his own blood relatives, and Tom's family no longer existed. Could Carr have done anything different that might have led to Susanna's rescue? Custer accomplished the safe release of his captives on the Sweetwater; could not Carr have done the same at Summit Springs? Might the Indians have negotiated if Carr had surrounded them? Was there anything that could have been done differently to save Susanna?

But what choices did Carr actually have? He basically matched the Dog Soldiers man for man while Custer outnumbered the Cheyenne at the Sweetwater two, if not three to one. Plus, Custer caught his village in the cold of the late winter, when the Indian pony herd was weak with hunger. Escape for the Indians there would have been unlikely, whereas the Dog Soldiers at Summit Springs would have had a much better chance escaping if they knew Carr's command was near. Indeed, the majority did escape when Carr charged the village. How easy it would have been for them to escape, if Carr had tried to first parley for the captives' release.

About the only two things similar between Custer's and Carr's villages were that each contained two white women captives and Dog Soldier Cheyenne comprised the majority of each camp. The circumstances were otherwise different and Carr had but little choice to do what he did. The charge into the village obviously was a gamble. If the soldiers were lucky, Susanna and Maria might have been rescued unharmed. Unfortunately, the captives were at the lower end of the village when it was attacked at the middle and upper ends. This gave vengeful Indians time to kill the captives before fleeing the village.

Now that Tom had lost his entire family he had no reason to remain in Lincoln County. He soon left, first moving to western Kansas and then eventually to Clinton County, Iowa, where he lived until 1886. While there, he married Mary Amelia Lepper in Delmar, August 17, 1873. With Mary, he had a second family. William Ira was born May 21, 1874; Alma Mable, July 29, 1877; Thomas F., September 9, 1880; Mary M., April 26, 1883; Ella Phylinda, May 29, 1885; Harry Eugene, November 6, 1888; John Henry, December 12, 1891, and Homer Bruce, November 18, 1894.[26]

While raising his family, Tom lived in several places in western Kansas and even for a short time in Missouri, but in 1891, the family settled in Milan, Kansas. Tom never moved from that area. In 1911, more than forty years after Susanna's capture, Tom revisited Lincoln County for the first time since the awful tragedy of 1869. It had been forty-two years since he had last been there. It was an emotional visit. He remarked to Adolph Roenigk that after he learned of Susanna's death, his mind went blank.[27] It was simply too much for him to live with. To go on, he blocked from his memory all those terrible events. Returning after all those years brought a gradual recall. The local newspaper reported his visit, noting that Tom said, "it feels like he has been dead these many years and resurrected and placed in a new and strange country."[28] His motive for returning to Lincoln County was to try to find the unmarked graves of John Daily and Frank Alderdice. He wanted to have their bodies removed to a cemetery. Although the landscape had changed that he could not remember anything of the area, it was thought that since the two dead boys were buried in boxes, the use of an augur would reveal the location of the bodies.[29] They were not found and Tom returned home to Milan, Kansas. He never returned to Lincoln County. The bodies of Susanna's two boys to this day remain undiscovered.

Tom encountered typical "red tape" when he tried to get the government to help find his wife in 1869. Late in his life, he experienced more "red tape." When he applied for his pension, he was denied because, first, he had served in the Confederacy before joining the Union service, and second, he served with the Union on the frontier, not in the War of the Rebellion. In 1907, he appealed and finally was awarded a pension. In his appeal he stated:

> When I enlisted in Co E 2nd US Vol. I was promised all the emoluments, all the benefits of other soldiers fighting the War of the Rebellion here and hereafter. If not why were we allowed the privilege of taking the Oath of Allegiance as citizens of US: This is what Col. Johnson Commandant of Rock Island told me at the time of enlistment, also Vice President Colfax when we escorted him from Fort Zarah to Fort Dodge Kans. If I am not entitled to pension I don't want one although my injuries ["falling disease" and a weak shoulder] were incurred in the service of United States.[30]

Tom died in Conway Springs, Kansas, May 29, 1925. An obituary for him noted that, until his last year, "he was often called upon to relate his Indian experiences to school students, Boy Scout meetings and upon other occasions, and the thrill that came to young listeners as the old warrior vividly lived over those old days was always something to be remembered."[31] Tom's passing was also noted in the national publication, *Winners of the West,* under the title "Kansas Survivor of Indian Battles Dies:"

> Thomas H. Alderdice, 80 years old, one of the three surviving pioneers of the battle of Beecher's Island, historic battle in western Kansas, against the Indians, died at his home here last night.
>
> Surviving the pioneer are a second wife and five children, all of whom live here. Alderdice's first wife and children were killed by Indians.[32]

Tom's granddaughter, Nina Pond (daughter of Ella Phylinda), took an interest in her grandfather's frontier experiences. There was much about her grandfather that she never knew, and thus she had to rely on family information that often led her astray. She did recall, however, that Tom never forgot Susanna: "In his last days he would call Mary Amelie, Susan (first wife). It was a blow to her and she [Mary] really whipped the ends of her big waist apron and retreated to the far end of the house."[33] Susanna was by then long gone, but not forgotten.

The story of Maria Weichel is more one of folklore than known history. When she arrived at Fort Sedgwick on July 15, she was admitted to the post hospital, where she remained until her discharge August 4.[34] After her discharge, differing accounts of her story are told. She is said to have married someone connected with her recovery at Summit Springs. Speculations have ranged from the hospital steward at Fort Sedgwick, an army surgeon, a soldier in the 5th Cavalry, the first person she met when rescued at Summit Springs, an Infantry soldier at Fort Sedgwick, and a blacksmith, either at Sedgwick or with Carr's 5th Cavalry.[35] Her new married name was never recorded in any of the pioneer reminiscences.

When Maria first came to Lincoln County with her husband, George Weichel, she was described as having many possessions, unlike the typical Kansas pioneer, who usually had little money and few possessions. C. Bernhardt remembered that she was "the proud possessor of twenty-four silk dresses."[36] J. J. Peate remembered "forty fine dresses."[37] Ferdinand Erhardt remembered her and her husband George as "educated people, and by their clothing and other goods which they brought with them, one could readily see that they were well-to-do. It was on account of some financial trouble in the Old World, that they came over to this country."[38] What these later pioneer reminiscences did not record, however, was the actions of a few rogue settlers who, after Maria was captured and her husband killed, entered the Lauritzen home, where the Weichels were temporarily living at the time of the raid, and stole her possessions.

The Indians who raided the Saline River valley on May 30 did not enter the unoccupied house of the Lauritzens. The Lauritzens had been murdered away from the house, as were both Fred Meigerhoff and Otto Peterson. When George was killed and Maria taken captive a few miles south of the Lauritzen place, the only surviving member left of the Lauritzen household was the young Lauritzen boy. But he had been removed, along with the Christensen family, to the Schermerhorn Ranch several miles down Spillman Creek and east across the Saline River. From there they went to Fort Harker. The Lauritzen boy was then sent to Chicago to be raised by relatives there, and thus the Lauritzen household had no occupants. Indeed, no one returned to the Denmark, Kansas settlement on Spillman Creek for more than a year and a half.[39] The possessions of everyone who had been living in the Lauritzen house at the time of the raid remained undisturbed until self-serving settlers took it upon themselves to retrieve the household goods for their own use.

The house was apparently broken into shortly after the raid. While Maria was still being held captive, the *Kansas Daily Commonwealth* reported that the "goods belonging to the Trichell [Weichel] family have been since stolen by some devils with no less moral principle than the savages themselves."[40] George Green, one of the scouts who served with Tom Alderdice and Eli Zeigler at Beecher Island, and whose wife made the valiant defense at the Hendrickson home, tried to protect the goods in the Lauritzen house. He was appointed as administrator of the estate "and went to the dugout cabin . . . and took possession of two large boxes of dry goods and retained them in his possession until the claimant [Maria] returned and then delivered them to her."[41] When he went to the dugout, he found that the house had been ransacked. Soon, he "traced some of the goods to the possession of a man by the name of Johnston and to a man by the name of Johnny-Come-Lightly white settlers [unknown persons] and recovered them and restored them to the claimant."[42] The white robbers at first resisted returning the stolen goods, so Green went to Ellsworth and received a warrant for their arrest. Now, escorted by the marshal from Ellsworth, Green returned to where the thieves lived and retrieved, under threat of arrest, the items stolen from Maria. The men were not arrested because they claimed "to have taken the goods to save them for claimant."[43]

When Maria returned to Lincoln County, it had been almost a year since her capture. She stayed only a few days to retrieve what George Green had so dutifully worked to recover. Bernhardt said that Maria visited a few times in the ensuing years and returned in 1909, "negotiating with the old settlers around Salina for evidence through which to secure damages from the government for losses sustained at that time."[44] She was said to have lived on a farm in eastern Kansas, western Kansas, western Nebraska, and even Lincoln, Nebraska.[45] If Bernhardt is correct about Maria returning to Lincoln County in 1909, she in all probability was still living when her daughter, Mrs. Minnie Wurthman, wrote to the adjutant general's office in Topeka, Kansas, to request information about her mother's captivity in 1869. A typescript of the request states that Minnie was born in an Omaha hospital and that after her birth, Maria "went away and never returned."[46] Minnie's purpose in contacting the authorities was to "verify the statement made by her mother at the hospital at Omaha in 1869."[47]

Minnie's statement is a bit ambiguous, for it leaves open the possibility that she was left for adoption after being born. But the more likely interpretation is that she was not given for adoption, for she also says she wants to verify the statement her mother made at the hospital when she was born. She must have known of that statement and wished to compare that with the official information about the raid. How would she have known that if she was adopted? Further, it will be recalled that Maria was pregnant by her first husband, George, when she was captured. Her child born in Omaha, if this is where her first child was born, would not have been from a pregnancy caused by a Dog Soldier. Consequently there would be little incentive to give the baby up for adoption, especially if she was at this time married to the man "connected with her recovery."

But strong evidence shows that Minnie is Maria's second child, her first with her second husband. The typescript at the Kansas State Historical Society of her request lists Minnie's address in San Francisco. The U. S. Census records for 1900 show a Minnie Wurthman living in San Francisco. She was born in Omaha, but in December 1870, not the fall of 1869, which would had to have been if she actually were Maria's first child. The December 1870 birth date fits the time period when Maria could have a second child. The 1900 census further verifies that Minnie's mother was from Germany, which was the case with Maria. Additionally, the census states that Minnie's father was born in England. Given that her first husband, George Weichel, was from Germany, this then, supports the idea that Minnie is the first child from Maria's second marriage.

The 1900 census also shows that Minnie had three children, all born in California. Harry was born in August 1888; Minnie was born in July 1891, and George was born in June 1894.[48] The 1920 U. S. Census shows Harry living in California with a new daughter, Frances.[49] An obituary appears in 1986 in Yuba City for a George Wurthman who was born in 1894 and was a native of San Francisco. This is in all likelihood Minnie's son, and quite possibly Maria's grandson. He retired in 1957 after a long career with the Oakland Police Department. He was a veteran of World War I, as was Susanna Alderdice's only grandson, James Daily. George Wurthman died November 20, 1986. Wurthman had a son, Donald G. Wurthman, of Live Oak, California; a daughter, Gwen Wurthman, of Walnut Creek;

and another daughter, Rhoda J. Robinson, of Yuba City. It is quite possible that these are the great-grandchildren of Maria Weichel, the wounded survivor of the fight at Summit Springs.[50] In addition to these three children, George also had four grandchildren and four great-grandchildren.

Settlers in Lincoln County, principally under the leadership of Christian Bernhardt, erected a monument in honor of those pioneers who suffered loss of life or captivity as a result of the Indian raids that so devastated the Lincoln County settlements in 1864, 1868 and 1869. The monument remains impressive today. The May 30, 1909 unveiling was an auspicious occasion, and was solemn in its honor of those pioneers who gave their lives to the conquest of the prairie and the grand settlement of the West. Mrs. Mary Edwards of Cedron Township, Lincoln County, performed the unveiling.[51] Mary was a niece of Susanna. Susanna's family was well represented. Eli Zeigler was present, and it is believed that Willis and his family were also present.[52] Near the bottom on one side of the monument is the inscription "Remember the days of old."

After the monument unveiling, Willis continued to farm in Blue Rapids, Kansas. He was soon blessed with grandchildren. The three oldest grandchildren spent many summers in Blue Rapids with their grandfather Willis, and grandmother, Mary. About 1917, Willis began to have problems with one of his legs. He is said to have had a slight limp from his arrow wounds, and it was first believed that his new problems were related to his old wounds. He was never one to talk about his experiences in 1869. His daughter Anna vividly remembered "Daddy never talked about it but I have seen the 5 big arrow scars on his back many times."[53] His leg problem turned out to be far worse than a mere reoccurrence of his arrow wounds bothering him. He was diagnosed with cancer. Three separate trips to a hospital in Rochester, Minnesota, where each time a part of his leg was amputated, failed to arrest the cancer. The third operation took his leg off at the hip, but by then the cancer had spread to the rest of his body.

He suffered greatly in his last days, but he suffered with the patience of a man who had been through enormous traumas in the past. Perhaps his thoughts in his final days brought him back to his mother, brothers, and sister. He was soon to join them in his next journey. On the evening of June 16, his daughter Elsie's twenty-ninth birthday, and the day after his wife's fifty-third birthday, Willis finally succumbed to his cancer. He died in his home outside Blue Rapids. His obituary stated that Willis "was dearly beloved by a large circle of friends, and while suffering for more than three years with sarcoma tumor, he was always patient and cheerful, bearing his great suffering with remarkable fortitude."[54] His patience, cheerfulness, and fortitude are moral virtues that defined his life. His funeral was one day before his granddaughter Berniece's eighth birthday. He was brought back to Lincoln County, for burial, and laid to rest at Spillman Cemetery outside Ash Grove, Kansas. Spillman Cemetery is barely two miles east of where Willis was raised by his grandparents. Mary Daily died on October 11, 1948. She was laid alongside Willis and next to her parents. It would be hard to imagine another child paying a higher price than did Willis in the settlement of the West. He remains one of the unsung pioneer heroes of the wild Kansas frontier. Susanna would have been proud. *One* of her dreams did not die in 1869. Today this dream still beats in the hearts of the many living descendants of Willis and Susanna Zeigler Daily Alderdice, pioneer mother.

Picture of the arrowhead taken from the back of Willis Daily.
Courtesy of Lincoln County Historical Society.

Appendix I

On Locating Susanna's Grave

8:00 a.m. Burial service read over the murdered white woman, whose grave was made in the midst of the village.[1]

As I began my research on the Summit Springs battle, I wrote to the Summit Springs property owner, Gary Ramey. I explained to him my interest in trying to locate Susanna's unmarked grave. Mr. Ramey responded to my request, informing me that he would fully support my efforts to locate her. All possibilities existed regarding what I might do. If I found her grave and her descendants wanted to rebury her in Kansas, to rest alongside her son Willis, he would support that. If her grave would be marked and located on his property, he would support that, too. If a new marker would be erected alongside the other markers on the dirt roundabout that brings visitors to the battle site, he also would support that. In short, Gary Ramey allowed me carte blanche in trying to locate Susanna's grave. At the battle site roundabout are four markers, two visible above the ground, and two lying flat on the ground. One is an original marker from 1933, when it was first placed at the battlefield. Another was erected in 1970 and is a marker honoring the Indians. The other two markers are lying flat on the ground; one briefly stating that Mrs. Alderdice was found dying on the battlefield, and the other noting the location of Tall Bull's tepee. Both ground markers are alleged to mark the respective spots where these events occurred on July 11, 1869.

In talking with Gary, however, he shared some rather startling information. The battlefield has been in his family's possession for more than a half a century. But when the roundabout was made in the late 1960s, to accommodate persons desiring to visit the battle site, these markers, which had been in place since 1933, were removed from where they had originally been placed in order to put them within the roundabout. The two flat markers replaced lost wooden markers. Gary met me at the roundabout, and proceeded to walk me up the hill to the north nearly four hundred yards. On top of the highest hill to the west of the springs is where he led me. Somewhere up there, he said, was where he remembered the markers to have been set prior to their removal to their present location about 1968.

A trip to the Colorado Historical Society revealed photographs taken prior to the construction of the roundabout. The original stone marker is visible in a panoramic series of photographs. Surprisingly, it appears not to be north of the present marker site, as Gary had shown me, but rather east, much closer to where Tall Bull was killed at the mouth of the ravines. A trip to the Nebraska State Historical Society brought me to even older photographs, which confirmed that the original markers had been placed just to the west of the mouth of the warrior death ravines. These older photographs were taken when the markers were originally placed on the battle site. Captain Luther North stands alongside them. It appears then, if Gary's memory serves him correctly, that the markers were located in at least two other locations before finally being placed where they currently reside.

Summit Springs was a forgotten battle site until Luther North visited it with members of the Nebraska State Historical Society in 1929, a full sixty years after the fight. A subsequent visit by this same group of men in 1933 located the places where the original battle markers were first erected. The three 1933 markers included two wooden ones with brass inscriptions, along with the stone battle marker that survives in the present-day roundabout. One marker stated where North found Susanna on the ground, dying. The other marker denoted where Tall Bull's tepee was found. The third marker

206

was the stone marker that was removed to the roundabout about 1968. At that time the two wooden markers were replaced with brass inscriptions encased in concrete and now lie flat on the ground within the present-day roundabout. Why, and by whom, the markers were moved is unknown.

There is an obvious problem in locating Susanna's grave site, given these different site locations and the distance in time from when the fight occurred and when the battle site was rediscovered. This is compounded when turning to written statements made by those who were there in 1869. What emerges is no clear consensus as to where she lies today. What is clear, however, is that Susanna is not buried near or on the hillside where the modern marker indicates she was buried.

The best possibility for success is to work off of where the wooden marker had originally been placed, and then study the primary source accounts that comment on Susanna's burial. The original marker, erected in 1933, states "This marks the spot where the body of Mrs. Alderdice was found by Luther H. North on July 11, 1869. *She was buried on a hill above.*" (italics added)

This would mean that Susanna was probably buried on a hillside near the location of the modern reservoir, nearly a half a mile northeast from the modern roundabout, as that would be the location corresponding to where the original marker was placed. This small reservoir was constructed in 1962. There is a modern day addendum to this likely site, based on a conversation with Joe Montgomery, a long-time ranch hand for the Ramey family. But first, let us look to the primary source accounts.

Carr's official report of the fight states: "We wrapped her in lodge skins and robes, and dug a deep grave; the officers and soldiers were assembled, and the burial service was read over her. A head board marks the grave with an inscription stating that we knew of her."[2] This is not helpful in locating where Susanna was buried. However, in Carr's unpublished memoirs, he wrote, "we dug a grave on a hill above the village and buried Mrs. Alderdice, the surgeon reading the service."[3] Mrs. Mary Carr, General Carr's wife, wrote her unpublished memoirs, and therein she reports Carr saying, "We buried Mrs. Alderdice in a knoll above camp, Dr. Tesson reading the service."[4]

There is yet another citation from Carr. In a letter to Lincoln County, Kansas resident Washington Smith, dated February 24, 1887, Carr wrote: "We buried Mrs. Alderdice on a little bluff, which overlooks Summit Springs, with such religious services as we were able to perform."[5] Hercules Price, an enlisted man who fought with Carr at Summit Springs, wrote in 1907: "Her burial was made a special one and we buried her on the rise of the hill in the best buffalo robe we could find and gave her a burial with military honors."[6] Teamster J. E. Welch, also with Carr in 1869, wrote in 1904:

> Our first duty next was to bury the poor woman they so foully murdered the day before. Not having a coffin, we wrapped her in a buffalo robe. General Carr read the funeral service and the cavalry sounded the funeral dirge, and as the soft, mournful notes died away many a cheek was wet that had long been a stranger to tears.[7]

All of the above accounts, however, do not show precisely where Susanna was buried. We only learn that she was buried on a bluff or a small hill, or the rise of a hill that overlooked the village. We are not told which side of the village or which end of the village she was buried. These accounts do not rule out the traditional site near the present-day roundabout. At this traditional site the marker states that Susanna was buried on the hill above the roundabout.

There are other accounts, however, when taken together with the ones already noted, that make it no longer plausible to believe Susanna was buried on the hillside at the present-day roundabout. The most significant account comes from Lieutenant Volkmar, the only eyewitness who wrote his account on the day Susanna was buried. As Carr's itinerary officer, he wrote on July 12, 1869, eight o'clock in the morning: "Burial service read over the murdered white woman, *whose grave was made in the midst of the village.*"[8]

If Volkmar was correct, and there is every reason to believe he was, she cannot be buried near the roundabout, as that is, at best, the end of the village and not the middle. The task then, is to understand exactly how the village was set out on the day of the fight. Surprisingly, no battle participants left accounts denoting the length of the village except Hercules Price, who gave his account more than forty years after the fight. A study of his map, however, shows terrain more like what is found at the Elephant Rock fight of May 13 than the Summit Springs fight of July 11. His memory of the terrain at the two fights apparently got mixed up after more than forty years.

Larry Finnell of Fort Collins, Colorado, however, has done extensive research at the battle site since 1982. Using a metal detector, he has carefully recorded each of his battle-related finds, which total over 2,000 artifacts. Once displayed at the museum at the Colorado State Historical Society in Denver, they are now in Larry's possession.[9] Mr. Finnell developed the panoramic picture of the Summit Springs battlefield that appears elsewhere in *Dog Soldier Justice*. He superimposed tepees onto the picture at spots where he located significant artifacts. Writes Larry: "In general, the Indian Village appears to have been on both sides of White Butte Creek [the small stream formed by runoff from the springs], ranging downstream for at least a mile from the origin of Summit Springs itself."[10]

The south end of the village, according to Finnell's research, roughly ends at the roundabout on the west end, and the ravines where Tall Bull was killed on the east end. If Susanna was buried in the midst of the village, she would not be near the roundabout. Larry's research indicates that the middle of the village is right at the man-made reservoir.[11] If Volkmar is right and Carr is also right in saying Susanna was buried on a hill or knoll, this knoll would be at or near the reservoir. And indeed, there are three such knolls, two of which are at opposite ends at the south end of the dam. When the reservoir was constructed in the early 1960s, dirt was piled in order to join these two knolls together to contain the water in the reservoir.

If one stands beyond the reservoir at its south end, Susanna could be buried at either knoll at the west and east ends of the dam. A third knoll rises at the northeast front of the reservoir. It is also possible Susanna could be buried there. Given Volkmar's report, it is unlikely that Susanna could be buried anywhere else on the battlefield.

During one of my visits at Summit Springs in early summer 2001, Pam Milavec accompanied me when we met ranch hand Joe Montgomery. In sharing with him our desire to locate Susanna's grave, he told us an interesting story regarding the man who built the dam. This man, Bill Lively, after finishing it, told Gary Ramey's father, Bill, an incident that occurred during the ground dozing for the dam. Both Bill Ramey and Bill Lively are now deceased, and the story is left for Joe Montgomery to tell, as he remembers it.

While cutting into the ground, along one of the knolls, Bill Lively uncovered what he thought to be an Indian grave. As no one except himself had discovered the body, Bill decided to rebury it and build the dam, working around it. After he finished, he told Bill Ramey of the Indian body he had uncovered and that he had reburied it. And he wasn't going to tell anyone where it was because he didn't want anyone coming out there and digging up bones from an old Indian grave.

This story, if true, is intriguing for several reasons. First, how would he have known it was an Indian grave? There must have been some markings associated with the grave to cause him to believe it was an Indian grave. Plains Indians did not bury their dead in the ground. They were mounted on scaffolds. Occasionally an Arapahoe Indian, after being dead a long time on a scaffold, would have his bones buried; but, bones alone, if that is all that Bill Lively uncovered, would not indicate the body was that of an Indian.[12] All other dead Indians would have been exposed to the elements of the harsh prairie. What, then, might Bill have seen that convinced him it was an Indian he uncovered?

Susanna was wrapped in lodge skins (treated buffalo hide) and the best buffalo robe found in the village. She was buried in a deep grave. Is it possible that Bill Lively uncovered Susanna, and misidentified her as an Indian because of the buffalo leather in which she was wrapped? Is it possible that leather stays preserved in a deep grave for that length of time? The answer to both questions is yes.

Recent discoveries at the 1879 Milk Creek battlesite in western Colorado uncovered a nearly complete leather saddlebag under about four feet of dirt, which had remained buried for a longer period of time than Susanna, if her body was uncovered in 1962.[13] If Bill Lively did discover Susanna, she would have been in her grave for 93 years. The preserved leather saddlebag found at Milk Creek was in the ground 122 years. It should be remembered, too, that Bill Lively did not know the history of the Summit Springs fight. In 1962, outside of teamster Welch's account in Brady's *Indian Fights and Fighters*, published accounts of Summit Springs said nothing about Susanna's burial in a buffalo robe, nor that she had been buried in the middle of the village. Further, no one knew then that the spot designated for the new reservoir was the middle of the 1869 Dog Soldier village.

Given Joe Montgomery's memory of what Bill Lively said around 1962, it is plausible that Susanna was briefly discovered and reburied then. If true, she remains buried near where Bill Lively had first found her. I do not believe she is presently under water, for if that were the case, Bill would have reported this and not stated that he reburied her, worked around her, and no one was going to know where he reburied the body. And no one did learn where he reburied the body, for Lively died several years ago. Further, this modern account fits well with the location of the original marker placed near the ravines where Tall Bull was killed.

Luther North has an account of finding Susanna on the day of the fight that fits this scenario. North wrote that he was standing near the ravine where Tall Bull was killed when he spotted a saddled horse "up the creek." He went to retrieve the horse and "had only gone a short way when he saw before him

211

a dead white woman."[14] When standing on top of the dirt walkway at the south end of the reservoir and looking to the south in the direction of the ravines where Tall Bull was killed, one can easily see the scar of the old stream as it meandered down past and around the ravines. The construction of the reservoir changed the course of the water flow. It now flows through the west end of the dam. If North's memory is correct, Susanna was found near the stream (he went *up* the stream after the saddled horse) about where the modern dam now is. This fits well with Bill Lively's story of finding a grave.

Is it possible that modern technology might be utilized to locate Susanna's grave? The answer is yes and no. Yes, modern technology makes it possible to locate anomalies in disturbed ground, which is just what a grave would show. But, no, the Summit Springs battleground rests atop several springs that run throughout the ground underneath, which would produce hundreds of ground anomalies. I have seen over the past few years where small springs will show in one area one season and in another area the next. There is even one account of the Summit Springs battle that says at the time of the fight there were seven springs at the battle site.[15] Today there are three, all north of the reservoir, two of which are right next to each other. Modern technology used at Summit Springs would reveal underground anomalies all over the place. Because of this, finding Susanna's grave via modern technology would probably be unfruitful.

Another possibility in locating Susanna's grave comes from old fashioned "witching" rods. There has always been success in using divining rods to locate water. In some cases, the rods turn in an opposite direction when standing over a grave. It seems, when this works, that it is the bones inside the grave that cause the rods to move.

In May 2001, Lowell Larson and Lee Modrow from Lincoln County, Kansas, tried the use of divining rods in locating Susanna's grave. Extremely wet, stormy weather did not permit the men entering the battle area until their last day of a three-day visit to the site. In a short time they both located what they positively felt was a grave. Surprisingly, the grave was on the hillside just to the northwest of the modern roundabout. Pam, her son Mitch, and I took turns digging the "grave" over the next two weekends. First, we dug down about eight feet, and then, finding nothing, we covered the hole. After consultation with Lee Modrow, it was decided to again dig the same grave, only deeper this time. This we did. After digging twelve feet, we gave up. If Susanna was placed in a deep grave, it was not twelve feet! But I am willing to dig another grave or two near the reservoir, and that area has yet to be thoroughly scouted with divining rods.

If Susanna's body can be found at the Summit Springs battlefield, what will that mean? Well, if her descendants desire, Susanna can be removed back to Kansas, to rest alongside Willis at the Spillman Cemetery near Ash Grove. Symbolically, it will end her captivity ordeal and return her home. When Willis died in 1920, his family purchased seven cemetery plots. Only his wife was buried next to him in 1948, leaving five empty plots next to Willis. Should Susanna be found and returned to Spillman Cemetery, perhaps Willis' two brothers' unmarked graves could be located near Beverly, Kansas, and symbolically reunited with Willis and their mother.

What happens if Susanna's bones are found but her descendants do not want them removed? The answer is simple. They will remain where they are found. But the Summit Springs property owner, Gary Ramey, has assured me that he is willing to allow a marker to be placed denoting the spot where she is buried, and another marker to be placed at the roundabout explaining what the visibly distant marker denotes.

Before any further searches are conducted for Susanna, however, a larger upright memorial marker needs to be placed at the roundabout at Summit Springs. The inscription should tell her story.

Mrs. Susanna Alderdice murder site at Summit Springs. The inscription on the plaque reads: "This marks the spot where the body of Mrs. Alderdice was found by Luther H. North on July 11, 1869. She was buried on a hill above." Courtesy of Colorado Historical Society.

Modern marker alleged to note where Susanna was murdered. In fact, the marker is several hundred yards from her murder and burial site. (See pages 205 - 212.) Author's collection.

Appendix 2

Epilogue

What is Past is Prologue[1]

When delving into the past there are two important considerations to which the historian needs to be sensitive. The first is to get the facts correct. The second is to interpret those facts to make a coherent picture. Both of these tasks are difficult. When interpreting history, there is a tendency to distort facts by taking them out of context. By that I mean the reader is sometimes made to see the events of yesterday through a current perspective in such a way that the past is lost in the present.

In recent years a new perspective lens, called New Western History, has developed. This is a paternalistic view, believing that today's historian can better understand the history of yesterday than those who lived through those events. Pioneers living through the Kansas events of 1868-1869, for example, were not in a position to understand their struggles, nor where their future was taking them. Today, some argue, historians can better know what the pioneer really experienced. Judging events of the 19th century by the standards of today's perspective can cause the loss of any meaningful understanding of what the pioneer really experienced. Historians have an obligation to explain what happened in the context of the times, but they should avoid judging those events by standards contrary to those of the era studied. I have been very sensitive to this issue and have consciously sought *not* to enter this modern perspective of New Western History. My attempt has been to enhance an understanding of the Kansas pioneers who were violently confronted with the raiding Dog Soldiers.

This does not mean that someone today should completely avoid using any contemporary perspective when viewing yesterday's history. But the major obligation is to explain what happened and, insofar as possible, why it happened and what its significance appears to have been, then and now. While it is true that today's historian cannot remove themselves from the contemporary world when they write, nor could a long dead pioneer likewise remove themselves from their era, one can be sensitive and not try and force this world's contemporary perspective upon yesterday's history. That is what I have tried to do in *Dog Soldier Justice*. I am not trying to make radical interpretations of history, such as is the case with New Western Historians.

I do believe, for philosophical considerations, that the individual moral and spiritual nature of yesterday's humanity is equal to the individual nature of today's humanity. That is, those today that are descended from yesterday's pioneer have the same human emotions and spiritual natures, as did their ancestors. And the same can be said of today's Indian. Further, the Indian's human nature is the same as the pioneer's human nature. Roenigk knew this when he said, "Enlightened, or savage, human nature is much the same."[2] It has not changed from yesterday to today, nor do I expect it to change tomorrow. The person living today has the same inner struggles with his or herself, as did the person of yesterday. We are all on a mysterious journey called life, and we all recognize that our human nature is far from what it ought to be and what it potentially can be. This is a basic understanding present in all major world faiths, and I believe it was also present in yesterday's pioneer and Indian.

This mysterious soul-making journey is fraught with challenges, sprinkled liberally with setbacks and seasoned with occasional triumphs. We wonder about the mysteries of life, but we nevertheless live within this journey of mystery, with an unformed moral and spiritual nature in which we are all equally responsible for the steps taken, both forward and backward, during this lifetime.[3] If I am correct in this assumption, the person of yesterday loved family no less and no more than the person of today. For that matter, the capacity for hatred and forgiveness remains the same, as it does for desires, hopes, and dreams. During the struggles of yesterday, the Indian was confronted with loss of home, loss of lifestyle, and the very real threat of loss of family. In this struggle, the Dog Soldier's capacity for hatred was equal, say, to an 1860s Southern family's hatred of northern Yankees.

During this conflict on the Plains, the pioneer settler had a similar struggle. Neither side had a monopoly in particular human virtues or vices. All humans bleed the same emotions as our brothers and sisters, regardless of time, race, and place. My focus in *Dog Soldier Justice* has been to make clearer our understanding of the pioneer's struggle, focusing when possible on the experiences of one family in particular.

Summit Springs was a justified battle on the part of the United States military, unlike Sand Creek, and there should be no grievance against the death of a single Dog Soldier at that fight.[4] Susanna Alderdice's death at this battle was unfortunate, tragic, and wholly unnecessary. It should not have happened. She was not an unlucky civilian in the line of fire. No, her death was an unjustified murder by an unknown Indian who was driven by the vice of hatred.

I began this epilogue with two considerations. It is now time to revisit the first consideration, namely, getting the facts correct. To do that, we have to rely on those who were there, but this is where the problem begins. People who were there and who did write about their experiences often said contradictory things about the same event. Who should we believe?

Unlike today where we have audio and video means to record facts, yesterday's documents consisted of still photographs, drawings, or written accounts. There were no photographs taken of the Spillman Creek raid or the battle at Summit Springs. There were no drawings either, other than the possibility of perhaps three of the pictographs found in the ledgerbook at Summit Springs. That leaves us, then, with only the written eyewitness accounts.

There are roughly three ways in which these accounts can be recorded. There were accounts written right at or close to the time the events occurred. There were accounts written years later, and there were accounts written either early or later for the newspapers. Newspaper accounts, unless written by the person present, were always written reports from verbal accounts of people who were there. Consequently, they can be inaccurate on several points. They should be accepted with caution and rejected when a primary source account contradicts them, unless good reasons can be given why the primary source account should be rejected. Still, newspaper accounts are important sources for reporting history and should not be ignored. My research revealed that many newspaper accounts of the Kansas Indian raids matched very well with the affidavits discovered in the individual depredation claims in the National Archives. They also accurately reported military reports written at or near the same time.

Primary source accounts written at or close to the time of the event should be accepted when contradicting a primary source account written years later, again, unless a good reason exists to reject it. Considering those accounts written years later, they can be either written by a participant, as was the case with much of Roenigk's *Pioneer History of Kansas*, or they can report the claims of those who were there, as was the case with Barr's *A Souvenir History of Lincoln County, Kansas* and

Bernhardt's *Indian Raids in Lincoln County, Kansas, 1864 and 1869.* These accounts, along with Spark's *Reckoning at Summit Springs*, where he culls his facts mostly from the above sources, are really the only books available to consider when sorting out the facts of May 30, 1869.

Alongside these are the military and newspaper reports. The military reports, stored at the National Archives, along with individual pioneer Indian depredation claims, served to fill in the gaps in the history of the area in question. I am unaware of any other historian who has sought to assimilate relevant testimonies found in individual Indian depredation claims.[5] I believe these pioneer affidavits constitute a substantial contribution to our understanding the facts about the Indian raids in 1868 and 1869. I did not use all of the testimonials I found in the National Archives. Nor did I find all that exists dealing with this period of Kansas history. Perhaps a more complete story could have been told had these files been located, but I feared any further delay in writing *Dog Soldier Justice* might have caused a permanent delay.

Considering the pioneer reminiscences listed earlier, the challenge of determining which statements to accept as fact lies mostly in analyzing the conflicts found in Barr, Bernhardt, and Roenigk. What follows in the rest of this chapter repeats much information presented in *Dog Soldier Justice.* The purpose of this repetition, however, is to summarize the facts surrounding the persons and events associated with the Spillman Creek raid, and then give my reasons as to which claims ought to be accepted as fact. After discussing these I will do a similar analysis with some of the discrepancies found in the Republican River Expedition and battle at Summit Springs. In this way I hope to settle once and for all some contemporary disputes occasionally raised by people who have carefully studied this history. It was the discovery of an affidavit or written document in the National Archives that led me to a proper sorting of the facts. The moral is that the published books alone cannot educate us to the true facts.

Did her family and friends know Mrs. Alderdice by the name of Susan or Susanna? When I developed my interest in Mrs. Alderdice's tragic story, I only knew her as Susanna. It did not seem right to refer to her as Susan. Judy Magnuson Lilly is the first contemporary author to call her Susan.[6] She did this with good reason. Both the marriage certificate certifying Susanna's marriage to Tom Alderdice and the 1865 Kansas State Census record list Susanna as Susan. In my research I found information to support Lilly's discoveries. The original letter Tom Alderdice wrote to the military while visiting Fort Leavenworth, now located at the National Archives, mentions his wife as Susan Alderdice, not Susanna. Further, the pension file for James Daily, filled out by Susanna's father Michael for his grandson Willis, often lists her as Susan instead of Susanna. But she was also referred to as Susanna in the pension files. From these records, therefore, I conclude that to her family and friends Mrs. Alderdice was known as both Susan and Susanna. Throughout *Dog Soldier Justice* I have chosen to refer to her as Susanna.

What were the ages and names of Susanna's four children? The correct answer to this question would probably elude the reader if one merely relied on published pioneer reminiscences such as found in Barr, Bernhardt, and Roenigk. If we look to them we find claims that Willis was eleven years of age when wounded, and that his brother John was the younger. Other claims say that Willis was seven or even five. Elizabeth Barr does not mention the ages of Susanna's children. The Pioneer monument in Lincoln, Kansas, lists John Daily as seven, Frank as two, and Alice as three months old.

The age of Alice Alderdice is easily settled in Tom Alderdice's Fort Leavenworth letter of June 21, 1869. There he states that his wife was captured with an eight-month old baby. Certainly Tom would have known the age of his own daughter, and his letter is definitive in settling the issue of the age of Alice. Alice was eight-months old when she was killed. The Pioneer Monument is in error in stating her age.

There is also no controversy regarding Willis's age. His gravestone, as well as the Daily pension file, lists his birth as October 5, 1864. That would have made him four years, seven months and twenty-five days at the time of the May 30, 1869 raid.

The pension file also lists John Daily's birthday as July 1, 1863. These various papers were filled out by Michael Zeigler, Susanna's father, and should be taken as definitive regarding the age of John. This makes John one month short of turning six when killed. The Pioneer Monument is again wrong, in stating the ages of two of Susanna's children, John and Alice.

Frank Alderdice is the one child whose age at the time of his death must be surmised. Tom and Susanna married on June 28, 1866. Making the safe assumption that Frank was born about ten months later, this would mean late April or early May 1867. Thus, he was barely two at the time of his death.

With Alice being eight-months old on May 30, she would have been born around the middle of September 1868. Her birth, then, was at the time Tom was involved with the Forsyth Scouts and the battle at Beecher Island. Susanna probably conceived for the fifth time around January 1869. This would give her a respite between Alice's birth and her next conception of about four or five months, which would be normal. If she began her last pregnancy around January 1869, she would have been about five months pregnant when captured, depending on when in January she conceived. Susanna had to be showing her pregnancy for Carr to note it in his report, otherwise he could not have known this fact. Maria didn't speak English, so she couldn't have been aware of Susanna's pregnancy either, unless Susanna was visibly pregnant. Susanna, then, must have been visibly pregnant when killed. And, as noted in *Dog Soldier Justice*, this was what was reported by teamster J. E. Welch, when he said she "had the appearance of being far gone in pregnancy."[7] She was probably at least seven months pregnant with her fifth child when murdered.

Regarding other facts uncovered in my research, we now know the name of Susanna's first husband as James Alfred Daily. This was not stated in any other accounts. Daily's pension file, as already noted, uncovered a wealth of new information about Susanna's family. Where Susanna and James married, when they married, the ages of their two children, the fact that Susanna's parents raised Willis after his family was killed, how James died, when he died and where he served is all new information in detailing Susanna's sad ordeal.

It was also at the National Archives that I discovered Tom Alderdice had a pension file. It revealed he was a "galvanized Yankee," having first served in the Confederate Army before being taken prisoner in battle and ultimately taking the Oath of Allegiance and then joining Union service. Also found was the letter Tom wrote at Fort Leavenworth after Susanna was captured. This letter gave a brief description of Susanna, which is new information. She was of medium build, fair complexion, blue eyes and had light brown hair.[8] Putting that with Barr's claim that Susanna and Maria Weichel were both "beautiful, refined women," and Washington Smith's claim that Susanna was "of an amiable disposition and endowed with great delicacy," I think it is appropriate to picture Susanna as Barr and Smith did.[9]

From pioneer accounts, especially that of Susanna's brother, Eli Zeigler, the military received a negative review regarding the Spillman Creek raid. Col. Ray Sparks was the first author to question this claim, producing three letters written by Lieutenants March and Law of Company G, 7th Cavalry, showing definitively that the military did assist the settlers right after the raid. My research added to this understanding. But Sparks rejected the claim that an army surgeon refused to aid Willis after he was found gravely wounded.[10] He was wrong. The detailed newspaper accounts noted in *Dog Soldier Justice* state the truth regarding the refusal of Dr. Renick to treat Willis Daily. Further, a friend of the surgeon admitted Renick did not treat him: "I am told that Dr. Renick did not go to see the Alderdyce [sic] boy, although twice called upon the camp not a half mile distant, and the arrow was drawn from the boy's body twenty-four hours afterward by Mr. W. Smith, a farmer who lives near."[11] This newspaper account is contemporary to the times and therefore ought to be accepted as truthful. I believe if Sparks had been made aware of these newspaper accounts, he would have amended his claim and admit that a military surgeon refused to treat Willis.

Regarding the wounds Willis received on May 30, accounts vary from one arrow wound to four arrow wounds, five arrow wounds, two gunshot wounds, and a lance wound, either in his hand or in his back.[12] I am not sure about the gunshot wounds or the lance wound, but am inclined to accept them. However, I feel positive that Willis had no less than five arrow wounds in his back. The first detailed account reported in the *Leavenworth Times and Conservative* on June 20, 1869, stated that Willis had five arrow wounds. There is more definitive evidence showing this to be true. In 1965, Sparks finally found the descendants of Willis Daily, after searching for nearly forty years. He sent a detailed questionnaire to Mrs. Anna Watters, Willis's daughter. In a letter dated September 27, 1965, Sparks asked her about her father's wounds. Anna wrote back saying she remembers distinctly that Willis had five big scars on his back from his arrow wounds. That he recovered is simply remarkable. In a conversation with Willis's granddaughter, Berniece Horton, the last person, so far as I know, still living to have known Willis during his lifetime, she told me that he was a very kind, gentle, and good man.

Another interesting fact I uncovered in my research was that Tom Alderdice trailed the Dog Soldiers to their village, which he noted in his Fort Leavenworth letter. It was a telegraphed copy of this letter that was given to Carr in late June when the supply wagons arrived at Carr's camp from Fort McPherson. And it was this letter that informed the command that the Indians they were trailing held two women captives. I am unaware of any published account detailing Carr's pursuit of Tall Bull that does not mention the command having discovered a woman's shoe print in an abandoned Indian village, thereby alerting them to the knowledge that a woman captive was with the Indians. While it is a wonderfully imaginative account that paces the heart when read, it is not a fact. I tried to straighten that out in *Dog Soldier Justice*.

Regarding the Summit Springs battle, I found that the command did not loop to the northwest and thereby surprise Tall Bull's village. From the journal of Lieutenant William Volkmar, substantiated by the anonymous account in the August 7, 1869, *Army and Navy Journal*, it was learned that the command approached the village from the northeast, not the northwest. I am aware of no contemporary publications that state this. I accept Volkmar's account as fact.

There are other issues of fact throughout *Dog Soldier Justice* that need no mention here. I hope that what I have detailed in this epilogue will be acknowledged in future mention of the events relating to the life of Susanna Zeigler Daily Alderdice.

Appendix 3

Susanna's Monument

Proposed inscription for monument at Summit Springs

Mrs. Susanna Alderdice was the only non-Indian casualty of the Summit Springs fight on July 11, 1869. Born Susanna Zeigler in Ohio in 1840, she married James A. Daily in Missouri in 1860, and shortly thereafter moved to Salina Kansas. She had two sons with James before he volunteered for Union service in 1864. Daily died of typhoid fever at Ft. Leavenworth. In 1866, Susanna married Tom Alderdice, a "galvanized Yankee." She then settled on a homestead along the Saline River near present-day Lincoln, Kansas, where she had a son and daughter with Tom. On May 30, 1869, while her husband was away, Tall Bull's band of Dog Soldiers raided homesteads near Lincoln, killing nine settlers and capturing Susanna, her eight month-old daughter, Alice, and Mrs. Maria Weichel, whose husband was killed. The dead in this raid included Susanna's five-year old son, John Daily, and two year-old son, Frank Alderdice. Alice was strangled in the Indian village three days later. Susanna and Maria remained in captivity 42 days until July 11, when Brevet General Carr's 5th U.S. Cavalry and Pawnee Indians attacked Tall Bull's village here at Summit Springs. Susanna was tomahawked in the face at the beginning of the fight. She was found dead by Capt. L. North. At 8 A.M. on July 12, she was buried in the middle of the battlefield. Her burial spot remains today unknown. She is likely buried somewhere near the reservoir, about a third of a mile to the northeast of this marker. Incredibly, Susan's four-year-old son, Willis Daily, was found alive, alongside his dead brothers, the day after the Kansas raid. His injuries included five arrows in his back, one of which had to be removed with a bullet-mold used as pliers, as it was firmly stuck in the back of his sternum. Raised by Susanna's parents, Willis died June 16, 1920, and is buried in the Spillman Cemetery near Ash Grove, Kansas. He had three children and five grandchildren.

Endnotes

Preface
Pages xxix - xxxvi

[1] Roenigk, Adolph, *Pioneer History of Kansas* (Self-published, 1933), 358.

[2] Dunn, William R., *War Drum Echoes: A Narrative History of the Indian Wars in Colorado* (Self-published, 1979), 87. Nye, Wilbur S., *Plains Indian Raiders* (Norman, OK: University of Oklahoma Press, 1968), 148.

[3] Dunn, *War Drum Echoes*, 87. See also Brown, Dee, *Bury My Heart at Wounded Knee: An Indian History of the American West* (Toronto, New York and London: Bantam Books, 1971), 167-168.

[4] Watson, Elmo Scott, "The Battle of Summit Springs," *The Chicago Westerners Brand Book* (Vol. VII, No. 7, September, 1950), 50.

[5] At the time I purchased these books on the Internet I did not know that they have all been reprinted at very reasonable cost by the Lincoln County Historical Society in Lincoln, Kansas.

[6] Indian Depredations Claims Division, Record Group 123; National Archives Building, Washington, D.C.

[7] "Depredations" Report, Department of the Interior, Office of Indian Affairs. Entry 96, Letters Sent, 1890, 18-19, Record Group 75, National Archives Building, Washington, D.C.

[8] "Depredations," 19.

[9] "Depredations," 21.

[10] "Depredations," 19-24.

[11] "Public Act No. 139, for the adjudication of claims arising from Indian depredations." The Carl Albert Center, The University of Oklahoma, Sidney Clarke Collection, Box 6, Folder 32, Norman, Oklahoma.

[12] Peter Ulbrich Indian Depredation Claim #6220. Indian Depredations Claims Division, Record Group 123; National Archives Building, Washington, D.C.

[13] Margareth Kalus Indian Depredation Claim #454. Indian Depredations Claims Division, Record Group 123; National Archives Building, Washington, D.C.

[14] For a study on the complicated legal issues involved with Indian depredation claims, see Scogen, Larry, *Indian Depredation Claims, 1796-1920* (Norman and London: University of Oklahoma Press, 1996).

[15] See Monnett, John, *The Battle of Beecher Island and the Indian War of 1868-1869* (Niwot, CO: University Press of Colorado, 1992); Hoig, Stan, *The Battle of the Washita* (Garden City, NY: Doubleday & Co., Inc., 1976). A better anaylsis of the Washita fight is in a recent Ph.D. dissertation. See Sarf, Wayne M., *A Winter Campaign: General Philip H. Sheridan's Operations on the Southern Plains, 1868-9* (Ann Arbor, MI: UMI Microfilm 9997119, 2001). See also Greene, Jerome, *Washita: The U.S. Army and the Southern Cheyennes, 1867 - 1869* (Norman, OK: University of Oklahoma Press, 2004)

Beginnings
Pages 1 - 6

[1] Rister, Carl Coke, *Border Captives; The Traffic in Prisoners by Southern Plains Indians, 1835-1875* (Norman, OK: University of Oklahoma Press, 1940), x.

[2] 1840 United States Census, Green Township, Ohio. Census Records, National Archives Building, Washington, DC.

[3] Ray Sparks Research—Manuscript Collections in the possession of Orvel Criqui, Lawrence, Kansas.

[4] Letter to Ray Sparks from Luella Zigler, Eli's youngest daughter. Sparks files. By the time of Luella's birth Eli had changed the spelling of his last name to Zigler.

[5] James A. Daily Military Service Record and Pension File, Record Group 94, National Archives Building, Washington, DC.

[6] Daily Pension File.

[7] 17th Kansas Volunteer Regiment, Enlistment Roster. Kansas Room, Salina Public Library, Salina, Kansas.

⁸ 17ᵗʰ Kansas Regiment.

⁹ Report of Colonel Samuel Drake, Commander of the 17ᵗʰ Kansas Volunteer Infantry, January 29, 1865. Kansas Adjutant General's Office, Volunteer Regiment Files, Kansas State Historical Society, Topeka, Kansas.

¹⁰ Report of Col. Drake.

¹¹ Report of Col. Drake.

¹² 1865 Kansas Census. Census Records. Kansas State Historical Society, Topeka, Kansas. The census fails to mention William Zeigler living at the home at this time. Perhaps he had by then moved away.

¹³ Thomas Alderdice Military Service Record and Pension File. Record Group 94, National Archives Building, Washington, DC.

¹⁴ Certificate from Soldiers and Sailors Historical Benevolent Society, Washington, DC, September 17, 1907. Copy in Sparks Files.

¹⁵ Copy of Marriage Certificate in the possession of Janie Alderdice Trotter, Tom's great-granddaughter. See also Lilly, Judy Magnuson, The marriage is also noted in Tom Alderdice's pension file. "Susan's Story," *Kanhistique*, April 1986, 11.

¹⁶ Roenigk, Adolph, *Pioneer History of Kansas* (Self-published, 1933), 299.

August 1868 Raids
Pages 7 - 34

1 Julia A. Marshall Indian Depredation Claim #3361. Indian Depredations Claims Division, Record Group 123, National Archives Building, Washington, DC.

2 Lt. General P. H. Sheridan, *Record of Engagements with Hostile Indians within the Military Division of the Missouri, from 1868 to 1882* (Washington: Government Printing Office, 1882. Facsimile Edition, Old Army Press, 1969), 8. James Malin, in "Dust Storms, Part Two, 1861-1880," implies that 1868 was not a drought year in Kansas. He cites the *Manhattan Independent*, August 29, 1868 as his source (268), where the paper there reports rain. However, nearly all of the 1868 Indian Depredation Claims that included crop losses reported that the year 1868 was extremely dry, and that the crops

would have been lost to the drought had the Indians not destroyed them. Because of this, destroyed crops were barred from compensation. Malin, I believe, was mistaken. See *Kansas Historical Quarterly*, Vol. XIV, No. 3, August, 1946, 268.

3 Garfield, Marvin, "Defense of the Kansas Frontier 1868-1869," *Kansas Historical Quarterly*, Volume I, No. 5, November, 1932 , 454.

4 John Nance Indian Depredation Claim #612. Depredation Claims Division, Record Group 123, National Archives Building, Washington, DC, italics added.

5 David Lucas Indian Depredation Claim #1169. Depredation Claims Division, Record Group 123, National Archives Building, Washington, DC.

6 Garfield, "Defense," 454-455. See also Crawford, Samuel J., *Kansas in the Sixties* (Chicago: A. C. McClure & Co., 1911), 289.

7 Aaron Grigsby Indian Depredation Claim #601. Depredation Claims Division, Record Group 123, National Archives Building, Washington, DC.

8 Grigsby Indian Depredation Claim.

9 Patrick O'Bryne Indian Depredation Claim #604. Depredation Claims Division, Record Group 123, National Archives Building, Washington, DC.

10 Hubert Pappan Indian Depredation Claim #179. Indian Depredations Claims Division, Record Group 123, National Archives Building, Washington, DC.

11 McAfee, J. B., "Report of the Adjutant General of the State of Kansas For The Year 1868," 4. Kansas State Historical Society, Topeka, Kansas.

12 Grigsby Indian Depredation Claim. Wynkoop's report is in the Grigsby Indian Depredation file.

13 Grigsby Indian Depredation Claim.

14 Berthrong, Donald, *The Southern Cheyennes* (Norman, OK: University of Oklahoma Press, 1963), 305.

15 Sheridan, P. H., *Personal Memoirs of P. H. Sheridan, Vol. II* (New York, NY: Charles L. Webster & Company, 1888), 289.

16 Garfield, "Defense," 455-456. Agent Wynkoop would later deny that the Indians causing the August depredations had just been

issued their arms, claiming they were issued arms at Fort Larned just hours before the outbreak, which occurred more than a day's journey to the north along Spillman Creek. Thus it was impossible for the Indians receiving arms to be guilty of the depredations. See Hoig, Stan, *The Battle of the Washita* (Garden City, NY: Doubleday & Co., 1976), 44-46. But Hoig also reports from a letter from General W. B. Hazen to General W. T. Sherman in which the Indians admit having their newly issued arms at the time of the raid and that they were trading them for other items *up until the day of the outbreak*, supposedly proving that the Indians were not planning a raid. It seems likely, then, that the issuance of arms by Wynkoop commenced earlier than August 9. Perhaps the last of the arms were finally given on August 9. The arms probably commenced being issued to the Indians on August 3. It was the band of Indians first receiving their arms that were responsible for the deadly raids in Lincoln and Mitchell Counties in August.

[17] *Junction City Weekly Union*, November 28, 1868.

[18] Crawford, *Kansas in the Sixties*, 291.

[19] Crawford, *Kansas in the Sixties*, 456.

[20] Berthrong, *Southern Cheyennes*, 306.

[21] P. H. Sheridan's Report to the Secretary of War, *Report of the Secretary of War, Volume 1* (Washington: Government Printing Office, 1869), 47.

[22] Sheridan's Report to the Secretary of War, 47. This implication of Black Kettle goes against modern day understandings, where Black Kettle is revered as perhaps the most significant of the Cheyenne Peace Chiefs. See e.g., Hoig, Stan, *The Peace Chiefs of the Cheyennes* (Norman, OK: University of Oklahoma Press, 1980), 104-121.

[23] Frost, Lawrence A., *The Court-Martial of General George Armstrong Custer* (Norman, OK: University of Oklahoma Press, 1967), 17-24.

[24] Sherman, General W.T., "The Report of the General-In-Chief." *Executive Documents of the House of Representatives During the Third Session of the Fortieth Congress* (Washington, DC: Government Printing Office, 1869), 3, emphasis added.

[25] *Junction City Weekly Union*, November 28, 1868.

[26] Elizabeth Barr, *A Souvenir History of Lincoln County, Kansas* (self-published, 1908), 31. The U.S. Census Report for 1870 gives Mrs. A. Bacon's age as twenty-nine, which would have made her twenty-seven during her ordeal. She was apparently just pregnant with her daughter at the time of the attack, as the girl is two years old in 1870. It is possible, however, that the daughter was a newborn on August 10, and this was the baby with her during her ordeal.

[27] Barr, *Souvenir History*, 31.

[28] Simeon Shaw Indian Depredation File, Claim #6441. Indian Depredation Claims Division, Record Group 123, National Archives Building, Washington, DC.

[29] Barr, *Souvenir History,* 31.

[30] Joseph T. Smith Indian Depredation Claim #7695, testimony of Benjamin Smith. Indian Depredation Claims Division, Record Group 123, National Archives Building, Washington, DC.

[31] Barr, *Souvenir History*, 31.

[32] Roenigk, Adolph, *Pioneer History of Kansas* (Self-published, 1933), 94-95.

[33] Sherman, "The Report of the General-In-Chief," 3.

[34] Sheridan, P. H., "Report of Major General P. H. Sheridan." *Executive Documents of the House of Representatives During the Third Session of the Fortieth Congress* (Washington, DC: Government Printing Office, 1869), 11.

[35] Sheridan, "Letter to General Sherman." Report of the Secretary of War, *Messages and Documents of the Second Session of the Forty-First Congress, Volume I* (Washington, D.C.: Government Printing Office, 1869), 48.

[36] Osborne, V. B., "Letter to Governor Crawford," August 13, 1868. Governor's Papers, Kansas State Historical Society, Topeka, Kansas. 1870 U.S. Census.

[37] Peterson, Rachel Wild, *The Long-Lost Rachel Wild or, Seeking Diamonds In The Rough* (Denver, CO: Reed Publishing Company, 1905), 16.

[38] William Wild Indian Depredation Claim #3482. James Wild Indian Depredation Claim #3779, Indian Depredation Claims

Division, Record Group 123 and 75, National Archives Building, Washington, DC.

[39] Barr, *Souvenir History*, 30.

[40] Information on events relating to the Bell, Bogardus, Springs, Farrow families taken from the following depredation claims: Martha Springs (#3704, Record Group 75), Hester Ann Snow, widow of David Bogardus (#3704, Record Group 75), Mary Bell (#3532, Record Group 75), Martha Gallop (#3542, Record Group 75), James Farrow (#2195, Record Group 75). Indian Depredation Claims Division, National Archives Building, Washington, DC.

[41] Martha Gallop—Springs Indian Depredation Claim.

[42] Mary Bell Indian Depredation Claim.

[43] Hester Ann Snow Indian Depredation Claim.

[44] *The Emporia News*, August 21, 1868.

[45] McAfee, J. B., *Report of the Adjutant General of the State of Kansas For The year 1868*, 5. Kansas Room, Salina Public Library, Salina Kansas.

[46] Hester Snow Indian Depredation Claim.

[47] Houghton, Alan, *The Frontier Aflame* (Beloit, KS: The Beloit Daily Call, 1958), 7.

[48] Hester Ann Snow Indian Depredation Claim.

[49] Hester Ann Snow Indian Depredation Claim. Barr says in *Souvenir History* that the girls remained at William Hendrickson's place for about a week until their father picked them up (31). This must be an error. They probably remained there a day or two until the soldiers took them to Fort Harker, where Aaron Bell retrieved them.

[50] Sheridan, *Personal Memoirs*, 291.

[51] Carroll, John M, Ed., *Cavalry Scraps: The Writings of Frederick W. Benteen* (no city: The Guidon Press, 1979), 3.

[52] Crandall letter, May 12, 1914, Microfilm 3, 2404, Elizabeth Bacon Custer Manuscript Collections, Little Bighorn Battlefield National Monument, Research Library, Crow Agency, Montana.

[53] Barr, *Souvenir History*, 30.

[54] Roenigk, *Pioneer History*, 96.

[55] Bernhardt, *Indian Raids in Lincoln County, Kansas, 1864 and 1869* (Lincoln, KS: The Lincoln Sentinel Print, 1910), 42-43.

[56] Martha Springs Indian Depredation Claim.

[57] Hester Ann Snow Indian Depredation Claim.

[58] Mary Bell Indian Depredation Claim.

[59] Hester Ann Snow Indian Depredation Claim.

[60] Hester Ann Snow Indian Depredation Claim.

[61] Martha Springs Indian Depredation Claim.

[62] Cornelius Reed Indian Depredation Claim #3681. Indian Depredation Claims Division, Record Group 75, National Archives Building, Washington, DC.

[63] Cornelius Reed Indian Depredation Claim.

[64] John S. Smith Indian Depredation Claim #3746 & 3748. Indian Depredation Claims Division, Record Group 75, National Archives Building, Washington, DC.

[65] Abraham Whitehurst affidavit, Lyman and Marvin Randall Indian Depredation Claim. Indian Depredation Claims Division, Record Group 75, National Archives Building, Washington, DC.

[66] Hester A. Snow affidavit, Lyman and Marvin Randall Indian Depredation Claim.

[67] Lyman and Marvin Randall Indian Depredation Claim.

[68] Julia A. Marshall Indian Depredation Claim #3361. Indian Depredation Claims Division, Record Group 123, National Archives Building, Washington, DC.

[69] Lena Baertoche Indian Depredation Claim #3530. Indian Depredation Claims Division, Record Group 123, National Archives Building, Washington, DC.

[70] Nancy Hewitt Indian Depredation Claim #333. Indian Depredation Claims Division, Record Group 123, National Archives Building, Washington, DC.

[71] Lena Baertoche Indian Depredation Claim.

72 Lena Baertoche Indian Depredation Claim.

73 Nancy Hewitt Indian Depredation Claim.

74 Bazil Saunders Indian Depredation Claim #3698. Indian Depredation Claims Division, Record Group 75, National Archives Building, Washington, DC.

75 Nathaniel Brooks Indian Depredation Claim #3538. Indian Depredation Claims Division, Record Group 75, National Archives Building, Washington, DC.

76 Custer, General G. A., "Report to General Sheridan, March 21, 1869." Record Group 393, Department of the Missouri, Part 1, Letters Received 1869, Entry 2601, National Archives Building, Washington, DC.

77 Hollibaugh, Mrs. E. F., *Biographical History of Cloud County, Kansas* (Logonsport, IN: Wilson, Humphrey & CO, 1903), 49.

78 Spotts, David L., *Campaigning With Custer and the Nineteenth Kansas Volunteer Cavalry* (Los Angeles, CA: Wetzel Publishing Company, 1928), 211-212.

79 Bazil Saunders Indian Depredation Claim.

80 Alfred Schull Indian Depredation Claim #10348. Indian Depredation Claims Division, Record Group 123, National Archives Building, Washington, DC.

81 George Shafer Indian Depredation Claim #5073. Indian Depredation Claims Division, Record Group 123, National Archives Building, Washington, DC.

82 George Shafer Indian Depredation Claim.

83 Clark, Mrs. Olive A., "Early Days Along the Solomon Valley," *Collections of the Kansas State Historical Society 1926-1928* (Vol. XVII, 1928), 719-730.

84 Clark, "Early Days," 724.

85 Clark, "Early Days," 723.

86 James W. McConnell Indian Depredation Claim #3643. Indian Depredation Claims Division, Record Group 123, National Archives Building, Washington, DC.

[87] Julia A. Marshall Indian Depredation Claim #3361. Indian Depredation Claims Division, Record Group 123, National Archives Building, Washington, DC. I preserved Julia's spelling rather than correct it or note it with [sic].

[88] Julia Marshall Indian Depredation Claim.

[89] Bickerdyke, Hiram, "Letter to Brother," Manuscript Collections, Kansas State Historical Society, Topeka, Kansas.

[90] Julia Marshall Indian Depredation Claim.

[91] *Forty-first Congress, 2nd Session, House of Representatives,* Mis. Doc. 20, #1431 (Washington, D. C., Government Printing Office, 1869), 3-7.

Beecher Island Battle
Pages 35 - 44

[1] Petree, Frank, "The Battle of Beecher Island and Recollections of Some of the Men Engaged in it," Robert Lynam, ed., *The Beecher Island Annual, Sixty-Second Anniversary of the Battle of Beecher Island Sept. 17, 18, 1868* (Wray, CO: The Beecher Island Battle Memorial Association, 1930), 110.

[2] Forsyth, George A., *The Story of the Soldier* (New York, NY: D. Appleton and Company, 1900), 210.

[3] Barr, Elizabeth, *A Souvenir History of Lincoln County, Kansas* (Lincoln, KS: privately published, 1908), 33.

[4] Eli Zeigler Military Records and Pension File. Record Group 94, National Archives Building, Washington, DC.

[5] Monnett, John H., *The Battle of Beecher Island and the Indian War of 1868-1869* (Niwot, CO: University Press of Colorado, 1992), 131-180.

[6] In my research on this fight I came across a map drawn in 1873 (map filed January 21, 1874, Surveyor General's Office, Denver, C.T. Bureau of Land Management Office, Denver, CO) that indicates the actual battle site rests almost four miles away from where the site was in 1898 "rediscovered" by three men associated with the fight in 1868, and where the present memorial site is located. At the time of

this writing a preliminary study has begun to establish whether this other location is the actual battle site. Doug Scott, Chief of the Rocky Mountain Research Division, Midwest Archeological Center, National Park Service, Lincoln, Nebraska, is coordinating the preliminary steps necessary to conduct this study.

7 Address of Dr. C. A. Brooks, *The Beecher Island Annual*, 112-113.

8 Roenigk, Adolph, *Pioneer History of Kansas* (Self-published, 1933), 365.

9 There should be no dispute regarding Eli's age at the time of Beecher Island. His Military Records and Pension File, which includes a copy of his death certificate, is consistent in listing his birth date as June 12, 1852. Eli was sixteen years and three months old when engaged at Beecher Island.

10 Forsyth, *Story of the Soldier*, 211.

11 Forsyth, *Story of the Soldier*.

12 Forsyth, *Story of the Soldier*, 215.

13 Zigler, Eli, "Story of the Beecher Island Battle as Told by Scout Eli Zigler," *The Beecher Island Annual*, 61.

14 Zigler, "Story."

15 Zigler, "Story."

16 Zigler, "Story." 63.

17 Forsyth, General George A., *Thrilling Days in Army Life* (New York and London: Harper & Brothers, 1900), 37.

18 *The Beecher Island Annual*, 27.

19 *The Beecher Island Annual*.

20 Zigler, "Story," 63.

21 Zigler, "Story."

22 Zigler, "Story."

23 Zigler, "Story," 64.

24 Zigler, "Story."

25 Zigler, "Story."

[26] Zigler, "Story."

[27] Zigler, "Story."

[28] Zigler, "Story."

[29] Zigler, "Story," 65.

[30] Zigler, "Story."

[31] Zigler, "Story."

[32] Zigler, "Story."

[33] Zigler, "Story," 66.

[34] Zigler, "Story."

[35] Zigler, "Story."

[36] Zigler, "Story."

October Raids
Pages 45 - 56

[1] Mary E. Smith Indian Depredation Claim #3736. Indian Depredations Claims Division, Record Group 75, National Archives Building, Washington, DC.

[2] Sheridan, P. H., "Letter to General Sherman, October 15 (sic) 1868." *Executive Documents printed by order of The House Of Representatives during the Third Session Of The Fortieth Congress 1868-'69* (Washington: Government Printing Office, 1869), 20.

[3] Carr, Eugene A., "Letter to William F. Cody, July 2, 1906." Box 3, Eugene A. Carr Papers, U.S. Army Military History Institute, Carlisle, PA.

[4] Montgomery, Mrs. Frank C., "Fort Wallace and its Relation to the Frontier," *Collections of the Kansas State Historical Society 1926-1928* (Vol. XVII, 1928), 235.

[5] Carr Letter to Washington Smith, dated March 17, 1887, Washington Smith Indian Depredation Claim #3951. Indian Depredation Claims Division, Record Group 75, National Archives Building, Washington, DC.

[6] Criqui, Orvel, *Fifty Fearless Men* (Marceline, MO: Walsworth Publishing Company, 1993), 290.

[7] Montgomery, "Fort Wallace," 234.

[8] Indian Depredation Files for the following persons: Hannah Howard, Robert W. Smith, Mary Smith (wife of Alexander Smith), William McDowell, Peter Hansen, John Virtue, Milton Keller, George Karnes, William Abbott, Edward Abbott, Samuel McBride, John S. Smith, James McBride, James Morgan, Thomas Misell, David Mortimer, William Abbott, L. W. Jones, E. L. Fisher. Indian Depredations Claims Division, Record Group 123 and Record Group 75, National Archives Building, Washington, DC.

[9] James Morgan Indian Depredation Claim #3644. Indian Depredation Claims Division, Record Group 75, National Archives Building, Washington, DC.

[10] Robert W. Smith Indian Depredation Claim #3301. Indian Depredation Claims Division, Record Group 123, National Archives Building, Washington, DC.

[11] Samuel Boyd Indian Depredation Claim #10344. Indian Depredation Claims Division, Record Group 123, National Archives Building, Washington, DC.

[12] Mary E. Smith Indian Depredation Claim #3736. Indian Depredations Claims Division, Record Group 75, National Archives Building, Washington, DC.

[13] Mary Smith Indian Depredation Claim.

[14] Milton Keller deposition, John S. Smith Indian Depredation Claim #10346. Indian Depredation Claims Division, Record Group 123, National Archives Building, Washington, DC. See also Milton Keller Indian Depredation Claim #3603, Record Group 75, and John Virtue Indian Depredation Claim #3765, Record Group 75.

[15] Peter Hansen Indian Depredation Claim #3562. Indian Depredations Claims Division, Record Group 75, National Archives Building, Washington, DC.

[16] William McDowell Indian Depredation Claim #3637. Indian Depredations Claims Division, Record Group 75, National Archives Building, Washington, DC.

[17] Jacob Studt Indian Depredation Claim #3704. Indian

Depredations Claims Division, Record Group 123, National Archives Building, Washington, DC.

[18] David Mortimer Indian Depredation Claim #3630. Indian Depredations Claims Division, Record Group 75, National Archives Building, Washington, DC.

[19] William Abbott Indian Depredation Claim #3498. Indian Depredations Claims Division, Record Group 75, National Archives Building, Washington, DC.

[20] William and Edward Abbott Indian Depredation Claim #3506. Indian Depredations Claims Division, Record Group 75, National Archives Building, Washington, DC.

[21] Thomas Misell Indian Depredation Claim #3629. Indian Depredations Claims Division, Record Group 75, National Archives Building, Washington, DC.

[22] Thomas Misell Indian Depredation Claim.

[23] Thomas Misell Indian Depredation Claim.

[24] "Mrs. Louise Davenport Lincoln biography of Mrs. Morgan from letters written to her from Mrs. Morgan in 1893." Misc. Manuscript Collections, Box Moo-Mou, Anna Brewster Morgan Folder, Kansas State Historical Society, Topeka, Kansas, 1.

[25] Spotts, David L., "Sketch of the Life of Mrs. Anna Belle Morgan," *Campaigning With Custer and the Nineteenth Kansas Volunteer Cavalry* (Los Angeles, CA: Wetzel Publishing Company, 1928), 207.

[26] Mrs. Lincoln, "Letters from Mrs. Morgan,"

[27] Spotts, *Campaigning With Custer*, 208.

[28] George Karnes Indian Depredation Claim #3602. Indian Depredations Claims Division, Record Group 75, National Archives Building, Washington, DC.

[29] Milton Keller Indian Depredation Claim #3603. Indian Depredations Claims Division, Record Group 75, National Archives Building, Washington, DC.

[30] George Karnes Indian Depredation Claim.

[31] James S. Morgan Indian Depredation Claim.

32 Spotts, *Campaigning With Custer*, 209.

33 Mrs. Lincoln, "Letters from Mrs. Morgan," 2.

34 James Morgan Indian Depredation Claim. Letter by Samuel J. Crawford in Morgan file.

35 Crawford, Samuel J., *Kansas in the Sixties* (Chicago, IL: A. C. McClurg & Co., 1911), 330.

36 Milton Keller Indian Depredation Claim. See also Morgan testimony in George Karnes Indian Depredation Claim.

37 Sherman, Lieutenant General W. T., "The Report of the General-In-Chief." *Executive Documents of the Second Session of the Fortieth Congress, With the Reports of the Heads of Departments* (Washington, DC: Government Printing Office, 1867), 378.

38 Broome, Jeff, "On Locating the Kidder Massacre Site of 1867." *The Denver Westerners Roundup* (Vol. LVI, No. 4, July—August, 2000), 10. See also Broome, "Custer, Kidder and Tragedy at Beaver Creek," *Wild West* (June, 2002), 46.

39 Poole, Captain D.C., *Among the Sioux of Dakota: Eighteen Months Experience as an Indian Agent* (New York, NY: D. Van Nostrand, Publisher, 1881), 104, emphasis added.

40 Dodge, Colonel Richard Irving, *Our Wild Indians: Thirty-Three Years Personal Experience Among the Red Men of the Great West* (New York, NY: Archer House, Inc., reprint, 1959), 530.

41 *The Kansas City Star*, Sunday, March 4, 1934.

Washita Battle
Pages 57 - 70

1 Letter from General Sherman to General Sheridan, January 18, 1869. Headquarters, Military Division of the Missouri, Part 1, E2601, Department of the Missouri, Letters Received, 1869. Record Group 393, National Archives Building, Washington, DC.

2 Frost, Lawrence A., *The Court-Martial of General George Armstrong Custer* (Norman, OK: University of Oklahoma Press, 1967), 266-267.

3 Sheridan, General P. H., "Report to General W. T. Sherman, November 1, 1869." Report of the Secretary of War, Forty-First Congress 2d Session, Volume I, Executive Document, Pt 2 (Washington, DC: Government Printing Office, 1869), 44.

4 Sheridan, "Report,"

5 Sheridan, Report," 45.

6 Sheridan, "Report," 46.

7 Custer, George A., "Report in the Field, November 28, 1868." Carroll, John M., ed., *General Custer and the Battle of the Washita: The Federal View* (Byron, TX: Guidon Press, 1978), 37.

8 Utley, Robert, ed., *Life in Custer's Cavalry: Diaries and Letters of Albert and Jennie Barnitz, 1867-1868* (New Haven and London: Yale University Press, 1977), 216. Edmund Tuttle, *Three Years on the Plains: Observations of Indians 1867-1870*, forward by Jerome Greene (Norman, OK: University of Oklahoma Press, 2002), 60.

9 Custer, "Report in the Field," 38.

10 Custer, "Report in the Field." Sheridan's report dated November 29, 1868, states there were fifty-three women and three children taken captive, 42.

11 Hoig, Stan, *The Battle of the Washita* (Garden City, NY: Doubleday & Company, Inc., 1976), 183.

12 Custer, "Report in the Field," 38.

13 Sheridan, "Report in the Field," 47.

14 "In Memoriam: Brevet Major Louis McLane Hamilton," 23. Microfilm #2778, Yale University. McCracken Research Library, Buffalo Bill Historical Center, Cody, Wyoming.

15 When the bodies of Elliott and his men were found, there were sixteen men with Elliott. One soldier was never found, and it is not known if he accompanied Elliott's party or not. Hoig, *Battle of the Washita*, 204-207.

16 Custer, George A., *My Life on the Plains, or, Personal Experiences with Indians* (New York, NY: Sheldon and Company, 1874), 189-190.

17 Sheridan, "Report in the Field, December 19, 1868." *General Custer and the Battle of the Washita*, 50. The death of Elliott's small

command caused a rift in the 7th Cavalry that divided the loyalties of certain officers against Custer, some feeling that Elliott was abandoned by Custer, and others defending Custer's actions, Captain F. W. Benteen representing the former view and Lieutenant E. S. Godfrey the latter. Sources are numerous to cite this rift. Perhaps the Elliott pages noted in the index of Graham's *The Custer Myth: A Source Book in Custeriana,* would be a good start to examine this controversy. (Harrisburg, PA: The Stackpole Company, 1953).

18 Sheridan, P. H., "Report To The General of the Army, November 1, 1869." *Report of the Secretary of War of the Second Session of the Forty-First Congress,* Volume I (Washington, DC: Government Printing Office, 1969), 46.

19 Richard Blinn Indian Depredation Claim #1564. Indian Depredations Claims Division, Record Group 123, National Archives Building, Washington, DC.

20 Justus, Judith P., "The Saga of Clara Blinn and the Battle of the Washita." *Research Review, The Journal of the Little Big Horn Associates* (Vol. 14, No. 1, Winter, 2000), 11.

21 Justus, "Saga of Clara Blinn." See also Richard Blinn Indian Depredation Claim.

22 Richard Blinn Indian Depredation Claim.

23 Richard Blinn Indian Depredation Claim.

24 Carroll, *General Custer and the Battle of the Washita,* 51-52.

25 Carroll, *General Custer and the Battle of the Washita,* 50, 69.

26 When Susanna was killed the following summer at Summit Springs, General Carr elected not to bring her to Fort Sedgwick for burial. It is not clear why in the one instance, in harsh winter conditions, Clara and her son were brought over 150 miles to be buried, while Susanna was not. There were plenty of buffalo robes and salt to preserve her body, and wagon space to carry her to Fort Sedgwick, a distance not half as far as Clara Blinn was brought.

27 *New York Times,* March 21, 1869.

28 *New York Times.*

29 Custer, "Report in The Field, December 22, 1868," 70.

30 Sheridan, "Report," 49.

31 Custer, *My Life on the Plains,* 190.

32 Custer, "Report in the Field, December 22, 1868," 71-72.

33 Sheridan, "Report," 49.

34 Sheridan, "Report," 50.

35 Custer, "Report In The Field, March 21, 1869." Part 1, E2601, Department of the Missouri, Letters Received, 1869, Record Group 393, National Archives Building, Washington, DC.

36 Custer, "Report March 21," 3-4.

37 Custer, "Report March 21," 6.

38 Custer, "Report March 21," 7-8.

39 Custer, "Report March 21," 8.

40 Custer, "Report March 21," 8-9.

41 Custer, "Report March 21," 10.

42 Custer, "Report March 21,"

43 Custer, "Report March 21," 11.

44 Custer, "Report March 21," 12-13.

45 Custer, "Report March 21, " 13-15.

46 "A. L. Runyon's Letters From the Nineteenth Kansas Regiment," *Kansas Historical Quarterly*, Vol. IX, Number 1, February, 1940, 74. It is possible that Sarah White either wasn't pregnant or miscarried, as there is no further evidence of her having an Indian baby. See Dixon, David, "Custer and the Sweetwater Hostages," *Custer and His Times, Book Three*, ed. G. Urwin and R. Fagan (no city noted, University of Central Arkansas Press and the Little Big Horn Associates, 1987), 107.

47 *Winners of the West*, Vol. XX, Number 7, July 28, 1943. McCracken Research Library, Don Russell MS NO 62, Box 2, Buffalo Bill Historical Center, Cody, Wyoming.

Carr's First Fight With Tall Bull
Pages 71 - 88

[1] Carr, Eugene A., "Reminiscences of Indian Wars," Carr Papers, Box 3, United States Military History Institute, Carlisle, PA.

[2] Carr, "Reminiscences."

[3] Sheridan, P. H., "Report To The General of the Army." *Report of the Secretary of War, Forty-First Congress 2d Session, Volume I, Executive Document, Pt. 2* (Washington, DC: Government Printing Office, 1869), 50. Exactly who Tall Bull was predominantly associated with and where he was before his clash with Carr is difficult to ascertain from primary source accounts. They seem about equally divided between his being among the Southern Cheyenne and thus active in depredations conducted by that band of Indians, and likewise with the Northern Cheyenne. The *Leavenworth Times and Conservative*, June 3, 1869, states that Tall Bull was not with the Southern Cheyenne, but rather came from the north. Yet the same newspaper on June 10 declares that he came from the area of the Washita (south) and did his May raids in retaliation for Custer's having the Washita captives at Fort Hays. In the *Kansas Daily Tribune*, June 10, Sheridan is said to believe Tall Bull came down from the Powder River Country, yet his report cited in the text states he escaped from Custer. The same paper reports on June 4 and again on June 17 that Tall Bull came from the north. Tall Bull, of course, is not mentioned by name. Rather, the raiding Indians are mentioned. It was not known until July 11 just who these raiding Indians were. My position is that Tall Bull indeed was with the Southern Cheyenne but came north and was joined by Whistler and Pawnee Killer from the Spotted Tail Agency in northwest Nebraska. Thus, both claims are correct, that is, Indians came from the north and Indians (Tall Bull's escaping band, and thus the Indians caught later at Summit Springs) came from the south.

[4] Sherman, W. T., "Letter to Sheridan January 18, 1869, Headquarters, Military Division of the Missouri." Part 1, E2601, Department of the Missouri, Letters Received, 1869. Record Group 393, National Archives Building, Washington, DC.

[5] *Chronological List of Actions, Ec., with Indians from January 15, 1837 to January, 1891*, Adjutant General's Office (Old Army Press, 1979), 40. See also Carr, "Report, May 22, 1869." Part 1, Entry

3731, Department of the Platte, Letters Received 1869, Record Group 393, National Archives Building, Washington, DC.

[6] Carr, E. A. "Report to General G. D. Ruggles, Camp at Fort McPherson, May 22, 1869." Part 1, Entry 3731, Department of the Platte, Letters Received 1869, 2, Record Group 393, National Archives Building, Washington, DC.

[7] Carr, "Report to Ruggles," 2-3.

[8] Carr, "Report to Ruggles," 4.

[9] *Chronological List of Actions.*

[10] Carr, "Report to Ruggles," 4.

[11] Sheridan, P. H., *Personal Memoirs of P. H. Sheridan*, Vol. II (New York, NY: Charles L. Webster & Company, 1888), 301.

[12] Carr, "Report to Ruggles."

[13] Carr, "Report to Ruggles."

[14] *The Medal of Honor of the United States Army* (Washington, DC: United States Government Printing Office, 1948), 210.

[15] Carr, letter dated February 24, 1887 to Washington Smith, Washington Smith Indian Depredation Claim #3951. Indian Depredations Claims Division, Record Group 75, National Archives Building, Washington, DC.

[16] Rister, Carl Coke, *Border Captives: The Traffic in Prisoners By Southern Plains Indians, 1835-1875* (Norman, OK: University of Oklahoma Press, 1940), 29.

[16] Rister, *Border Captives*, 31.

[18] Winsor, M. and Scarbrough, James A., *History of Jewell County, Kansas, With a Full Account of its Early Settlements, and The Indian Atrocities Committed Within its Borders* (Jewell City, KS: "Diamond" Printing Office, 1878), 12. The Indian Depredation Claims noted in the Jewell County raid reveal historical inaccuracies in this work of Winsor and Scarbrough. Tanner, for instance, accompanied the Buffalo hunters' burial detail and was not at his home when it was raided. At the Dahl house it was not Johnny Dahl who was shot and later died. Rather it was the Dahl brothers' nephew, Thomas Voarness.

[19] McAfee, J. B., "Report of the Adjutant General of the State of Kansas for the year 1868." *Reports of the Adjutant General of the State of Kansas, For the Years 1862, 1865, 1866, 1867, 1868* (Topeka, KS: W. Y. Morgan State Printer, 1902), 13.

[20] Charles N. Hogan Indian Depredation Claim #3119. Indian Depredations Claims Division, Record Group 123, National Archives Building, Washington, DC.

[21] Eliza M. Burke Indian Depredation Claim #10553. Indian Depredations Claims Division, Record Group 123, National Archives Building, Washington, DC.

[22] Peter Tanner Indian Depredation Claim #9807. Indian Depredations Claims Division, Record Group 123, National Archives Building, Washington, DC.

[23] Tanner Indian Depredation Claim.

[24] Hogan Indian Depredation Claim.

[25] Hogan Indian Depredation Claim.

[26] Maria Winklepleck Indian Depredation Claim #10100. Indian Depredations Claims Division, Record Group 123, National Archives Building, Washington, DC. Later newspaper accounts of this event note that the party of buffalo hunters had a two day running fight with the Indians before they ran out of ammunition and were overtaken and killed. This however, contradicts the affidavits in the separate depredation claims filed later. See, for example, *Emporia News*, June 11, 1869. The newspaper does report that Mr. Burke left a wife and eight children, all young daughters. Mr. Winklepleck left a wife and six children. Both women were destitute after their husbands' murders.

[27] Winklepleck Indian Depredation Claim.

[28] *Kansas Daily Tribune*, June 1, 1869.

[29] Roenigk, Adolph, *Pioneer History of Kansas* (Self-published, 1933), 171.

[30] Roenigk, *Pioneer History*, 173.

[31] Roenigk, *Pioneer History*, 173-174.

[32] Roenigk, *Pioneer History*, 175.

[33] Roenigk, *Pioneer History*, 176.

[34] *Kansas Daily Tribune*, June 1, 1869.

[35] *Leavenworth Times and Conservative*, June 4, 1869.

[36] *Leavenworth Daily Commercial*, June 4, 1869.

[37] *Junction City Weekly Union*, June 5, 1869.

[38] Roenigk, *Pioneer History*, 170.

[39] Report of Brevet Major General C.C. Augur, Omaha, October 23, 1869. Don Russell Manuscript Collection. Manuscript No 62, Series I:D, Box 5, File Folder 12, McCracken Research Library, Buffalo Bill Historical Center, Cody, WY.

[40] Napoleon B. Alley Indian Depredation Claim #3503. Indian Depredations Claims Division, Record Group 123, National Archives Building, Washington, DC. A later account says the men camped on Covert Creek, which, if correct, would put the camp somewhere between present-day Covert and Osborne, Kansas. "Jack Peate Wins Fame on the Frontier as a Scout," undated newspaper account of Jack Peate, in the possession of Loa Page, Lincoln, Kansas. Humbarger's account of this incident, in Roenigk, *Pioneer History* (222) says the raid occurred June 2, not May 29. This is in error in that it contradicts the affidavits of himself, Earle and Alley, given in their individual depredation claims made decades earlier. Obviously, years later Humbarger forgot the precise date he was severely wounded. Actually it was June 2 that he was rescued, not wounded.

[41] Napolean Alley Indian Depredation Claim.

[42] William V. F. Earle Indian Depredation Claim #840. Indian Depredations Claims Division, Record Group 123, National Archives Building, Washington, DC.

[43] Earle Indian Depredation Claim.

[44] *Kansas Daily Commonwealth*, June 20, 1869.

[45] Earle Indian Depredation Claim. Alley and Humbarger would eventually marry sisters and become brothers-in-law.

[46] Earle Indian Depredation Claim.

[47] *Beverly Tribune*, June 17, 1926. In the possession of the late Joe Greene, Beverly Kansas.

Captured!
Pages 89 - 106

[1] Rister, Carl Coke, *Border Captives: The Traffic in Prisoners by Southern Plains Indians 1835-1875* (Norman, OK: University of Oklahoma Press, 1940), 31.

[2] Homan, Dorothe, *Lincoln – That County in Kansas* (Lindsborg, KS: Bardos Printing, 1979), 62. In 1872 John Haley would become embroiled in a land dispute with a neighbor and the neighbor would kill him. Vigilantes would then kill the neighbor while he was under arrest. See Homan, 61-63.

[3] Hendrickson, C. C., "Memories," *The Lincoln-Sentinel Republican*, February 1, 1934.

[4] Bernhardt, Christian, *Indian Raids in Lincoln County, Kansas, 1864 and 1869* (Lincoln, KS: The Lincoln Sentinel Print, 1910), 35.

[5] "Indian Depredations," *41st Congress, 2nd Session, House of Representatives*, Mis. Doc. 20, #1431 (Washington, D. C., Government Printing Office, 1869), 5.

[6] Timothy Kine Indian Depredation Claim #3598. Indian Depredation Claims Division, Record Group 123, National Archives Building, Washington, DC. Bernhardt, *Indian Raids*, 30, says Tom Alderdice was in Junction City at the time of the raid. Timothy Kine notes in his depredation claim that he himself returned from the Land Office in Junction City on May 31, the same day Tom returned. Eli Zeigler recalls that Tom was in Salina during the raid (Bernhardt, *Indian Raids*, 35). The *Leavenworth Times and Conservative*, June 20, 1869, indicates Tom was returning from Salina. The question whether Tom was in Junction City or Salina during the raid can be settled by placing him with Timothy Kine in Junction City but at Salina just before their return at the time of the raid. They were probably picking up supplies to bring home. That Timothy Kine makes a sworn affidavit that he was returning from Junction City, and since Tom and Timothy returned at the same time, would indicate they traveled together. This especially makes sense when it is also noted that their wives were staying together at the Haley house. I would like the reader to here allow me to interject a personal note. In January 1967, when I was fourteen, I was sent from my home in Littleton, Colorado, to St. John's Military School in Salina, Kansas. I graduated from St. John's in 1971. I have remained

an active alumnus with St. John's since my graduation. In October 2002, I gave a talk to the cadets at St. John's about the Spillman Creek raid and the research I was doing for *Dog Soldier Justice*. The faculty member who picked me up at the airport that lonely and cold Sunday night when I first arrived at St. John's in 1967 later became my teacher in history. Major Virgil Loy, now retired, had come back to St. John's to hear my talk. Afterward, I learned that his great-grandfather was the same Michael Haley, in whose house Susanna was staying at when captured by the Indians. He told me that he grew up as a little boy hearing the many stories of his family's involvement in the Indian raids of Lincoln County. He also has vivid memories of Jack Peate sharing thrilling stories to Virgil when he was a young boy living in Beverly. Little could we know that years after introducing me to American history, I would be writing this book, which involves his family. And while I was a cadet at St. John's, on warm spring weekends I used to walk along the creeks that are on the south end of Elm Creek Township, visualizing myself hiding from Indians in the 1860s. Elm Creek Township was where Susanna and James Daily first homesteaded, and where her first two sons were born.

[7] Bernhardt, *Indian Raids*, 31.

[8] Bernhardt, *Indian Raids*, 35. Eli recalls that his dinner was at Susanna's home, but this is a mistake. He wrote his account almost forty years after the events in question, and thus had forgotten this minor detail. Nicholas Whalen makes an affidavit in Eli Zeigler's depredation claim, and notes that he saw Eli and John when they started to the claim up Spillman Creek. As he was also staying at the Haley house, it certainly makes more sense to believe Susanna's lunch with her brother was not at her home but rather at the Haley home, where she was staying at the time. Eli Zeigler Indian Depredation Claim #3796, Indian Depredations Claims Division, Record Group 75, National Archives Building, Washington, DC.

[9] Bernhardt, *Indian Raids*, 35.

[10] Bernhardt, *Indian Raids*, 36.

[11] Bernhardt, *Indian Raids*, 36-37.

[12] Eli Zeigler Indian Depredation Claim.

[13] *Leavenworth Times and Conservative*, June 3, 1869. This statement is not entirely true, as will be seen as a fuller account of the

Spillman Creek raid is developed in this chapter. Nevertheless, this statement is in principle true, and is generally true of the type of warfare that accompanies Indian raids into settlements. First, there is not the time available during a raid to engage in a shot-for-shot battle, as the purpose of the raid is to strike quick and then leave. Second, the loss of a single Indian warrior in battle was a hardship unlike the loss of the Indian's white enemy. If a soldier is killed, another man is available to enlist. If a settler is killed, another pioneer is available to settle the home. If a warrior is killed, a tribe must await the time it takes for a young Indian boy to mature into a warrior. The Indians could not afford to engage in shot-for-shot battles. Still, such tactics as employed by the Indians during a raid upon a settlement were cold, cruel and heinous, which, of course, is what often happens in active warfare.

[14] It is also possible that their son was already playing at the Christensen home and his parents were on their way to retrieve him when they were surprised and killed. If this story is true then the Lauritzen boy was not with his parents when discovered by the Indians.

[15] Sorensen, Ruth, *Beyond the Prairie Wind: History, Folklore and Traditions From Denmark, Kansas* (Hillsboro, KS: Partnership Book Services, 1998), 11.

[16] Barr, Elizabeth, *A Souvenir History of Lincoln County, Kansas* (privately printed, 1908), 39; Carr, E. A., "Republican River Expedition Report." Part 1, Department of the Platte, Letters received, 1869, Record Group 393, National Archives Building, Washington, DC. Bernhardt is explicit in noting that they were not from Germany but rather were from Switzerland (*Indian Raids*, 27 & 45). However, Ray Sparks, a descendant of Lincoln County, Kansas pioneers, who spent more than forty years of his life researching this history, noted in private correspondence that Bernhardt was wrong, and that the records in Junction City, Kansas, which Bernhardt allegedly consulted, clearly state that the Weichels came from Hanover.

[17] Roenigk, Adolph, *Pioneer History of Kansas* (Self-published, 1933), 113; Carr, E. A., Letter to William F. Cody, July 2, 1906, Box 3, E. A. Carr Papers, U.S. Army Military History Institute, Carlisle Barracks, PA; Hercules Price Letter, Kansas State Historical Society, Topeka, Kansas.

18 Roenigk, *Pioneer History*, 113.

19 Roenigk, *Pioneer History*.

20 Bernhardt, *Indian Raids*, 45.

21 Bernhardt, *Indian Raids*, 40. This comes from Eli Zeigler's account of the raid. Bernhardt believed Otto Peterson was found on the same side of Spillman Creek as the Lauritzens, 28. I accept Zeigler's account on the basis that Peterson was not found when the Lauritzens were found, plus the fact that the Lauritzen cabin was on the west side of Spillman Creek and the cabin was not raided by the Indians. Peterson thus had to be some distance from the cabin when he was overcome and killed by the Indians.

22 *Kansas Weekly Tribune*, June 10, 1869.

23 Bernhardt, *Indian Raids*, 34.

24 Bernhardt, *Indian Raids*, 29.

25 Carr, letter to Cody.

26 Timothy Kine Indian Depredation Claim.

27 Timothy Kine Indian Depredation Claim.

28 Bridget Kyne obituary, *Lincoln Republican Sentinel*, May 23, 1913. It should be noted that the Indian depredation claim of Timothy Kine spells his last name "Kine" and not "Kyne." Timothy there signs his name "Kine." Bridget cannot spell and an "x" marks her signature. Apparently, as they lived in Lincoln County, they came to later spell their name "Kyne." The 1906 court matter (see endnote 39) regarding Bridget's insanity has her name spelled "Kyne." I have chosen the name "Kine" as apparently that was the way it was spelled in 1869.

29 Barr, *Souvenir History*, 38-39.

30 Kyne Obituary.

31 Kyne Obituary. Roenigk, *Pioneer History*, 213. Barr, *Souvenir History,* 38-39, says that Bridget crossed the river. Bernhardt, *Indian Raids,* 31, says she escaped to the river. I follow the Roenigk claim that she hid in the river, which is consistent to what is said in Bridget's obituary.

32 Petree, Frank, "Correction to 'Square' Scout With Comrades –

Last of the Indian Raids in Kansas," undated newspaper article from the J. J. Peate Scrapbook, in the possession of Loa Page, Lincoln, Kansas.

33 Barr, *Souvenir History,* 39.

34 McMullen, Thelma, "Hats Off to the Builders of Lincoln County," *The Lincoln Sentinel Republican,* November 16, 1939. If this account is accurate, it indicates, perhaps, that some white men were among the Dog Soldiers. It would be a mistake to use this claim as evidence that Indians were not the perpetrators of this devastating raid.

35 McMullen, "Hats Off."

36 Bernhardt, *Indian Raids,* 31.

37 Roenigk, *Pioneer History,* 213. For Roenigk to have known this regarding Susanna's capture is only possible if this is what Bridget had seen and later reported. Barr, *Souvenir History* (39), says Susanna was "overcome with terror, sat down on the ground, as she could not escape with her children." Other accounts have Susanna asking for Bridget's help, with Bridget responding that she could only save herself. See Smith, Washington, *Saline Valley Register,* July 5, 1876, and *The Lincoln Republican,* February 3, 1886. This account has been reprinted in Weingardt, Richard, *Sound the Charge, The Western Frontier: Spillman Creek to Summit Springs* (Englewood, CO: Ajacqueline Enterprises, Inc., 1978), 126.

38 Bernhardt, *Indian Raids,* 31.

39 "Report of Commission and Judgment in the Probate Court of Lincoln County, Kansas," February 23, 1906, 104. A. Artman, Probate Judge. Copy in the personal papers of Craig Walker, Lincoln, Kansas.

40 "Report of Commission and Judgment," 106.

41 *Lincoln Sentinel,* April 24, 1913.

42 *Republican Daily Journal,* June 4, 1869.

43 *Emporia News,* June 11, 1869.

44 *Leavenworth Times and Conservative,* June 30, 1869.

45 Barr, *Souvenir History,* 39.

46 Barr, *Souvenir History.*

[47] 1870 Mortality Schedule of Kansas notes that Schmutz died August 12, 1869. Denver Public Library, Western History Collections, Denver, Colorado.

[48] 1870 Mortality Schedule. Coincidentally, Arthur was taken to the same hospital (Fort Harker) that Adolph Roenigk, author of *Pioneer History of Kansas*, was recovering from his wounds suffered at Fossil Creek two days earlier.

[49] Smith, "Historical Sketch."

[50] *Leavenworth Times and Conservative*, June 20, 1869.

[51] Hendrickson, C. C., "Memories," *The Lincoln-Sentinel Republican*, February 1 & 8, 1934.

[52] *Manhattan Standard*, June 12, 1869.

[53] *Kansas Weekly Tribune*, June 24, 1869.

[54] Bernhardt, *Indian Raids*, 31.

[55] Bernhardt, *Indian Raids*, 39-40.

[56] Peate, J. J., "Historical Sketches, From the Scrapbook of J. J. Peate," undated newspaper account in the possession of Loa Page, Lincoln, Kansas.

[57] Homan, *Lincoln*, 47-48.

[58] *Leavenworth Times and Conservative*, June 1, 1869. This story was repeated in the *Kansas Daily Tribune*, June 2 & 3, 1869.

[59] *Junction City Weekly Union*, June 5, 1869.

[60] *New York Times*, June 2, 1869, 5.

[61] Schofield, General John, "Letter to General Sheridan, June 5, 1869." Records of the U.S. Army Continental Command, Headquarters Records, Department of the Missouri, Letters Sent, Entry 2575, Record Group 393, National Archives Building, Washington, DC.

[62] March, Thomas Jefferson, "Letter to Lt. Edward Law." Letters Received, Department of the Missouri, 1869, Entry 2601, Record Group 393, National Archives Building, Washington, DC.

[63] Jacob Shafer Indian Depredation Claim #3715. Indian Depredation Claims Division, Record Group 123, National Archives Building, Washington, DC.

[64] Timothy Kine Indian Depredation Claim.

[65] Timothy Kine Indian Depredation Claim.

Aftermath of May 30 Raid
Pages 107 - 126

[1] McCarter, Margaret Hill, *The Price of the Prairie: A Story of Kansas* (Chicago: A. C. McClurg, 1910).

[2] Roenigk, Adolph, *Pioneer History of Kansas* (self-published, 1933), 94.

[3] Bridget Kyne Obituary, *Lincoln Sentinel*, May 23, 1913.

[4] Hendrickson, C. C., "Memories," *The Lincoln-Sentinel Republican*, February 15, 1934.

[5] Vincenta Ivy Indian Depredation Claim #3589fi. Indian Depredations Claims Division, Record Group 75, National Archives Building, Washington, DC.

[6] *Junction City Weekly Union*, July 10, 1869.

[7] *Leavenworth Times and Conservative*, July 3, 1869

[8] *Junction City Weekly Union*, February 19, 1870.

[9] Law, Lt. Edward, "Letter Written From the Schermerhorn Ranche, May 31, 1869." Letters Received, Department of the Missouri, Part 1, Entry 2601, 1869, Record Group 393, National Archives Building, Washington, DC.

[10] Conversation with Bernice Graepler, whose grandfather survived the May 30 raid, November 19, 2000.

[11] Law, Lt. Edward, 2nd letter dated May 30. Letters Received, Department of the Missouri, Part 1, 1869, Record Group 393, National Archives Building, Washington, DC.

[12] Law, Lt. Edward, "Letter from Camp at Mouth of Asher Creek and Solomon River, June 2, 1869." Letters Received, Department of the Missouri, Part 1, 1869, Record Group 393, National Archives Building, Washington, DC.

[13] Law, "Letter June 2."

[14] Robert Watson Indian Depredation Claim #3787. Indian Depredations Claims Division, Record Group 75, National Archives Building, Washington, DC.

[15] *Kansas Daily Tribune*, June 13, 1869.

[16] Hollibaugh, Mrs. E. F., *Biographical History of Cloud County, Kansas* (Indiana: Wilson, Humphrey and Company, 1903), 53.

[17] Hollibaugh, *Biographical History*, 54.

[18] Hollibaugh, *Biographical History*.

[19] Adolph Schultz Indian Depredation Claim #3699. Indian Depredations Claims Division, Record Group 123, National Archives Building, Washington, DC.

[20] James McHenry Indian Depredation Claim #7219. Indian Depredations Claims Division, Record Group 123, National Archives Building, Washington, DC.

[21] Law, Lt. Edward, "Letter from Mouth of Asher Creek and Solomon River, June 10, 1869." Letters Received, Department of the Missouri, Part 1, 1869, Record Group 393, National Archives Building, Washington, DC.

[22] Law, Lt. Edward, "Letter from Camp at Mouth of Asher Creek and Solomon River, June 11, 1869." Letters Received, Department of the Missouri, Part 1, 1869, Record Group 393, National Archives Building, Washington, DC.

[23] August Ernest Indian Depredation Claim #841. Indian Depredations Claims Division, Record Group 123, National Archives Building, Washington, DC.

[24] Nancy Hewitt Indian Depredation Claim #333. Indian Depredations Claims Division, Record Group 123, National Archives Building, Washington, DC.

[25] Law, Lt. Edward, "Letter from Mouth of Asher Creek and Solomon River, June 12, 1869." Letters Received, Department of the Missouri, Part 1, 1869, Record Group 393, National Archives Building, Washington, DC.

[26] *Junction City Weekly Union*, January 15, 1870.

[27] Alderdice, Tom, "Letter dated June 21, 1869." Part 1, E2601,

Department of Missouri, Letters Received, 1869, Record Group 393, National Archives Building, Washington, DC.

[28] *Leavenworth Daily Commercial*, June 24, 1869; *Leavenworth Times and Conservative*, June 24, 1869.

[29] *Leavenworth Daily Commercial*, June 20, 1869, emphasis added.

[30] Custer, Elizabeth Bacon, *Following the Guidon* (New York, NY: Harper and Brothers, 1890), 224-225. Custer detractors might be tempted to use this passage by Libbie as an instance of Custer's cruelty in having his wife listen to a story that he knew would upset her. But such interpretations ignore the training Custer received at West Point, where a major exam was given in moral philosophy prior to the last year of study. Custer well knew the teachings of Aristotle. Aristotle's position was that people acquire the virtue of sympathy by being exposed to situations where sympathy can be developed in one's character. Thus it was important for one's moral training to be exposed to situations that foster virtues. Custer's desire to have his wife listen to Tom's story was more likely the result of his training at West Point and had nothing to do with a desire to cause stress in his wife.

[31] *Leavenworth Times and Conservative*, June 20, 1869. See also *New York Times*, June 26, 1869.

[32] Alderdice, "Letter."

[33] *Atchison Daily Champion*, June 12, 1869.

[34] Endorsement Book, Department of the Missouri, Part 1, Entry 2586, Vol. 2 of 44, A 364, Vol. 1, 1869, Record Group 393, National Archives Building, Washington, DC.

[35] Endorsement Book.

[36] Carr, E. A., "Letter to Bill Cody, July 2, 1906, New York City." Box 3, E. A. Carr Papers, U.S. Army Military History Institute, Carlisle Barracks, PA. See also Carr, "Reminiscences of Indian Wars," Carlisle Barracks, 25.

[37] Carr, E. A., "Republican River Expedition Report, July 20, 1869." Record Group 94, National Archives Building, Washington, DC.

[38] Barr, *Souvenir History*, 39.

[39] Roenigk, *Pioneer History*, 212.

[40] Bernhardt, *Indian Raids*, 30.

[41] *Lincoln Republican Sentinel*, May 25, 1911. See also Roenigk, *Pioneer History*, 127.

Dog Soldier Captivity
Pages 127 -146

[1] Barnett, Louise, *Touched by Fire: The Life, Death, and Mythic Afterlife of George Armstrong Custer* (New York, NY: Henry Holt and Company, 1996), 171.

[2] Bradley, Lieutenant James H., *The March of the Montana Column: A Prelude to the Custer Disaster*, Ed. by Edgar I. Stewart (Norman, OK: University of Oklahoma Press, 1961), 113.

[3] Bridget Kyne Obituary, *Lincoln Sentinel Republican*, May 23, 1913.

[4] Hoebel, E. Adamson, *The Cheyennes: Indians of the Great Plains* (New York, NY: Holt, Rinehart and Winston, 1960), 95. See also with Llewellyn, Karl N., *The Cheyenne Way: Conflict and Case Law in Primitive Jurisprudence* (Norman, OK: University of Oklahoma Press, 1941), 202.

[5] Barnett, *Touched by Fire,* 172.

[6] Dodge, Col. Richard Irving *The Plains of the Great West and Their Inhabitants* (New York, NY: The Archer House, Inc., 1959), 395-396. First published in 1877.

[7] Derounian-Stodola, Katheryn, and Levernier, James, *The Indian Captivity Narrative, 1550-1900* (New York, NY: Twayne Publishers, 1993), 2-8.

[8] Dodge, Col. Richard Irving, *Our Wild Indians: Thirty-Three Years' Personal Experience Among the Red Men of the Great West* (New York, NY: Archer House, Inc., 1959), 530. Originally published in 1890.

[9] Rister, Carl Coke, *Border Captives: The Traffic in Prisoners by Southern Plains Indians, 1835-1875* (Norman, OK: University of Oklahoma Press, 1940), viii.

[10] Dodge, *Our Wild Indians*, 530.

[11] Examples of such accounts would include Kelly, Fanny, *Narrative of My Captivity Among the Sioux Indians* (Chicago, IL: R. R. Donnelley & Sons Company, ed. Clark and Mary Lee Spence, 1990), and Wakefield, Sarah F., *Six Weeks in the Sioux Tepees: A Narrative of Indian Captivity*, ed. June Namias (Norman, OK: University of Oklahoma Press, 1997). For a scholarly study of the entire history of white captivity among Indians, see Namias, June, *White Captives: Gender and Ethnicity on the American Frontier* (Chapel Hill and London: University of North Carolina Press 1993). Unfortunately, this study ignores the captivity of Susanna Alderdice. The picture developed in *White Captives* is a study that is a macrocosmic focus. The intent of the study in this chapter is a microcosmic focus. Thus, Namias's conclusions do not help understanding the experiences of Susanna and Maria.

[12] Peter Ulbrich Indian Depredation Claim #6220. Indian Depredations Claims Division, Record Group 123, National Archives Building, Washington, DC.

[13] Nancy Jane Morton Indian Depredation Claims #1642, 1892, 1194. Indian Depredation Claims Division, Record Group 75, National Archives Building, Washington, DC. See also Washburn, Wilcomb E., "Introduction," in Vaughan, Alden T., *Narratives of North American Indian Captivity: A Selective Bibliography* (New York and London: Garland Publishing Company, 1983), xlv.

[14] Nancy Morton Indian Depredation Claim.

[15] Trapp, Dan L., *Encyclopedia of Frontier Biography*, Vol. III (Glendale, CA: The Arthur H. Clark Company, 1988), 1239.

[16] Nancy Morton Indian Depredation Claim.

[17] Nancy Morton Indian Depredation Claim.

[18] Nancy Morton Indian Depredation Claim.

[19] Nancy Morton Indian Depredation Claim.

[20] Czaplewski, Russ,, *Captive of the Cheyenne: The Story of Nancy Jane Morton and the Plum Creek Massacre* (Kearney, NE: Morris Publishing), 1993.

[21] Czaplewski, *Captive*, Section One, 69.

22 Czaplewski, *Captive*, Section One, 70.

23 Czaplewski, *Captive*, Section Two, 16.

24 Czaplewski, *Captive*, Section One, 70.

25 Czaplewski, *Captive*, Section Two, 17.

26 Czaplewski, *Captive*, Section One, 71.

27 Meredith, Grace E., *Girl Captives of the Cheyennes: A True Story of the Capture and Rescue of Four Pioneer Girls 1874* (Los Angeles, CA: Gem Publishing Company, 1927), 31.

28 Dodge, *Plains of the Great West*, LI. A descendant of twelve-year-old Sophie German has written an excellent account of the captivity of the German sisters. See Jauken, Arlene Feldman, *The Moccasin Speaks: Living as Captives of Dog Soldier Warriors* (Lincoln, NE: Dageforde Publishing, Inc.), 1998.

29 Jauken, *The Moccasin Speaks*, 96.

30 Rister, *Border Captives*, 34.

31 *Nebraska Advertiser*, Brownville, Nebraska, August 1, 1867.

32 *Nebraska City News*, August 10, 1867. The paper did go on to state that the Danish girl "was pretty much stupid and speechless and little could be gained from her about anything," as if to imply her condition was a result of her stupidity and not her captivity. To the contrary, Veronica, as shown in her affidavit in her father's Indian depredation claim, was quite bright and intelligent, as are all descendants of the Ulbrich family today.

33 *Nebraska City News*, August 10, 1867.

34 The testimony in the depredation claim does not state that there were three other Ulbrich children safely in the house during the raid. Anna Ulbrich was eleven, Bernard was three and William was an infant about one. Bernard grew up to be a Catholic priest in Nebraska, dying in 1940 after serving the priesthood faithfully for several decades. See Ulbrick Obituary in *The Lincoln Star*, November 29, 1940. Veronica also lived until 1940. See Ulbrich Obituary in the *Talmage* [Nebraska] *Tribune*, May 2, 1940. She never remarried or had any children. Her captivity affected her the rest of her life. The family later changed the spelling of Ulbrich to Ulbrick.

35 Peter Kalus and Joseph Piexa were killed by the same Indians the day before the Ulbrich depredation. Peter left a wife and four small children. Peter Kalus was Veronica's uncle. See Margaretha Kalus Indian Depredation Claim #454, Indian Depredations Claims Division, Record Group 123, National Archives Building, Washington, DC.

36 Peter Ulbrich Indian Depredation Claim.

37 Campbell, John R., "An Indian Raid of 1867," *Collections of the Nebraska State Historical Society*, ed. by Albert Watkins, Volume XVII (Lincoln, NE: The Nebraska State Historical Society, 1913), 260.

38 Danker, Donald F., ed., *Man of the Plains: Recollections of Luther North, 1856-1882* (Lincoln, NE: University of Nebraska Press, 1961), 59.

39 Peter Ulbrich Indian Depredation Claim. The Nebraska Census for 1890 shows Mr. Megnin living alone as a single man. Perhaps he had learned of the truth regarding his wife's captivity shortly after the filing of the Indian depredation claim. On April 23, 1892 Alfred remarried a woman with his same last name, Sophronia E. Megnin. See Marriage Records, Nebraska State Historical Society, Lincoln, Nebraska.

40 Peter Ulbrich Indian Depredation Claim.

41 *Omaha Daily Herald*, September 21, 1867.

42 Powell, Father Peter John, *People of the Sacred Mountain: A History of the Northern Cheyenne Chiefs and Warrior Societies 1830-1879 With an Epilogue 1969-1974*, Volume II (San Francisco, CA: Harper & Row, Publishers, 1981), 717.

43 Stratton, Joanna L., *Pioneer Women: Voices From the Kansas Frontier* (New York, NY: Simon and Schuster, 1981), 123-125.

44 Stratton, *Pioneer Women*, 25.

45 Harrison, Emily Haines, "Reminiscences of Early days in Ottawa County," *Kansas Historical Collections, Vol. X, 1907-1908*, 627-628, emphasis added.

46 Custer, Elizabeth B., *Following the Guidon* (New York, NY: Harper & Brothers, 1890), 60-61.

[47] Custer, *Following the Guidon*, 62.

[48] Custer, Gen. G. A., *My Life on the Plains, or, Personal Experiences With Indians* (New York, NY: Sheldon and Company, 1874), 252.

[49] White, Lonnie J., "White Women Captive of the Southern Plains Indians, 1866-1875," *Journal of the West* (Vol. III, No. 3, July 1969), 351.

[50] Morgan Letter to Mrs. Louis Davenport Lincoln, June 9 and 27, 1893. Manuscript Collections, Misc. Moo-Mow, Morgan Folder, 3, emphasis added. Kansas State Historical Society, Topeka, Kansas.

[51] Morgan Letter, 4.

[52] *Delphos Republican*, July 18, 1902.

[53] Morgan Letter.

[54] Morgan Letter.

[55] Sidney Clarke Collection, Box 4, Folder 10, Carl Albert Congressional Research and Studies Center Congressional Archives, University of Oklahoma, Monnett Hall, Norman, Oklahoma, emphasis added.

[56] Rister, *Border Captives*, 65.

[57] Zimmer, William F., *Frontier Soldier: An Enlisted Man's Journal of the Sioux and Nes Perce Campaigns, 1877*, ed. Jerome A. Greene (Helena, MT: Montana Historical Society Press, 1998), 53.

[58] Morgan letter, 2.

Republican River Expedition
Pages 147 - 162

[1] Carr, Eugene A., "Letter to Washington Smith, February 24, 1887." Washington Smith Indian Depredation Claim #3951. Indian Depredations Claims Division, Record Group 75, National Archives Building, Washington, DC., 5.

[2] Carr, "Letter to Smith," 4.

[3] Carr, Eugene A., "Reminiscences of Indian Wars," Box 3, Indian Wars 1868-1892. Eugene A. Carr Papers, United States Army Military History Institute, Carlisle Barracks, PA. This account was earlier used in Buffalo Bill's program for his famous Wild West shows, when the Summit Springs battle was depicted. See, for example, Buffalo Bill's Wild West program booklet for 1884.

[4] Carr, "Reminiscences."

[5] Carr, Eugene A., "Report to General Ruggles from Camp on Medicine Lake Creek, June 11, 1869." Part 1, Entry 3731, Department of the Platte, Letters Received, 1869, Record Group 393, National Archives Building, Washington, DC.

[6] Company F Muster Roll, 5th Regiment of U. S. Cavalry. Record Group 94, 1869, National Archives Building, Washington, DC.

[7] Muster Rolls for 5th Regiment of U. S. Cavalry.

[8] Volkmar, Lieutenant William J., "Journal of the March of the Republican River Expedition." Department of the Platte, Letters Received, 1869, Record Group 393, National Archives Building, Washington, DC.

[9] Volkmar, "Journal Entry for June 12 and 13."

[10] Carr, Eugene A., "Republican River Expedition, Letter to General G. D. Ruggles, June 17, 1869." Part 1, Entry 3731, Department of the Platte, Letters Received, 1869, Record Group 393, National Archives Building, Washington, DC.

[11] Volkmar, "Journal Entry for June 15."

[12] Volkmar, "Journal Entry for June 15."

[13] Carr, "Letter to Ruggles, June 17."

[14] Volkmar, Journal Entry for June 16." Carr, Letter to General Ruggles, June 17."

[15] Carr, "Letter to Ruggles, June 17."

[16] Volkmar, "Journal Entry for June 21."

[17] Volkmar, "Journal Entry for June 25."

[18] Volkmar, "Journal Entry for June 26."

[19] Volkmar, "Journal Entry for June 26."

[20] Carr, Eugene A., "Letter to General Ruggles from Camp on Buffalo Head Creek, June 30, 1869." Part 1, Entry 3731, Department of the Platte, Letters received, 1869, Record Group 393, National Archives Building, Washington, DC.

[21] Carr, "Reminiscences," 15-16.

[22] Carr, "Letter to Ruggles, June 30."

[23] Volkmar, "Journal Entry for June 28."

[24] Carr, "Reminiscences," 15.

[25] Carr, "Letter to Ruggles, June 30."

[26] Price, George F., *Across the Continent With The Fifth Cavalry* (New York, NY: Antiquarian Press LTD, 1959, originally published in 1883), 136.

[27] Cody, William F., *The Life of Honorable William F. Cody Known as Buffalo Bill* (New York, NY: Indian Head Books, 1991. Originally published in 1879), 255. See also Wetmore, Helen Cody and Grey, Zane, *Last of the Great Scouts (Buffalo Bill)* (New York, NY: Grosset & Dunlap, 1918. Originally published in 1899), 183.

[28] Walsh, Richard J., *The Making of Buffalo Bill: A Study in Heroics* (Indianapolis, IN: The Bobbs-Merrill Company, 1928), 147.

[29] Russell, Don, *The Lives and Legends of Buffalo Bill* (Norman, OK: University of Oklahoma Press, 1960), 132.

[30] Nye, Wilbur, *Plains Indian Raiders* (Norman, OK: University of Oklahoma Press, 1968), 147. Nye is disappointing in that he credits George Price as his source for this claim. But Price makes no mention of footprints or Pawnees finding them, as is obvious in looking at his claim in the text of this chapter. But the usually reli-

able University of Oklahoma Press published Nye's book, and thus readers might not question his false claim.

[31] Price, Hercules, "Letter to Ferdinand Erhardt, January 19, 1908." Price Letters, Kansas State Historical Society, Topeka, Kansas.

[32] Box 3 of the Carr Papers at the United States Army Military History Institute in Carlisle Pennsylvania has a telegraphed copy of Tom's letter. Perhaps this is the very copy received by Carr during the Republican River Expedition.

[33] Volkmar, "Journal Entry for June 30."

[34] Volkmar, "Journal Entry for June 29-July 3."

[35] Carr, "Reminiscences," 16.

[36] Carr, "Reminiscences," 17.

[37] Volkmar, "Journal Entry for July 4."

[38] Carr, "Reminiscences," 17.

[39] Volkmar, "Journal Entry for July 7."

[40] Volkmar, "Journal Entry for July 5-8."

[41] Townsend, E. D., "Letter to Major General C. C. Augur, August 24, 1869." Adjutant General's Office, Washington, DC, Part 1, Entry 3731, Department of the Platte, Letters Received, 1869, Record Group 393, National Archives Building, Washington, DC.

[42] Townsend, "Letter to Augur, August 24."

[43] Danker, Donald F., ed., *Man of the Plains: Recollections of Luther North, 1856-1882* (Lincoln, NE: University of Nebraska Press, 1961), 125.

[44] King, James T., "The Republican River Expedition, June-July, 1869." *The Nebraska Indian Wars Reader 1865-1877*, ed. R. Eli Paul (Lincoln and London: University of Nebraska Press, 1998), 69.

[45] Riley, Paul D., "The Battle of Massacre Canyon," *Nebraska Indian Wars Reader*, 102.

[46] Danker, *Man of the Plains*, 119-120.

[47] Part 1, Entry 3731, Letters Received, 1869, Department of the Platte, Record Group 393, National Archives Building, Washington, DC.

48 Carr, Eugene A., "Letter to General Ruggles, from Headquarters Camp near Fort Sedgwick, July 20, 1869." Republican River Expedition, Part 1, Entry 3731, Department of the Platte, Letters Received, 1869, Record Group 393, National Archives Building, Washington, DC.

49 Carr, "Reminiscences," 19, emphasis added.

50 Muster Roll, Company M, 5th Regiment of Cavalry, June 30, 1869. Record Group 94, National Archives Building, Washington, DC. The Muster Roll lists Kile's name as "Kile," not "Kyle," as is recorded in Carr's report and in his recommendation for the Medal of Honor. I chose to accept the spelling as it appears in the muster roll of the 5th Cavalry.

51 Muster Roll, Company M, 5th Regiment of Cavalry, August 31, 1869. Record Group 94, National Archives Building, Washington, DC.

52 Ryan, John, *Ten Years With Custer: A 7th Cavalryman's Memoirs*, ed. Sandy Barnard (Terre Haute, IN: AST Press, 2001), 122.

53 Ryan, *Ten Years*, 123.

54 Volkmar, "Journal Entry for July 9," emphasis added.

55 Volkmar, "Journal Entry for July 10."

56 Volkmar, "Journal Entry for July 10."

57 Danker, *Man of the Plains*, 302.

58 Carr, "Reminiscences," 20.

59 Volkmar, "Journal Entry for July 8."

60 Volkmar, "Journal Entry for July 10."

61 Price, *Across the Continent*, 137.

62 Volkmar, "Journal Entry for July 11."

63 Carr, "Letter to Ruggles, July 20."

64 Price, *Across the Continent*, 137.

65 Volkmar, "Journal Entry for July 11." Carr, "Letter to Ruggles, July 20." In Carr's report, written eleven days after the fight at Summit Springs, he claims that he only took 244 men and one company of Pawnee scouts when he left camp on the morning of July 11, leaving the rest with fagged horses to accompany the wagon

train. If this were the case, however, when he divided his command at eleven-thirty he would have only had one hundred twenty-one men and twenty-five Pawnee scouts for his command. This is obviously an error. Lt. Volkmar notes in his journal for July 11 that a guard was left to accompany the fifty plus wagons as the command left with their five days of rations. A guard is much smaller than the approximately 175 men that would have been left if Carr's report is calculated against the approximate total number of men accompanying his expedition. The 5th Cavalry muster rolls for the companies involved in the Republican River Expedition reveal an average number of men per company of forty-six. That amount added to the 150 Pawnee scouts makes an aggregate command for Carr of about 465 men, not counting teamsters, etc., which probably fills out his total command at around 500 men. It seems highly unlikely that roughly half of these men would have been left with the wagon train on the morning of July 11. If Carr meant by his 244 soldiers and 50 Pawnees the men left with him after he divided his command on the way to Summit Springs, then Royall's command did not have quite half the command, and Carr had more. I interpret it this way. Thus, when the command rejoins just before the charge at Summit Springs, Carr had with him all of his command with the exception of the detail that remained with the wagons. I would estimate that about fifty soldiers plus teamsters remained back with the wagons. Everybody else participated in the Summit Springs fight.

The Battle of Susanna Springs (Summit Springs)
Pages 163 - 186

[1] Record of Events, Muster Roll, Company M, 5th U.S. Cavalry, July/August 1869. Record Group 94, National Archive Building, Washington, DC. The fight at Summit Springs was initially called by General E. A. Carr "Susanna Springs," as noted by several 5th Cavalry Muster Rolls. Carr later changed the name to "Summit Springs," when he learned the springs already had that name. The battle site also has been called "Battle Springs." I have chosen to refer to the fight only in this chapter as "Susanna Springs."

[2] Volkmar, Lieutenant William J., Journal of the March of the Republican River Expedition, Journal Entry for July 11, 1869. Department of the Platte, Letters Received, 1869, Record Group 393, National Archives Building, Washington, DC.

[3] Price, George F., *Across the Continent With The Fifth Cavalry*, (New York, NY: The Antiquarian Press, 1959. Originally published in 1883), 138.

[4] Carr, General Eugene A., "Republican River Expedition, Letter to General G. D. Ruggles, July 20, 1869." Department of the Platte, Letters Received, Part 1, Entry 3731, Record Group 393, National Archives Building, Washington, DC.

[5] *New York Herald*, July 26, 1869, 7. This copies an earlier publication in the *Winona Republican* (Minnesota), July 23, 1869.

[6] Volkmar, "Journal Entry for July 11;" Price, *Across the Continent*, 138; Carr, "Letter to Ruggles, July 20;" Carr, Eugene A., "Reminiscences of Indian Wars," Box 3, Indian Wars 1868-1892, 22. Eugene A. Carr papers, United States Army Military History Institute, Carlisle Barracks, PA; Muster Rolls, 5th Cavalry, August, 1869.

[7] Volkmar, "Journal Entry for July 11."

[8] Price, *Across the Continent*, 138-139. An unidentified 5th Cavalry officer wrote a detailed account of Carr's expedition and fight at Summit Springs for the *New York Times*. He reported the wind blowing from the south. *New York Times*, July 26, 1869.

[9] Carr, "Reminiscences," 22.

[10] Price, *Across the Continent*, 138.

[11] Danker, Donald F., ed., *Man of the Plains: Recollections of Luther North, 1856-1882*, (Lincoln, NE: University of Nebraska Press, 1961), 115.

[12] Price, *Across the Continent*, 139.

[13] Walker, Lieutenant Leicester, "Remarks," Muster Roll, Company H, 5th U. S. Cavalry, August 31, 1869. Record Group 94, National Archives Building, Washington, DC.

[14] *New York Times*, July 26, 1869.

[15] Carr, "Letter to Ruggles, July 20."

[16] Carr, "Letter to Ruggles, July 20."

[17] Carr, "Letter to Ruggles, July 20;" Volkmar, "Journal Entry for July 11."

18 Carr, "Letter to Ruggles, July 20."

19 Carr, Letter to Washington Smith, March 17, 1887, Washington Smith Indian Depredation Claim #3955. Indian Depredations Claims Division, Record Group 75, National Archives Building, Washington, DC.

20 Volkmar, "Journal Entry for July 11."

21 Russell, Don, *The Lives and Legends of Buffalo Bill* (Norman, OK: University of Oklahoma Press, 1960), 130-148.

22 Russell, *Lives and Legends*, 130. Russell notes nine different accounts, but since then another account has been published in *Camp on Custer: Transcribing the Custer Myth*, ed., Liddic, Bruce and Harbaugh, Paul (Spokane, WA: The Arthur H. Clark Company, 1995), 173.

23 Russell, *Lives and Legends*, 130.

24 Liddic and Harbaugh, *Camp on Custer*, 173. See also Danker, *Man of the Plains*, 117; Grinnell, George Bird, *Two Great Scouts and Their Pawnee Battalion* (Lincoln, NE: University of Nebraska Press, 1973), 198-199.

25 Brady, Cyrus Townsend, *Indian Fights and Fighters* (New York, NY: McClure, Phillips & Co., 1904), 177.

26 Carr, "Reminiscences," 28.

27 Brady, *Indian Fights and Fighters*, 177; Carr, "Letter to Ruggles, July 20."

28 Carr, "Reminiscences," 27.

29 Volkmar, "Journal Entry for July 11."

30 Carr, "Letter to Cody, July 2, 1906," Eugene A. Carr Papers, Box 3, United States Military History Institute, Carlisle Barracks, Carlisle, PA, italics added.

31 Carr's account of the Summit Springs fight as published in the 1907 pamphlet for Buffalo Bill's Wild West Show. Ironically, Carr's account is dated December 29, 1906, the same year he had earlier written to Cody and credited the Pawnees with killing Tall Bull. McCracken Research Library, Buffalo Bill Historical Center, Cody, WY.

32 Research Archives, Overland Trails Museum, Sterling, CO. Don Rickey, Junior discovered this letter in 1954. See Rickey, Don Jr., *Forty Miles a Day on Beans and Hay: The Enlisted Soldier Fighting the Indian Wars* (Norman, OK: University of Oklahoma Press, 1963), 64.

33 Cody, William Frederick, *The Life of Hon. William F. Cody, Known as Buffalo Bill, the Famous Hunter, Scout and Guide: An Autobiography* (Hartford, CT: F. E. Bliss, 1879), 261.

34 Anderson, Harry H., ed. pamphlet of Captain Charles King, *Summit Springs From Indian Campaigns*, published by the Old Army Press, undated, Sixth Annual Conference of Order of the Indian Wars; McCracken Research Library, Charles King Collection, Buffalo Bill Historical Center, Cody, WY, footnote 14.

35 Stevenson, John, alias Charles Abbott, unpublished memoirs of his long service during the Indian wars. This memoir is in the possession of Harry H. Anderson of Milwaukee, Wisconsin. This author appreciates the generosity of Mr. Anderson in sharing this important document with me.

36 Hyde, George, *Life of George Bent Written From His Letters* (Norman, OK: University of Oklahoma Press, 1968), 331-332.

37 Carr, "Reminiscences," 16-17.

38 Hyde, *Life of George Bent*, 332.

39 Hyde, *Life of George Bent*, 333.

40 Hyde, *Life of George Bent*, 331.

41 Carr, "Letter to Ruggles, July 20."

42 Volkmar, "Journal Entry for July 11."

43 Price, *Across the Continent*, 140.

44 *New York Herald*, July 26, 1869.

45 Carr, "Letter to Washington Smith, February 24, 1887," Washington Smith Indian Depredation Claim.

46 *Army and Navy Journal*, July 31 and August 7, 1869.

47 Hyde, *Life of George Bent*, 334.

48 Carr, "Reminiscences," 26-27.

49 Hyde, *Life of George Bent*, 333.

50 Grinnell, George Bird, *The Fighting Cheyennes* (Norman, OK: University of Oklahoma Press, 1956. Originally published in 1915), 313-316.

51 Cox, C. Jefferson, "Summit Springs," *Denver Westerners Roundup*, Vol. 26, #3, March 1970, 20.

52 Carr, "Letter to Ruggels, July 20."

53 *Kansas Daily Commonwealth*, July 16, 1869.

54 Carr, "Letter to Ruggles, July 20," italics added.

55 Volkmar, "Journal Entry for July 11."

56 *New York Times*, July 26, 1869.

57 Liddic and Harbaugh, *Camp on Custer,* 174.

58 Danker, *Man of the Plains,* 115-116.

59 Sorenson, Alfred, "General Carr's Campaign the Battle of Summit Springs, July 11, 1869," Manuscript Collections, Kansas State Historical Society, Topeka, KS, 13. Also reprinted in Weingardt, Richard, *Sound the Charge. The Western Frontier: Spillman Creek to Summit Springs* (Englewood, CO: Ajacqueline Enterprises, Inc., 1978), 105.

60 Roenigk, Adolph, *Pioneer History of Kansas* (self-published, 1933), 273. This account was also published by Reckmeyer, Clarence, "The Battle of Summit Springs," *Colorado Magazine*, Volume VI, #6, 1929, 213.

61 Brady, *Indian Fights and Fighters*, 176.

62 Carr, "Letter to Ruggels, July 20."

63 Carr, "Reminiscences," 25.

64 North, Luther, "Letter to Mr. Reckmeyer, April 18, 1932," italics added. Manuscript Collection 504, Nebraska State Historical Society, Lincoln, NE.

65 Cox, "Summit Springs," 21.

66 Volkmar, "Journal Entry for July 12." Volkmar makes the mistake of calling the site the "American or Wisconsin Ranch." These

were two separate stage stops on the South Platte Trail separated by nearly fifteen miles. Volkmar noted that the command marched almost eleven miles from Susanna Springs to the ranch. Both ranches are about that distance from the battlefield, however, American Ranch is almost directly west, while Wisconsin is due north. Given that their destination was Fort Sedgwick to the east, it makes more sense to have the command march north to Wisconsin Ranch rather than west to American Ranch. That would have required the command to march about fifteen additional miles to finally arrive at Fort Sedgwick. The column marched the next day an additional eighteen and a half miles to Riverside Ranche, which has recently been discovered on the present Bill Condon Ranch west of Crook, Colorado.

[67] Sorenson, "General Carr's Campaign," 14-15. Also Weingardt, *Sound the Charge*, 106-107.

[68] Carr, "Letter to Cody, July 2, 1906."

[69] Carr, "Letter to Washington Smith." Washington Smith Indian Depredation Claim.

[70] Price, Hercules, "Letter to Ferdinand Erhardt, December 6, 1907." Price Letters, Kansas State Historical Society, Topeka, KS. Company G Muster Roll, July/August, 1869. Record Group 94, National Archives Building, Washington, DC.

[71] Price, Hercules, "Letter to Ferdinand Erhardt, January 19, 1908."

[72] Nichols, Ronald H., ed., *Men With Custer: Biographies of the 7th Cavalry June 25, 1876* (Hardin, MT: Custer Battlefield Historical & Museum Association, 2000), 341.

[73] Volkmar, "Journal for July 11."

[74] "Record for the Month of July, 1869." Medical History of Posts, Fort Sedgwick, Record Group 94, National Archives Building, Washington, DC.

[75] Reckmeyer, "The Battle of Summit Springs," 216-217; Roenigk, *Pioneer History*, 275-276.

[76] Volkmar, "Journal Entry for July 11."

[77] Royall, Major W. B., "Camp, Republican River Expedition, July 11, 1869." Part 1, E3731, Department of the Platte, Letters Received,

1869, Record Group 393, National Archives Building, Washington, DC.

[78] Carr, "Letter to Ruggels, July 20."

[79] Copied from records in the National Archives, but not identified which Record Group. Ray Sparks Manuscript/Research Collections, in the possession of Orvel Criqui, Lawrence, Kansas.

[80] Ray Sparks Collection, emphasis added.

[81] Carr, "Letter to Ruggles, July 20;" Carr, "Reminiscence," 28-29.

[82] Afton, Jean; Halaas, David; and Masich, Andrew, *Cheyenne Dog Soldiers: A Ledgerbook History of Coups and Combat* (Niwot and Denver, CO: University Press of Colorado and Colorado Historical Society, 1997). The analytic study by the historians named in this book is extremely disappointing on two counts: One is their failure to identify any drawings beyond 1865. The Lieutenant Lyman S. Kidder massacre of July 2, 1867 is without question depicted on pictograph Plate 57. A search of all noted engagements from 1865 until 1869 shows only *one* encounter that involves eleven white men and an Indian with a horned scalp lock, and that is the Kidder massacre. (See *Chronological List of Actions, &c., With Indians from January 15, 1837 to January, 1891*, Adjutant General's Office, published in 1979 by Old Army Press, 29.) That the Colorado historians failed to acknowledge this irrefutable fact renders otiose their claim that none of the pictographs date past 1865. Thus, three pictographs are included in *Dog Soldier Justice* as possible depictions of the Dog Soldier Indian raids associated with the events of 1869. The second extremely disappointing aspect of their study of the ledgerbook is their Appendix A, which is alleged to portray a chronology of Cheyenne military actions from 1864-1869. If one bothers to pay attention to the many individual depredation files noted in *Dog Soldier Justice* and compare them to what these historians show in this appendix, one will quickly realize the disappointing results of their study at the National Archives that they portray in their appendix. I cannot explain their failure to uncover Indian Depredation claims against the Cheyenne and Sioux Indians guilty of creating the troubling conflicts between the Dog Soldiers and pioneers during the time period of this study. The National Archives contain more than ten thousand separate depredation claims. In the eighteen days I spent at the National Archives on two separate visits in 2001 and 2002 I found more than two hundred claims that were *ignored* in the analysis associated with the publication of this ledgerbook. I know I

only found a portion of the claims that exist which the Cheyenne are responsible for committing. Further, the Indian depredations they do list in Appendix A are not the violent ones I discovered in the National Archives, which might cause one to wonder if their neglect was intentional. If it was not intentional, it was professionally careless: and any reader who studies their publication should be aware of the inadequacies I have noted here. If it was intentional, I leave it to the reader to suggest why this was so. Having said that, the ledger-book is invaluable for what the Dog Soldiers left in the village at Susanna Springs.

83 Carr, "Letter to Ruggles, July 20;" Price, Hercules, "Letter of January 19, 1908."

84 "Officers Wagon, headquarters Republican Expedition, Camp in the Field, July 14, 1869." Copy in the possession of Steven G. Miller of Lake Villa, IL, which has been graciously shared with me.

85 "Statement Signed in Officer's Wagon, July 14." These documented amounts of money contradict North's claim in *Man of the Plains* that the Pawnees turned over $640.00 to Maria. See Danker, *Man of the Plains*, 119.

86 Price, Hercules, "Letter of January 19, 1908."

87 Volkmar, "Journal Entry for July 11."

88 Carr, "Letter to Washington Smith," Washington Smith Indian Depredation Claim.

89 Carr, Eugene A., "Letter to Custer, August 16, 1869." Swann Library, Little Bighorn Battlefield National Monument, Crow Agency, Montana.

90 Brady, *Indian Fights and Fighters*, 178; Carr, "Letter to Ruggles, July 20;" Volkmar, "Journal Entry for July 12;" Price, Hercules, "Letters of December 6, 1907, January 19, 1908, August 10, 1910."

91 Danker, ed., *Man of the Plains*, 141-142.

92 Price, Hercules, "Letter of August 10, 1910."

93 Eli Zeigler Pension File, Cert. #1174920. Recored Group 94, National Archives Building, Washington, DC.

94 Carr, "Reminiscences," 29.

The Rest of the Story
Pages 187 - 204

[1] Bernhardt, C., *Indian Raids in Lincoln County, Kansas 1864 and 1869* (Lincoln, KS: The Lincoln Sentinel Print, 1910), 45.

[2] *Kansas Weekly Tribune*, June 10, 1869; family story passed down to Berniece Graepler from her mother, Elsie Daily Horton, and her grandfather Willis, November 19, 2000.

[3] *Leavenworth Times and Conservative*, June 1, 2, 3, 20, 1869; *Junction City Weekly Union*, June 5, 1869; March, 2nd Lieutenant T. J., "Letter from Camp on Saline River, May 31, 1869." Part 1, Letters Received, Department of the Missouri, 1869, Record Group 393, National Archives Building, Washington, DC. "Letter from Anna Waters to Ray Sparks," Sparks Manuscript Research Collection, in the possession of Orvel Criqui, Lawrence, Kansas.

[4] *Lincoln Republican*, March 26, 1917. Another source indicates the year 1914. This story has been pasted into a scrapbook owned by J. J. Peate and titled "Historical Sketches," and is in the possession of Loa Page, Lincoln, Kansas.

[5] Hendrickson, C. C., "Memories," *The Lincoln-Sentinel Republican*, February 8, 1934.

[6] Peate, "Historical Sketches."

[7] Sparks, Colonel Ray, "Tall Bull's Captives," *The Trail Guide* of the Kansas City Posse of the Westerners, Vol. VII, March, 1962, Number 1, 16-17. This claim is repeated in Sparks, *Reckoning at Summit Springs* (Kansas City, MO: The Lowell Press, 1969), 36.

[8] Law, Lieutenant Edward, "Letter from Schermerhorn Ranch by Saline River, May 31, 1869." Part 1, Letters Received, Department of the Missouri, 1869, Record Group 393, National Archives Building, Washington, DC.

[9] "Orders to General Geo. A. Custer, Headquarters, Department of the Missouri, Fort Leavenworth, Kansas, May 24, 1869." Part 1, Letters Received, Department of the Missouri, 1869, Record Group 393, National Archives Building, Washington, DC.

[10] Law, Lieutenant Edward, "Letter from Camp at Mouth of Asher Creek, June 2, 1869." Part 1, Letters Received, Department of

the Missouri, 1869, Record Group 393, National Archives Building, Washington, DC.

11 March, Lieutenant Edward, "Letter from near Salt Creek, Kansas, June 1, 1869." Part 1, Letters Received, Department of the Missouri, Record Group 393, National Archives Building, Washington, DC.

12 Nichols, Ronald H., ed., *Men With Custer: Biographies of the 7th Cavalry June 25, 1876* (Hardin, MT: Custer Battlefield Historical & Museum Association, Inc., 2000), 353.

13 *Junction City Weekly Union*, June 12, 1869.

14 *Kansas Daily Commonwealth*, June 12, 1869.

15 *Kansas Daily Commonwealth*, June 12, 1869.

16 *Kansas Daily Commonwealth*, June 12, 1869.

17 Hendrickson, "Memories."

18 James Alfred Daily Civil War Pension File #187.771. Record Group 94, National Archives Building, Washington, DC. When I first began researching the National Archives there was no known record of the full name of Susanna's first husband, other than the last name "Daily." There was even discrepancy as to the correct spelling of Daily. When I learned that Willis named his son James Alfred Daily, I wondered why this name. On a hunch that perhaps this was the name of his father, I searched the pension records at the National Archives to see if there might be a file for a James Alfred Daily. Indeed there was, and when I read it I discovered that my hunch was correct. Not only did I discover the name of Susanna's first husband, but the records inside the pension file, filled out by Susanna's father Michael, included the birth date of Willis's brother, John, which was also not known until this discovery. Included in the file was a copy of the marriage certificate of Susanna and James, in Liberty, Missouri, October 28, 1860. This also had been unknown until this discovery. The pension file also revealed when and where James Daily died, another unknown event. In a subsequent visit to the Fort Leavenworth National Cemetery, I discovered the grave of Susanna's first husband. The marble marker, placed there in the early 1870s, had misspelled James' last name as "Dailey." I filled out necessary paperwork to correct this error, and in the fall of 2002, a corrected marker was placed on the grave of James Alfred Daily. It sits today about forty-

five paces away from the headstone marking the grave of Thomas Ward Custer, George Custer's younger brother, who died next to Custer at the Little Bighorn fight June 25, 1876. A similar search of the pension file for Thomas Alderdice revealed the date of his marriage to Susanna and the fact that he had been a Confederate soldier who had enlisted in the Union Army to gain release from a Union prisoner of war camp. Tom was a "galvanized" Yankee, something no one in his direct family apparently ever knew. They had always believed Tom served time in Andersonville, Georgia, the notorious Confederate prisoner of war camp housing Union prisoners. The moral of the story for the reader interested in doing historical research is always check your hunches, no matter how wild they may appear. I was earlier able to locate the descendants of Willis Daily by asking a reporter of the *Salina Journal*, who was interviewing me on the phone to write a story regarding a talk I was giving to the Lincoln County Historical Society on the Spillman Creek raid, to please include in her story my desire to locate descendants of Willis Daily. Her article, published in the *Salina Journal* November 7, 2000, highlighted my desire to locate descendants. A call from Wayne Little in Abilene, Kansas, led to my finding Willis' granddaughter, Berniece Horton. From that family came all the pictures of Willis, his family and his father in his Civil War uniform, taken shortly before he died. Researchers should always be thinking of creative ways to locate information that will bring more knowledge to the story one is interested in telling.

[19] James Daily Pension File. When Michael Zeigler filled out the paperwork for Willis' pension, he was spelling his name "Zigler" instead of the "Zeigler" that shows up in earlier records.

[20] In a letter to Ray Sparks, Anna Daily Watters said that she was born in Huem (Hume?), Missouri (Sparks Research/Manuscript Collection). If this is the case, Willis left Lincoln County after his son was born, and before his first daughter was born. At any rate, shortly after his last child was born, he settled in Blue Rapids, Kansas.

[21] *Kansas Daily Commonwealth*, July 16, 1869.

[22] Bernhardt, *Indian Raids*, 33.

[23] Farrier William McConnell Diary, Bates Collection, Little Bighorn Battlefield National Monument Library Collections. Copy also on file in Manuscripts Collections, Kansas State Historical Society, Topeka, Kansas.

[24] McConnell, "Entry for July 23, 1869," emphasis added.

25 Register of Letters Sent, Department of the Missouri, Part 1, Entry 2575, 450, Record Group 393, National Archives Building, Washington, DC.

26 Thomas Alderdice Civil War Pension File #1175-380. Record Group 94, National Archives Building, Washington, DC.

27 Roenigk, Adolph, "Letter to Clarence Reckmeyer, Aug. 26, 1926." Manuscript #504, Box 1, Folder 1929, Kansas State Historical Society, Topeka, Kansas.

28 *Lincoln Sentinel*, May 25, 1911.

29 *Lincoln Sentinel*, May 25, 1911.

30 Tom Alderdice Military Pension File.

31 Lyman, Robert, ed., *The Beecher Island Annual* (Wray. CO. The Beecher Island Battle Memorial Association, 1930), 105.

32 *Winners of the West* (Vol. II, No. 7, June, 1925), 7.

33 "History of Sumner County, KS. 1987 Vol. I," by the *Caldwell Messenger*. Copied for me by a reporter for the *Conway Springs Star and The Argonia Argosy*. In the Manuscripts Collections at the Kansas State Historical Society there is a rather large file on Tom Alderdice, comprising information collected by Nina Pond and other descendants of Tom and Mary Alderdice. It is rift with errors, including, for example, that Susanna was taken captive in 1868 and that this was the cause for Tom joining with Forsyth and fighting at Beecher Island, that his other son, William, was taken captive and raised by the Indians and that Tom hunted for him the rest of his life, that Tom was for several years a prisoner at Andersonville, etc. The file should be ignored by anyone interested in the truth about Tom Alderdice. In doing the research for this book, I have met many wonderful people. Mickie Alderdice is one. She married a grandson of Tom's. She told me a story that at about the time of World War II she met an old woman who, when young, knew Tom Alderdice in Conway Springs. This lady reported to Mickie that everyone knew Tom's sad tale of losing his first family in an Indian massacre. One of Tom's jobs then was a contract to deliver mail, and thus he knew well the county he lived in. The old lady recalled to Mickie that whenever an adult male Indian wandered into the county he disappeared. Everyone knew Tom had something to do with his disappearance, but nobody ever asked about the missing Indian.

34 "Letter to Clarence Reckmeyer from the Adjutant General's

Office, August 2, 1929." Manuscript Collection #504, Box 1, Folder 1929. Kansas State Historical Society, Topeka, Kansas.

35 Barr, Elizabeth, *A Souvenir History of Lincoln County, Kansas* (Self-published, 1908), 42; Roenigk, *Pioneer History*, 238;

36 Bernhardt, *Indian Raids*, 46.

37 Peate, "Historical Sketches."

38 Roenigk, *Pioneer History*, 113.

39 Bernhardt, *Indian Raids*, 29, 34.

40 *Kansas Daily Commonwealth*, June 20, 1869.

41 Lena Baertsche Indian Depredation Claim #3530. Indian Depredations Claims Division, Record Group 123, National Archives Building, Washington, DC. George Green makes his affidavit twenty-one years after the May 30 raid, and thus by this time confused the name of Maria Weichel with Lena Baertsche, whose husband had been killed during the August 13, 1868 raids in Mitchell County. It is clear however, in his testimony that he is speaking of Maria Weichel, for he says that Lena was the woman whose husband had been killed and she taken captive along with Mrs. Alderdice. He also locates Lena's residence seven miles northwest of Lincoln, which is where the Lauritzen cabin was and where Maria was living at the time of the raid.

42 Lena Baertsche Indian Depredation Claim.

43 Lena Baertsche Indian Depredation Claim.

44 Bernhardt, *Indian Raids*, 46.

45 Bernhardt, *Indian Raids*, 46.

46 Mrs. B. Worthman document under Weichel Manuscript Collection, Kansas State Historical Society, Topeka, Kansas. This document is typed, and not written by Minnie. It is a letter forwarding her request from the adjutant general's office to the Kansas State Historical Society. Her name was apparently misspelled as "Worthman" instead of the correct "Wurthman."

47 Worthman document. I was unable to discover what this statement was that Maria made.

48 1900 U.S. Census, San Francisco County, California, Vol. 31,

E.D. 132, Sheet 4, Line 36, Roll 103.

[49] Harry's last name is spelled as Worthman, not Wurthman. U. S. Census, Kern County, Bakersfield, California, Vol. 27, E.D., 92, Sheet 4, Line 89.

[50] George Wurthman Obituary, *Appeal Democrat*, November 22, 1986, Yuba City, California. George's wife was Rhoda H. Wurthman. She died in Palo Alto, California January 16, 2000. Social Security Death Index, Denver Public Library, Western History Department. All attempts to locate these descendants of George Wurthman have been unsuccessful at the time of this writing.

[51] Bernhardt, *Indian Raids*, 57.

[52] Hank Graepler, great-grandson of Willis Daily, has original pictures taken of the Pioneer Monument when it was first erected. They are displayed in this book. I am very grateful for his cooperation and enthusiasm during my writing of this book.

[53] Letter of Anna Watters to her cousin, September 15, 1965. Sparks Manuscript Collection. Copy with Joeleen Passow, Anna's granddaughter.

[54] *Blue Rapids Times*, June 24, 1920. I am not a person to read significance in coincidence, but I find it remarkable how dates involving Willis Daily correspond with me. For example, my mother was born June 15, 1920, Mary Daily's birthday, and one day before Willis died. My only nephew was born October 5, Willis' birthday. My only niece was born July 11, the day Susanna was killed. My brother was born October 13, 1946. Mary Daily died October 11, 1948, two years and two days apart.

Appendix 1
On Locating Susanna's Grave
Pages 205 - 214

[1] Volkmar, Lieutenant William, "Journal of the March, July 12, 1869." Department of the Platte, Letters Received, 1869, Record Group 393, National Archives Building, Washington, DC.

[2] Carr, General Eugene A., "Letter to General Ruggles, July 20, 1869." Republican River Expedition, Record Group 94, National Archives Building, Washington, DC.

[3] Carr, Eugene A., *Personal Memoirs*, unpublished manuscript on microfilm file, MS2688, Nebraska State Historical Society, Lincoln, NE, 221.

[4] Carr, Mrs. Eugene, *Memoirs*, unpublished manuscript on microfilm, Nebraska State Historical Society, Lincoln, NE, 34.

[5] Washington Smith Indian Depredation Claim #3951. Indian Depredations Claims Division, Record Group 75, National Archives Building, Washington, DC.

[6] Price, Hercules, "Letter dated December 6, 1907." Price Letters, Kansas State Historical Society, Topeka, Kansas.

[7] Brady, Cyrus Townsend, *Indian Fights and Fighters: The Soldier and the Sioux* (New York, NY: McClure, Phillips & Co., 1904), 178.

[8] Volkmar, "Journal Entry for July 12, 1869," emphasis added.

[9] These artifacts can be viewed at Larry's website, and can be found at http://www.metallocators.com/summit.htm.

[10] Werner, Fred H., *The Summit Springs Battle* (Greeley, CO: Werner Publications, 1991), 149.

[11] Conversation with Larry Finnell at Summit Springs, Summer, 2001.

[12] Conversation with Historian Nell Brown-Propst, August, 2002.

[13] Edwards, Brad, "New Thornburgh Battle Discoveries," *Western and Eastern Treasures*, Vol. 36, May 2002, 30. See also Edwards, "New Facts on the Battle of Milk Creek September 20 – October 5, 1879," *The Denver Westerners Roundup*, May-June 2002.

[14] Grinnell, George Bird, *Two Great Scouts and Their Pawnee Battalion* (Lincoln, NE: University of Nebraska Press, 1973. Originally published in 1928), 198.

[15] Cox, C. Jefferson, "Summit Springs," *Brand Book 1969 Silver Anniversary Addition*, Volume 25, ed., Martin Rist (Boulder, CO: Johnson Publishing Company, 1970), 300.

Appendix 2
Epilogue
Pages 215 - 224

[1] Inscription on outside of the National Archives and Records Administration Building, Washington, DC.

[2] Roenigk, Adolph, *Pioneer History of Kansas* (Self-published, 1933), 357.

[3] The view I express is summarized from the thesis developed in Hick, John, *Evil and the God of Love* (New York, NY: Harper and Row, publishers, 1966). See especially 279-400. See also Broome, James Jefferson, *The Theodicy of John Hick: A Critical Defense* (Ann Arbor, MI: UMI Dissertation Services, 1999).

[4] For a philosophical defense of this position, see French, Peter A., *The Virtues of Vengeance* (Lawrence, KS: University Press of Kansas, 2001).

[5] John ("Jack") D. McDermott did use eleven individual Indian depredation claims from the National Archives in *Forlorn Hope: The Battle of White Bird Canyon and the Beginning of the Nez Perce War* (Boise, ID: Idaho State Historical Society, 1978).

[6] Lilly, Judy Magnuson, "Susan's Story," *Kanhistique*, April, 1986.

[7] Brady, Cyrus Townsend, *Indian Fights and Fighters* (New York, NY: McClure, Phillips & Co, 1904), 176.

[8] Thomas Alderdice letter dated June 21, 1869. Letters Received 1869, Entry 2601, Department of the Missouri, Record Group 393, National Archives Building, Washington, DC.

[9] Barr, Elizabeth, *A Souvenir History of Lincoln County, Kansas* (privately printed, 1908), 39. Washington Smith, *Lincoln Republican*, Feb. 3, 1886.

[10] Sparks, Col. Ray, *Reckoning at Summit Springs* (Kansas City, MO: The Lowell Press, 1969), 36, 42.

[11] *Kansas Daily Commonwealth*, July 12, 1869. It should be noted that the arrow was in Willis's back for at least forty-eight hours, which includes the time he lay alone and wounded on the prairie. Dr. Renick refused treatment for a day after that before Washington Smith extracted the arrow with a bullet mold used as pliers. This metal arrow point is on display at the Lincoln County Historical Society Museum in Lincoln, Kansas.

[12] *Leavenworth Times and Conservative*, June 1, 2 and 20, 1869; March, Lt. T.J., "Letter to Lt. Edward Law, May 31, 1869." Part 1, Letters Received 1869, Department of the Missouri, Record Group 393, National Archives Building, Washington, DC.

Bibliography

Books & Magazines

Afton, Jean; Halaas, David Fridtjof; and Masich, Andrew E., *Cheyenne Dog Soldiers: A Ledgerbook History of Coups and Combat* (Niwot and Denver, CO: Colorado Historical Society and the University Press of Colorado, 1997).

Allred, B. W., et. al., *Great Western Indian Fights* (Garden City, NY: Doubleday and Company, Inc., 1960).

Andersen, Denise, "Indian Raids of 1867 in Jefferson County, Nebraska," (Fairbury: NE: The Jefferson County Historical Society, Nov., 2000), 1-15.

Anonymous, *General Sheridan's Squaw Spy and Mrs. Clara Blynn's Captivity* .... (Philadelphia, PA: Co-operative Publishing House), 1869. Reprinted as *Garland Library Narratives of North American Indian Captivity, Vol. 81* (New York and London: Garland Publishing Company, 1976).

Ayers, Nathaniel M., *Building A New Empire* (New York, NY: Broadway Publishing Co., 1910).

Barnard, Sandy, ed., *Ten Years With Custer: A 7ᵗʰ Cavalryman's Memoirs* (Terre Haute, IN: AST Press, 2001).

Barr, Elizabeth N., *A Souvenir History of Lincoln County, Kansas* (Self-published, 1908).

*The Beecher Island Annual: Ninety-third Anniversary of the Battle of Beecher Island September 17, 18, 186*8 (Beecher Island, CO: The Beecher Island Battle Memorial Association, 1960).

Bernhardt, Christian, "Camp Pliley," *Kansas State Historical Collections*, (Eighteenth Biennial Report, 1913), 52-60.

Bernhardt, Christian, *Indian Raids in Lincoln County, Kansas, 1864 and 1869* (Lincoln, Kansas: The Lincoln Sentinel Print, 1910).

Berthrong, Donald J., *The Southern Cheyennes* (Norman, OK: University of Oklahoma Press, 1963).

Blackburn, Forrest R., "The 18th Kansas Cavalry and The Indian War," (*The Trail Guide of the Kansas City Westerners*, Vol. IX, March, 1964, Number 1), 1-15.

Bradley, Lieutenant James H., *The March of the Montana Column*, ed., Stewart, Edgar I., (Norman, OK: University of Oklahoma Press, 1961).

Brady, Cyrus Townsend, *Indian Fights and Fighters: The Soldier and the Sioux* (New York, NY: McClure, Phillips & Co., 1904).

Brininstool, E. A., *Fighting Indian Warriors: True Tales of the Wild Frontier* (Harrisburg, PA: The Stackpole Company, 1953).

Broome, James Jefferson, *The Theodicy of John Hick: A Critical Defense* (Ann Arbor, MI: UMI Dissertation Services, 1999).

Broome, Jeff, "Libbie Custer's Encounter with Tom Alderdice ... The Rest of the Story," (*The Denver Westerners Roundup*, Vol. LVII, No. 4, July-August, 2001), 3-25. Slightly revised version in Hart, John, ed., *Custer and His Times, Book Four* (Honolulu, HI: Little Big Horn Associates, 2002), 63-93.

_____, "On Locating the Kidder Massacre Site of 1867," (*The Denver Westerners Roundup*, Vol. LVI, No. 4, July-August, 2000), 3-18.

_____, "Custer, Kidder and Tragedy at Beaver Creek," (*Wild West*, June, 2002), 38-46.

_____, "Death at Summit Springs: The Story of Susanna Alderdice," (*Wild West*, October, 2003), 38-45.

Brown, Dee, *Bury My Heart At Wounded Knee: An Indian History of the American West* (New York, NY: Bantam Books, Inc., 1971).

Burgess, Henderson L., "The Eighteenth Kansas Volunteer Cavalry, and Some Incidents Connected With Its Service On the Plains," (*Collections of the Kansas State Historical Society*, 1913-1914, Vol. XII), 534-538.

Burkey, Blaine, *Custer, Come at Once!* (Hays, KS: Society of the Friends of Historic Fort Hays, 2nd ed., 1991).

Campbell, John R., "An Indian Raid of 1867," (*Collections of the Nebraska State Historical Society*, 1913, Vol. XVII), 259-262.

Carlson, Paul H., *The Plains Indians* (College Station, TX: Texas A&M University Press, 1998).

Carroll, John M., ed., *Cavalry Scraps: The Writings of Frederick Benteen* (no city: Guidon Press, 1979).

_____, *General Custer and the Battle of the Washita: The Federal View* (Byron, TX: Guidon Press, 1978).

Chandler, Lt. Col. Melbourne C., *Of Garryowen in Glory: The History of the 7th U.S. Cavalry* (Annandale, VA: The Turnpike Press, Inc., 1960).

Chronological List of Actions, Etc., With Indians From January 15, 1837 to January, 1891, Introduction by Floyd, Dale E. (No town listed, Old Army Press, 1979).

Clark, Olive A., "Early Days Along the Solomon Valley," (*Collections of the Kansas State Historical Society, 1926-1928*, Vol. XVII), 719-730.

Cody, William F., *The Life of Hon. William F. Cody Known As Buffalo Bill, the Famous Hunter, Scout and Guide* (New York, NY: Indian Head Books, 1991. Originally published in 1879).

Collins, Dennis, *The Indians' Last Fight or The Dull Knife Raid* (Girard, KS: Press of the Appeal to Reason, no date).

Conklin, Emma Burke, *A Brief History of Logan County, Colorado With Reminiscences by Pioneers* (Denver, CO: Welch-Haffner Printing Co., 1928).

Cox, C. Jefferson, "Summit Springs," (*Denver Westerners Roundup*, Vol. 26, Number 3, March, 1970), 19-24. Reprinted in Rist, Martin, ed., *Brand Book 1969 Silver Anniversary Edition, Vol. 25* (Boulder, CO: Johnson Publishing Company, 1970).

Craig, Reginald S., "Tall Bull's Last Fight," (*Denver Westerners Roundup*, April, 1968), 17-25.

Crawford, Samuel J., *Kansas in the Sixties* (Chicago: A. C. McClurg & Co., 1911).

Criqui, Orvel A., *Fifty Fearless Men: The Forsyth Scouts & Beecher Island* (Marceline, MO: Walsworth Publishing Co., 1993).

Custer, Elizabeth B., *Following The Guidon* (New York, NY: Harper & Brothers, 1890).

Custer, Gen. G. A., *My Life on the Plains, or, Personal Experiences With Indians* (New York, NY: Sheldon & Co., 1874).

Czaplewski, Russ, *Captive of the Cheyenne: The Story of Nancy Jane Morton and the Plum Creek Massacre* (Kearney, NE: Morris Publishing, 1993).

Danker, Donald F., ed., "The Journal of an Indian Fighter – The 1869 Diary of Major Frank J. North," (*Nebraska History*, Vol. 39, Number 2, June, 1958), 87-177.

_____, ed., *Man of the Plains: Recollections of Luther North, 1856-1882* (Lincoln, NE: University of Nebraska Press, 1961).

_____, "The Pawnee Scouts and the North Brothers," (*The Trail Guide of the Kansas City Westerners*, Vol. XI, Number 1, March, 1966), 1-13.

Dawson, Charles, *Pioneer Tales of the Oregon Trail and of Jefferson County* (Topeka, KS: Crane & Company, 1912).

Derounian-Stodola, Kathryn Zabelle and Levernier, James Arthur, *The Indian Captivity Narrative 1550-1900* (New York, NY: Twayne Publishers, 1993).

Dixon, David, *Hero of Beecher Island: The Life and Military Career of George A. Forsyth* (Lincoln, NE: University of Nebraska Press, 1994).

Dixon, David, "Custer and the Sweetwater Hostages," *Custer and His Times, Book Three*, ed., Urwin, Gregory J. W., and Fagen, Roberta E. (No city listed: University of Central Arkansas Press and the Little Big Horn Associates, Inc.), 1987.

Dodge, Col. Richard Irving, *Our Wild Indians: Thirty-three Years' Personal Experience Among the Red Men of the Great West* (New York, NY: Archer House, Inc., 1959. Originally published in 1890).

_____, *The Plains of the Great West and Their Inhabitants* (New York, NY: Archer House, Inc., 1959. Originally published in 1877).

Dunn, Lt. Col. William R., *War Drum Echoes: A Narrative History of the Indian Wars in Colorado* (Self Published, 1979).

Edwards, Brad, "New Facts on the Battle of Milk Creek September 20 – October 5, 1879," (The Denver Westerners Roundup, May-June, 2000), 1-19.

_____, "New Thornburgh Battle Discoveries," (Western and Eastern Treasures, Vol. 36, May, 2000), 26-31.

Fairfield, S. H, "The Eleventh Kansas Regiment at Platte Bridge," (*Kansas State Historical Collections*, Vol. 8, 1903-1904), 352-362.

Farley, Alan W., ed., "Reminiscences of Allison J. Pliley Indian Fighter," (*The Trail Guide of the Kansas City Westerners*, Vol. 2, Number 2, June, 1957), 1-16.

_____, "The Pioneers of Kansas," (*The Trail Guide of the Kansas City Westerners*, Vol. XI, Number 2, June, 1966), 1-16.

Filipiak, Jack D., "The Battle of Summit Springs," (*The Colorado Magazine*, Vol. XLI, Number 4, 1964), 343-354.

Fisher, John R., "The Royall and Duncan Pursuits: Aftermath of the Battle of Summit Springs," (*Nebraska History*, Vol. 50, Number 3, Fall, 1969), 292-308.

Forsyth, George A., *The Story of the Soldier* (New York, NY: D. Appleton and Co., 1900).

_____, *Thrilling Days in Army Life* (New York, NY: Harper and Brothers, 1900).

Freeman, Winfield, "The Battle of the Arickaree," (*Kansas State Historical Collections*, Vol. 6, 1897-1900), 346-357.

Frost, Lawrence A., *The Court-Martial of General George Armstrong Custer* (Norman, OK: University of Oklahoma Press, 1967).

Fry, James B., *Army Sacrifices; or, Briefs From Original Pigeon-Holes* (New York, NY: D. Van Nostrand, Publisher, 1979).

Garfield, Marvin H., "The Military Post as a factor in the Frontier Defense of Kansas," (*The Kansas Historical Quarterly*, Vol. 1, No. 1, November, 1931), 50-62.

_____, "Defense of the Kansas Frontier, 1864-1865," (*The Kansas Historical Quarterly*, Vol. 1, No. 2, February, 1932), 140-152.

_____, "Defense of the Kansas Frontier, 1866-1867," (*The Kansas Historical Quarterly*, Vol. 1, No. 4, August, 1932), 326-344.

_____, "Defense of the Kansas Frontier, 1868-1869," (*The Kansas Historical Quarterly*, Vol. 1, No. 5, November, 1932), 451-473.

Goodrich, Thomas, *Scalp Dance: Indian Warfare On The High Plains 1865-1879* (Mechanicsburg, PA: Stackpole Books, 1997).

Graham, Colonel William A., *The Custer Myth: A Source Book in Custeriania* (Harrisburg, PA: The Stackpole Company, 1953).

Grinnell, George Bird, *Two Great Scouts and Their Pawnee Battalion: The Experiences of Frank J. North and Luther H. North*, forward by King, James T. (Lincoln, NE: University of Nebraska Press, 1973. Originally published in 1928).

_____, *The Fighting Cheyennes* (Williamstown, MA: Corner House Publishers, 1956. Originally published in 1915).

_____, *Pawnee Hero Stories and Folk Tales* (Lincoln, NE: University of Nebraska Press, 1961. Originally published in 1889).

Hall, J. N., "Colorado's Indian Troubles as I View Them," (*The Colorado Magazine*, Vol. XV, Number 4, July, 1938), 121-129.

Harrison, Mrs. Emily Haines, "Reminiscences of Early Days in Ottawa County," (*Kansas State Historical Collections*, Vol. 10, 1907-1908), 622-631.

Heitman, Francis B., *Historical Register and Dictionary of the United States Army, Vol. 1* (Washington, DC: Government Printing Office, 1903. Reprinted 1965, University of Illinois Press, Urbana).

Hick, John H., *Evil and the God of Love* (New York, NY; Harper and Row, Publishers, 1966).

Hoebel, E. Adamson, *The Cheyennes: Indians of the Great Plains* (New York, NY: Holt, Rinehart and Winston, 1960).

Hoig, Stan, *The Battle of the Washita* (Garden City, NY: Doubleday & Co., Inc., 1976).

_____, *Tribal Wars of the Southern Plains* (Norman, OK: University of Oklahoma Press, 1993).

_____, *The Peace Chiefs of the Cheyennes* (Norman, OK: University of Oklahoma Press, 1980).

Hollibaugh, Mrs. E. F., *Biographical History of Cloud County, Kansas* (Logonsport, IN: Wilson, Humphrey & Co., 1903).

Holmes, Louis A., *Fort McPherson, Nebraska, Fort Cottonwood, N.T.: Guardian of the Tracks and Trails* (Lincoln, NE: Johnson Publishing Co., 1963).

Homan, Dorothe Tarrence, *Lincoln – That County in Kansas* (Lindsborg: KS: Bardos Printing, 1979).

Humphrey, James, "The Country West of Topeka Prior to 1869," (*Kansas State Historical Collections*, Vol. 4, 1896-1890), 289-297.

Hutton, Paul Andrew, *Phil Sheridan and His Army* (Lincoln and London: University of Nebraska Press, 1985).

Hyde, George E., *Life of George Bent Written From His Letters* (Norman, OK: University of Oklahoma Press, 1968).

Jauken, Arlene Feldmann, *The Moccasin Speaks: Living as Captives of the Dog Soldier Warriors Red River War 1874-1875* (Lincoln, NE: Dageforde Publishing, Inc., 1998).

Jelinek, George, *90 Years of Ellsworth and Ellsworth County History* (no city: The Messenger Press, 1957).

_____, *Frontier Land: A Collection of Narratives of the Old West* (Ellsworth, KS: The Ellsworth Reporter, 1973).

Johnston, Terry C., *Black Sun: The Battle of Summit Springs, 1869* (New York, NY: St. Martin's Paperbacks), 1991.

Justus, Judith P., "The Saga of Clara Blinn and the Battle of the Washita," (*Research Review, The Journal of The Little Big Horn Associates*, Vol. 14, No. 1, Winter, 2000), 11-20.

Keenan, Jerry, *Encyclopedia of American Indian Wars 1492-1890* (Santa Barbara, Denver and Oxford: ABC-CLIO, Inc., 1997).

Keim, De B. Randolph, *Sheridan's Troopers on the Borders: A Winter Campaign on the Plains* (Williamstown, MA: Corner House Publishers, 1973. Originally published in 1870).

Kelly, Fanny, *Narrative of My Captivity Among the Sioux Indians*, ed. by Clark and Mary Lee Spence (Chicago, IL: R. R. Donnelley & Sons Co., 1990. Originally published in 1871).

King, James T., "The Republican River Expedition, June-July, 1869," Paul, R. Eli, ed., *The Nebraska Indian Wars Reader 1865-1877* (Lincoln and London: University of Nebraska Press, 1998), 31-70.

_____, *War Eagle: A Life of General Eugene A. Carr* (Lincoln, NE: University of Nebraska Press, 1963).

Kloberdanz, Timothy, *The Tragedy at Summit Springs From the Viewpoint of the Indians* (Self-published, no date, 2nd edition).

_____, *... As High as the Eagle Flies, Being an Account of the Recent Indian Struggle Which Occured* [sic] *at Summit Springs, Colorado July, 1969* (self-Published, April, 1970).

Kraft, Louis, *Custer and the Cheyenne: George Armstrong Custer's Winter Campaign on the Southern Plains* (El Segundo, CA: Upton and Sons, Publishers, 1995).

Lee, Wayne C. and Raynesford, Howard C., *Trails of the Smoky Hill: From Coronado to the Cow Towns* (Caldwell, ID: The Caxton Printers, LTD., 1980).

Levernier, James and Cohen, Hennig, ed., *The Indians and Their Captives* (Westport, CN & London: Greenwood Press, 1977).

Lilly, Judy Magnuson, "Susan's Story," (*Kanhistique*, April, 1986), 11.

Llewellyn, Karl N. and Hoebel, E. Adamson, *The Cheyenne Way: Conflict and Case Law in Primitive Jurisprudence* (Norman, OK: University of Oklahoma Press, 1941).

Longstreet, Stephen, *War Cries on Horseback: The Story of The Indian Wars of The Great Plains* (Garden City, NY: Doubleday & Co., Inc. 1970).

Luchetti, Cathy, *Children of the West: Family Life on the Frontier* (New York & London: W.W. Norton & Co., 2001).

Lynam, Robert, ed., *The Beecher Island Annual*, Vol. II, No. I, August, 1905 (Wray, CO: Wray Gazette. The Beecher Island Battle Memorial Association, 1905).

_____, *The Beecher Island Annual* (Vol. III, August, 1906).

_____, *The Beecher Island Annual* (Vol. IV, August, 1908).

_____, *The Beecher Island Annual* (Vol. V, September, 1917).

_____, *The Beecher Island Annual* (1930).

Mails, Thomas E., *Dog Soldiers, Bear Men and Buffalo Women: A Study of the Societies and Cults of the Plains Indians* (Englewood Cliffs, NJ: Prentice-Hall, Inc., 1973).

Malin, James C., "Dust Storms, Part Two, 1861-1880," (*The Kansas Historical Quarterly*, Vol. XIV, No. 3, August, 1946), 265-296.

Marsh, Fred Raymond, *Souvenir of Wray and of Vernon, Colorado* (no publisher, city or date).

McCarter, Margaret Hill, *The Price of the Prairie: A Story of Kansas* (Chicago, IL: A.C. McClurg & Co.), 1910.

McReynolds, Robert, *Thirty Years on the Frontier* (Colorado Springs, CO: El Paso Publishing Co., 1906)

Mead, James R., *Hunting and Trading on The Great Plains 1859-1875*, ed., Schuyler Jones (Norman, OK: Oklahoma University Press, 1986).

The Medal of Honor of the United States Army (Washington, DC: Government Printing Office, 1948).

Meredith, Grace E., ed., *Girl Captives of the Cheyennes: A True Story of the Capture and Rescue of Four Pioneer Girls 1874* (Los Angeles, CA: Gem Publishing Co., 1927).

Miner, Craig, *West of Wichita: Settling the High Plains of Kansas, 1865-1890* (Lawrence, KS: University Press of Kansas, 1986).

Monnett, John H., *The Battle of Beecher Island and the Indian War of 1868-1869* (Niwot, CO: University Press of Colorado, 1992).

Montgomery, Mrs. Frank C., "Fort Wallace and its Relation to the Frontier," (*Collections of the Kansas State Historical Society* 1926-1928, Vol. XVII, 1928), 189-282.

Moore, Horace L., "The Nineteenth Kansas Cavalry," (*Kansas State Historical Collections*, Vol. 66, 1897-1900), 35-47.

Namias, June, ed., and annotated, Wakefield, Sarah, *Six Weeks in the Sioux Tepees: A Narrative of Indian Captivity* (Norman, OK: Oklahoma University Press, 1997).

_____, *White Captives: Gender and Ethnicity on the American Frontier* (Chapel Hill and London: The University of North Carolina Press, 1993).

Nichols, Ronald H., ed., *Men With Custer: Biographies of the 7th Cavalry* (Hardin, MT: Custer Battlefield Historical & Museum Association, 2000).

Nye, Wilbur Sturtevant, *Plains Indian Raiders* (Norman, OK: University of Oklahoma Press, 1968).

O'Donnell, Jeff, *Blood on the Republican* (New York, NY: M. Evans & Company, Inc.), 1992.

_____, *Luther North Frontier Scout* (Lincoln, NE: J & L Lee Co., 1995).

O'Neal, Bill, *Fighting Men of the Indian Wars* (Stillwater, OK: Barbed Wire Press, 1991).

Paul, R. Eli, ed., *The Nebraska Indian Wars Reader* (Lincoln and London: University of Nebraska Press, 1998).

Peterson, Rachel Wild, *The Long-Lost Rachel Wild or, Seeking Diamonds in the Rough* (Denver, CO: The Reed Publishing Company, 1905).

Poole, Captain D. C., *Among the Sioux of Dakota* (New York, NY: D. Van Nostrand, Pub., 1881).

Powell, Father Peter John, *People of the Sacred Mountain: A History of the Northern Cheyenne Chiefs and Warrior Societies 1830-1879 With an Epilogue 1969-1974* (San Francisco: Harper and Row, Publishers, 1981).

_____, *Sweet Medicine: The Continuing Role of the Sacred Arrows, The Sun Dance, and the Sacred Buffalo Hat in Northern Cheyenne History* (Norman, OK: University of Oklahoma Press, 1969).

Price, Captain George F., *Across the Continent with the Fifth Cavalry* (New York, NY: Antiquarian Press LTD, 1959. Originally published in 1883).

Propst, Nell Brown, *Forgotten People: A History of the South Platte Trail* (Boulder, CO: Pruett Publishing Co., 1979).

Raine, William MacLeod, *Famous Sheriffs & Western Outlaws* (Garden City, NY: Doubleday, Doran & Company, Inc., 1929).

Reckmeyer, Clarence, "The Battle of Summit Springs," (*The Colorado Magazine*, Vol. VI, Number 6, 1929), 211-220.

Record of Engagements With Hostile Indians Within The Military Division of the Missouri From 1868 To 1882, Lieutenant-General P. H. Sheridan, Commanding (Washington: Government Printing Office, 1882; reprinted Fort Collins, CO: Old Army Press, 1972).

Rees, D. S., "An Indian Fight on the Solomon," (*Kansas State Historical Collections*, Vol. 7, 1901-1902), 471-472.

Rickey, Donald, Jr., *Forty Miles a Day on Beans and Hay: The Enlisted Soldier Fighting in the Indian Wars* (Norman, OK: University of Oklahoma Press, 1963).

Rister, Carl Coke, *Border Command: General Phil Sheridan in the West* (Norman: University of Oklahoma Press, 1944).

_____, *Border Captives: The Traffic in Prisoners by Southern Plains Indians, 1835-1875* (Norman, OK: Oklahoma University Press, 1940).

Roenigk, Adolph, *Pioneer History of Kansas* (Self published, 1933).

Ross, Harry E., *What Price White Rock? A Chronicle of Northwestern Jewell County* (Burr Oak, KS: The Burr Oak Herald, 1937).

Russell, Don, *The Lives and Legends of Buffalo Bill* (Norman, OK: University of Oklahoma Press, 1960).

Sarf, Wayne, *A Winter Campaign: General Philip H. Sheridan's Operations on the Southern Plains, 1868-9* (Ann Arbor, MI: UMI Dissertation Services, 2001).

Savage, I. O., *A History of Republic County, Kansas* (Beloit, KS: Jones & Chubbic, Art Publishers, 1901).

Sheldon, Addison Erwin, *History and Stories of Nebraska* (Lincoln-Chicago-Dallas: The University Publishing Co., 1922).

Sheridan, P. H., *Personal Memoirs of P. H. Sheridan, Volume II* (New York, NY: Charles L. Webster & Company, 1888).

Skogen, Larry, *Indian Depredation Claims, 1796-1920* (Norman and London: Oklahoma University Press, 1996).

Slotkin, Richard, *The Fatal Environment: The Myth of the Frontier in the Age of Industrialization, 1800-1890* (New York: Antheneum, 1985).

Sorensen, Alfred, "General Carr's Campaign The Battle of Summit Springs," (Manuscript Collections, Kansas State Historical Society, Topeka, Kansas), 1-22.

Sorensen, Ruth, *Beyond the Prairie Wind: History, Folklore and Traditions from Denmark, Kansas* (Hillsboro, KS: Partnership Book Services, 1998).

Sowell, Thomas, *Conquests and Cultures: An International History* (New York, NY: Basic Books, 1998).

Sparks, Col. Ray G., *Reckoning at Summit Springs* (Kansas City, MO: The Lowell Press, 1969).

_____, "Tall Bull's Captives," (*The Trail Guide of the Kansas City Westerners*, Vol. VII, Number 1, March, 1962), 1-29.

Spotts, David L, *Campaigning With Custer and the Nineteenth Kansas Volunteer Cavalry* (Los Angeles, CA: Wetzel Publishing Co., 1928).

Sratton, Joanna L., *Pioneer Women: Voices From the Kansas Frontier* (New York, NY: Simon and Schuster, 1981).

Trapp, Dan L., *Encyclopedia of Frontier Biography, Vol. III* (Glendale, CA: The Arthur A. Clark Company, 1988).

Utley, Robert M., *Frontier Regulars: The United States Army and the Indian, 1866-1891* (New York and London: Macmillan Publishing Co., Inc. and Collier Macmillan Publishers, 1973).

_____, *The Indian Frontier of the American West 1846-1890* (Albuquerque, NM: University of New Mexico Press, 1984).

_____, ed., *Life in Custer's Cavalry: Diaries and Letters of Albert and Jennie Barnitz, 1867-1868* (New Haven and London: Yale University Press, 1977).

Vaughan, Alden T., ed., *Narratives of North American Indian Captivity: A Selective Bibliography* (New York and London: Garland Publishing Company, 1983).

Vestal, Stanley, *Warpath and Council Fire: The Plains Indians' Struggle for Survival in War and Diplomacy 1851-1891* (New York, NY: Random House, 1948).

Walsh, Richard J., *The Making of Buffalo Bill: A Study in Heroics* (Indianapolis, IN: The Bobbs-Merrill Company, 1928).

Watson, Elmo Scott, "The Battle of Summit Springs," (*The Chicago Westerners Brand Book*, Vol. VII, No. 7, September, 1950), 49-51.

Weingardt, Richard, *Sound the Charge: The Western Frontier: Spillman Creek to Summit Springs* (Englewood, CO: Ajacqueline Enterprises, Inc., 1968).

Wellman, Paul I., *Death on Horseback: Seventy Years of War for the American West* (Philadelphia & New York: J. B. Lippincott Co., 1947).

Werner, Fred H., *The Summit Springs Battle July 11, 1869* (Greeley, CO: Werner Publications, 1991).

Wetmore, Helen Cody and Grey, Zane, *Last of the Great Scouts* (New York, NY: Grosset & Dunlap, 1918).

White, Lonnie J., "Indian Raids on the Kansas Frontier, 1869," (*Kansas Historical Quarterly*, Number 4, Winter, 1972), 369-388.

_____, "White Women Captives of the Southern Plains Indians," (*Journal of the West*, Vol. III, No. 3, July, 1969), 327-354.

Wilson, Hill P., "Black Kettle's Last Raid – 1868," (*Kansas State Historical Collections*, Vol. 8, 1903-1904), 110-117.

Windbarger, J.W., *Indian Depredations in Texas* (Austin, TX: Hutchings Printing House, 1989).

Winsor, M. and Scarbrough, James A., *History of Jewell County, Kansas, With a Full Account of its Early Settlements and the Indian Atrocities Committed Within its Borders* (Jewell City, KS: "Diamond" Printing Office, 1878).

Woodward, Arthur, ed., and annotated, *Man of the West: Reminiscences of George Washington Oaks 1840-1917* (Tucson, AZ: Arizona Pioneers' Historical Society, 1956).

Wynkoop, Edward W., *The Tall Chief: The Unfinished Autobiography of Edward W. Wynkoop, 1856-1866*, ed., Gerboth, Christopher B., (Denver, CO: The Colorado Historical Society, Monograph 9, 1993).

Zimmer, William F., Greene, Jerome A. ed., *Frontier Soldier: An Enlisted Man's Journal of the Sioux and Nez Perce Campaigns, 1877* (Helena, MT: Montana Historical Society Press, 1998).

Newspapers

Appeal Democrat, Yuba City, California, 1986.

Army and Navy Journal, 1869.

Atchison Daily Champion, Atchison, Kansas, 1869.

Beverly Tribune, Beverly, Kansas, 1926.

Blue Rapids Times, Blue Rapids, Kansas, 1893-1954.

Conway Springs Star, Conway Springs, Kansas, 1925.

The Daily Nebraska Press, Nebraska City, Nebraska, 1867-1869.

Delphos Republican, Delphos, Kansas, 1902.

The Denver Post, Denver, Colorado, 1914.

Doniphan County Republican, Doniphan, Kansas, 1869.

The Emporia News, Emporia, Kansas, 1868-1869.

Journal Advocate, Sterling, Colorado, 1965.

Junction City Daily Union, Junction City, Kansas, 1868-1869.

Junction City Weekly Union, Junction City, Kansas, 1868-1869.

The Kansas Daily Commonwealth, Topeka, Kansas, 1869.

The Kansas Daily Tribune, Lawrence, Kansas, 1869.

The Kansas City Star, Kansas City, Kansas, 1934.

The Kansas State Record, Topeka, Kansas, 1868-1869.

Kansas Weekly Commonwealth, Topeka, Kansas, 1869.

The Kansas Weekly Tribune, Lawrence, Kansas, 1868-1869.

Leavenworth Daily Commercial, Leavenworth, Kansas, 1869.

Leavenworth Times and Conservative, Leavenworth, Kansas, 1868-1869.

The Lincoln Republican, Lincoln, Kansas, 1886, 1917.

The Lincoln Republican Sentinel, Lincoln, Kansas, 1911.

The Lincoln Sentinel Republican, Lincoln, Kansas, 1933-34, 1939.

The Lincoln Star, Lincoln, Nebraska, 1940.

The Manhattan Homestead, Manhattan, Kansas, 1869.

The Manhattan Standard, Manhattan, Kansas, 1868-1869.

Nebraska Advertiser, Brownville, Nebraska, 1867-1869.

The Nebraska City News, Nebraska City, Nebraska, 1867-1869.

New York Herald, New York, New York, 1869.

New York Times, New York, New York, 1869.

Omaha Daily Herald, Omaha, Nebraska, 1867-1869.

Omaha World Herald, Omaha, Nebraska, 1933.

Republican Daily Journal, Lawrence, Kansas, 1869.

Rocky Mountain News, Denver, Colorado, 1869;

Saline Herald, Salina, Kansas, 1876.

Talmage Tribune, Talmage, Nebraska, 1940.

Winners of the West, St. Joseph, Missouri, 1925.

Unpublished References

Carr, Mary P. M., *Memoirs of Brevet Major General Eugene A. Carr by his wife* (Lincoln, NE: Microfilm copy, Nebraska State Historical Society, 1961).

Carr, Eugene A., "Reminiscences of Indian Wars Service," (Lincoln: NE: Microfilm copy, Nebraska State Historical Society, 1961).

Dixon, David, "'A Fate More Dreadful Than Death:' Women, Indian Captivity and Frontier Military Policy," Paper read before The Western History Association, 1993.

Hancks, Elizabeth H., *The Life and Activities of James Jared Peate* (Thesis Presented to the Graduate Faculty of the Fort Hays State College), undated, in the possession of the Lincoln County Historical Society, Lincoln, Kansas

Peate, James Jared, "Scrapbook," in the possession of Loa Page, Lincoln, KS.

Ray Sparks Research/Manuscript Collections, in the possession of Orvel Criqui, Lawrence, KS.

Research Institutions, Museums and Libraries

Blue Rapids Public Library, Blue Rapids, KS.

Buffalo Bill Museum and Grave, Golden, CO.

Colorado State Historical Society, Denver, CO.

Denver Public Library, Western History Department, Denver, CO.

Kansas State Historical Society, Topeka, KS.

Lincoln County Historical Society, Lincoln, KS.

Little Bighorn Battlefield National Monument Research Library, Crow Agency, MT.

McCracken Research Library, Buffalo Bill Historical Center, Cody, WY.

Nebraska State Historical Society, Lincoln, NE.

Salina Public Library, Kansas Room, Salina, KS.

Overland Trails Museum, Sterling, CO.

United States Army Military History Institute, Carlisle Barracks, PA.

University of Oklahoma, The Carl Albert Center, Sidney Clarke Collection, Norman, OK.

U.S. Government Documents

House Executive Documents, 41st Congress, 2nd Session, 1869-1870.

Record Group 75, Indian Depredations Claims.

Record Group 94, Military Pensions.

Record Group 94, 5th U. S. Cavalry, Muster Rolls, 1869.

Record Group 94, Republican River Expedition.

Record Group 123, Indian Depredations Claims.

Record Group 393, Department of the Missouri, Letters Received, 1869.

Record Group 393, Department of the Missouri, Letters Sent, 1869.

Record Group 393, Department of the Platte, Letters Received, 1869.

Report of the Adjutant General of the State of Kansas, for the Years 1862, 1865, 1866, 1867, 1868, 1869.

Senate Executive Documents, 40th Congress, 3rd Session, 1869.

Senate Executive Documents, 40th Congress, 2nd Session, 1867-1868.

United States Census Report, 1840, 1870, 1890, 1900, 1910, 1920, 1930.

U.S. Secretary of War, *Annual Reports*, 1867-1870.

Index